Popper and Economic Methodology

It is generally acknowledged that Sir Karl Popper 'had a greater influence on postwar economic methodology than any other single philosopher' (Wade Hands, 2001). However, since his death in 1994, there has been widespread resistance to Popper's notion of critical rationalism, in the light of other twentieth century developments in philosophy. Boylan and O'Gorman have gathered essays that seek to reassess Popper's contribution to the methodology of the social sciences and in particular economics, in both a positive and negative fashion.

The particular Popperian themes addressed in this volume include: the three-world thesis; the concept of rationality; his use of open-systems and his anti-inductivism. These particular themes are critically analysed in the context of the philosophy of economics. Arising from this analysis, it is argued that there is a compelling need to acknowledge and re-evaluate the role of realism in Popperian economic methodology. This has major implications for the construction of models in economic theorising.

This book will be of great interest to students engaged with economic methodology and the philosophy of economics, as well as anyone interested in new readings of the work of Popper.

Thomas A. Boylan is Personal Professor of Economics in the Department of Economics at the National University of Ireland, Galway.
Paschal F. O'Gorman is Personal Professor of Philosophy in the Department of Philosophy at the National University of Ireland, Galway.

Routledge INEM Advances in Economic Methodology

Series edited by Esther-Mirjam Sent, University of Nijmegen, the Netherlands

The field of economic methodology has expanded rapidly during the last few decades. This expansion has occurred in part because of changes within the discipline of economics, in part because of changes in the prevailing philosophical conception of scientific knowledge, and also because of various transformations within the wider society. Research in economic methodology now reflects not only developments in contemporary economic theory, the history of economic thought, and the philosophy of science; but it also reflects developments in science studies, historical epistemology, and social theorising more generally. The field of economic methodology still includes the search for rules for the proper conduct of economic science, but it also covers a vast array of other subjects and accommodates a variety of different approaches to those subjects.

The objective of this series is to provide a forum for the publication of significant works in the growing field of economic methodology. Since the series defines methodology quite broadly, it will publish books on a wide range of different methodological subjects. The series is also open to a variety of different types of works: original research monographs, edited collections, as well as republication of significant earlier contributions to the methodological literature. The International Network for Economic Methodology (INEM) is proud to sponsor this important series of contributions to the methodological literature.

1 **Foundations of Economic Method, 2nd edition**
A Popperian perspective
Lawrence A. Boland

2 **Applied Economics and the Critical Realist Critique**
Edited by Paul Downward

3 **Dewey, Pragmatism and Economic Methodology**
Edited by Elias L. Khalil

4 **How Economists Model the World into Numbers**
Marcel Boumans

5 McCloskey's Rhetoric
Discourse ethics in economics
Benjamin Balak

6 The Foundations of Paul Samuelson's Revealed Preference Theory
A study by the method of rational reconstruction, revised edition
Stanley Wong

7 Economics and the Mind
Edited by Barbara Montero and Mark D. White

8 Error in Economics
Towards a more evidence-based methodology
Julian Reiss

9 Popper and Economic Methodology
Contemporary challenges
Edited by Thomas A. Boylan and Paschal F. O'Gorman

Popper and Economic Methodology

Contemporary challenges

Edited by
Thomas A. Boylan and Paschal F. O'Gorman

Routledge
Taylor & Francis Group
LONDON AND NEW YORK

First published 2008
by Routledge

2 Park Square, Milton Park, Abingdon, Oxfordshire OX14 4RN

Simultaneously published in the USA and Canada
by Routledge

711 Third Avenue, New York, NY 10017

First issued in paperback 2014

Routledge is an imprint of the Taylor & Francis Group, an informa company

Typeset in Times New Roman by
HWA Text and Data Management, Tunbridge Wells

British Library Cataloguing in Publication Data
A catalogue record for this book is available from the British Library

Library of Congress Cataloging-in-Publication Data
Popper and economic methodology : contemporary challenges / edited by Thomas A. Boylan and Paschal F. O'Gorman.
p. cm. (Routledge INEM advances in economic methodology)
Includes bibliographical references and index.
1. Popper, Karl Raimund, Sir, 1902–1994. 2. Economics–Methodology.
I. Boylan, Thomas A. II. O'Gorman, Paschal F. (Paschal Francis), 1943–
HB135.P64 2007
330–dc22 2007005433

ISBN 978–0–415–32339–0 (hbk)
ISBN 978–0–415–75868–0 (pbk)
ISBN 978–0–203–35653–1 (ebk)

We would like to dedicate this book to the memory of our siblings, Hugh and Shaun Boylan and Maura McMahon (nee O'Gorman), whose sojourn among us was all too short.

Contents

Contributors

Thomas A. Boylan is Personal Professor of Economics in the Department of Economics at the National University of Ireland, Galway.

Giulio Giorello is Professor of Philosophy of Science at the University of Milan.

Tony Lawson is Reader in Economics in the Faculty of Economics and Politics at the University of Cambridge.

John McCall is Professor of Economics in the Department of Economics at the University of California.

Matteo Motterlini is Professor of Philosophy of Science at the Università San Raffaele, Milan.

Paschal F. O'Gorman is Personal Professor of Philosophy in the Department of Philosophy at the National University of Ireland, Galway.

K. Vela Velupillai is John E. Cairnes Professor of Economics at the National University of Ireland, Galway. He is also Professor of Economics at the University of Trento, and a Fellow of Girton College and University Lecturer in Economics, University of Cambridge.

Preface

The origins of this book arose from an International Symposium that was held at the National University of Ireland, Galway in September 2002. The occasion was to mark the centenary of Sir Karl Popper's birth in 1902. The symposium was held under the auspices of the Royal Irish Academy and the Austrian Embassy in Ireland, who invited the editors to undertake its organisation. Centenaries are normally the occasion that motivate the organisation of such celebratory activities as conferences and symposia, which undertake the reassessment of the contribution and influence of a leading figure in a particular field of intellectual endeavour, and in the case of Popper the centenary of his birth provided such an occasion. While there was no 'visible hand' directing the division of labour as to which aspect of Popper's work should be addressed on this occasion, we felt that a significant area of Popper's work that warranted attention was his contribution to economic methodology. Consequently a number of international experts, working at the frontiers of theoretical research in economics along with a number of economic methodologists who are developing new approaches to economic methodology were brought together in Galway to explore the significance of Popper's writings for contemporary economic methodology.

The chapters in this volume explore a number of major issues central to Popper's work and provide a critical reassessment of his work in the light of developments in twentieth-century philosophy and mathematics. Among the principal themes addressed in this volume are a number of major tensions in Popper's contribution to economic methodology. More specifically these tensions result from two divergent trends in Popper's thought. One trend emerges from his demarcation criterion as contained in his doctrine of falsifiability. In this prescriptive doctrine, if economics is a science then it must be falsifiable. The alternative trend is contained in Popper's situational analysis, his highly prescriptive approach to the social sciences, which is embedded in his rationality principle. The rationality principle privileges a conception of rationality, which underlies orthodox neoclassical economics. The realist ground for Popper's rationality principle is explored. This realist ground, we argue, has not received sufficient attention in the economic methodology literature. In this connection a range of anti-realist critiques are presented.

The second major issue explored is based on a critical reading of Popper's later work. In this later work the universe is perceived as an open system, untainted by determinism. Under the shadow of this Popperian thesis, orthodox economics is the only social science to have attained the maturity of Newtonian physics. The implications of Popperian open systems for economic methodology have been ignored to-date in the literature on economic methodology. This challenge is addressed, and in the examination of this issue, the hegemony of orthodox economics, based as it is on a methodological foundation of closed-systems theorising, is rigorously interrogated and found to be wanting.

A third major issue addressed is the Popperian critique of induction, which was the motivation and starting point of a great part of Popper's contribution to the philosophy of science. As is well known, Popper traced the problem of induction back to Hume and he distinguished between the logical and psychological dimensions of Hume's problem. Popper agreed with Hume's negative answer to the logical problem of induction, namely: are we rationally justified in reasoning from repeated instances which we have experienced to other instances of which we have no experience? Popper, however, disagreed with Hume's psychological position, namely, that rational people, based on custom and habit, expect that the instances of which they have no experience will conform to those of which they have had experience. For Popper induction does not exist. This Popperian thesis is fundamentally reassessed in two major contributions to this volume, whereby recourse to the conceptual reservoir of metaphor, similarity, search processes, Bayesian frameworks and de Finetti's concept of exchangeability, along with developments in contemporary mathematical recursion theory, from which a challenging, rigorous and innovative defence of induction is presented. These particular contributions represent a significant addition to the field of Popperian scholarship.

In organising an international symposium and forging its contents into a book there are inevitably many debts of gratitude incurred. We would like to thank the Royal Irish Academy and the Austrian Embassy in Ireland for extending the invitation to organize the symposium on the occasion of the centenary of Popper's birth. Funding from the Millennium Research Fund at the National University of Ireland, Galway, helped to defray the costs of organising the symposium and for that we would like to record our appreciation. To all the contributors we are deeply grateful for their contributions and participation in the symposium. But a special work of thanks must go to our cherished and esteemed colleague, Professor Vela Velupillai, who was instrumental in securing the contribution of Professor John McCall from the University of California at San Diego, and at a later stage in soliciting the contribution of Giulio Giorello and Matteo Motterlini, when one of the original contributors was unable to contribute. For the latter's generous response at short notice we would like to record our most sincere gratitude. Terry Clague and later Taiba Batool at Routledge have yet again produced a 'heroic' display of patience, cheerfulness and utter civility in the face of protracted delays, arising from a concatenation of events that conspired to unduly extend the gestation period of this project. For their steadfast encouragement and unwavering assistance at every juncture we are profoundly grateful. Finally, we would like to thank Imelda Howley and Claire Noone for all their assistance, and in particular Claire for her extraordinary efficiency and customary cheerfulness in typing various drafts of a difficult manuscript and ensuring its safe electronic and other form of transfer to Routledge.

Introduction

Popper's influence in the social sciences, including economics, has been pervasive, certainly as reflected in the attention that has been devoted to analysing and interpreting his prescriptive philosophy of science. But his prescriptions also bear a deeply ambiguous relationship to the actual practice of social scientists. This ambivalent position has been well rehearsed within the literature on economic methodology and is addressed in a number of the chapters of this volume. Given the voluminous body of literature that Popper's work has generated within economics, a reasonable question to pose to yet another volume in this area, is: what is distinct, or to invoke the economic nomenclature, what is the 'value-added' of another addition to the literature? Apart from the celebratory motivation of acknowledging the centenary of Popper's birth, which was the original rationale for undertaking this project, the more substantive rationale was to avail of the occasion to reflect and reconsider fundamental aspects of Popper's work in the light of major developments in twentieth-century philosophy. In particular the emergence of the realist/anti-realist debate, which we consider to be among the most significant developments in both twentieth-century philosophy and philosophy of science. Conjoined with this has been the continuing debate on the induction/anti-induction issue, so central to Popper's whole philosophical project. Therefore our central focus in this volume is the re-examination of Popper's work in the light of these major debates.

Arising from these considerations, the informing debates that have influenced and shaped the two central themes around which this collection of essays can be grouped are the inductive/anti-inductive debate and the realist/anti-realist debate. Both of these debates we consider as central to enriching and deepening our appreciation of Popper's reflections on economics and the social sciences. In our view the inductive/anti-inductive debate is not just a series of technical issues surrounding developments in the calculus of probability or on how to apply probability theory to either science or philosophy. Rather it concerns our view of human knowledge. Popper was clearly aware of this. His anti-inductivism is rooted in his view of knowledge as conjectural but objective, which cannot be justified by any use of probability theory. Thus Popper is at the other end of the spectrum to the numerous epistemologists who view human knowledge as *justified* or true belief, where probability can, as it were, specify the degree of confirmation of our beliefs. Indeed for Popper, human knowledge is objective and exists apart from human beliefs. In this fashion his Platonic realist view of knowledge is crucial to his deep-seated opposition to recourse to probability theory as the core of a theory of confirmation. However, as the parameters of the inductive/anti-inductive debate are generally well known, we do not propose to rehearse them here. These parameters, however, are central to some of the challenging essays in this collection.

What is less familiar but, in our view, equally important in appreciating Popper's reflections on economics, both positively and negatively, is the realism/anti-realism debate. For purposes of ease of discussion, we distinguish between the realism/anti-realism debate in 'pure' or general philosophy, and this debate as it unfolded in the philosophy of science. While one may, prima facie, see the relevance of the realist/anti-realist debate in philosophy of science to Popper's reflections on economics, it is less evident how this debate in pure philosophy could impinge on either economics or economic methodology. One would have sympathy with any economist interested in economic methodology maintaining that, while the realist/anti-realist debate may be crucial to professional philosophers interested in abstract metaphysical questions, these issues either do not impinge at all or are very peripheral to economics and its methodology.

But as we argue in an extended opening chapter what we call the 'early' Popper had more than just sympathy with such a position. However, after his reading of Tarski's work on truth, he changed his mind. This Popper we call the 'later' Popper. According to the later Popper the realism/anti-realism debate, especially the specific variety of realism worked out by Popper himself, plays an indispensable role in both economics and in economic methodology.

In this connection there is some overlap between Popper's analysis of what one might call 'the economics-realism nexus' and that of Mäki's adjustment of realism to economics, a programme on which Mäki has been working on for a number of years. While this is undoubtedly the case, we contrast Popper's rich and sophisticated version of realism with 'the weak conception of realism' (Mäki 2002: 92) used by Mäki in elucidating this economics–realism nexus.

In particular, we look at three aspects of how Popper applied his realism in pure philosophy to economics and to economic methodology. First, we look at his interpretation of Tarski on truth and how he uses this to counteract relativist moves in methodology in general and economic methodology in particular. Second, we address what Popper calls his realist reading of logic and argue that such a reading is indispensable to the mathematical modelling of the economy in general equilibrium theory. We further argue that, if one adopts an anti-realist approach to logic, then this general equilibrium, mathematical model must be rejected. Popper's realist reading of logic prohibited him from appreciating the possibility of mathematically modelling an economy compatible with the intuitionist, non-realist logic, introduced by Brouwer and developed by Dummett. In short, in tune with the early Popper's belief that there are good arguments for anti-realism, an intuitionist anti-realism necessarily limits our mathematical modelling of an economy to what has come to be called finitist mathematics, where the core neoclassical notions of rationality and equilibrium are seriously challenged. Thus a Popperian realist is an indispensable under-labourer for an Arrow-Debreu type, infinitist mathematical model of an economy, whereas an intuitionist non-realist will under-labour for finitist mathematical models. Thus Popper was correct in noting the significance of logical realism for economics and its methodology. The realist/anti-realist debate on pure philosophy matters to the range and list of mathematical models available to economists.

Finally we turn to another indispensable pillar of Popperian realism, namely his Three-World Thesis. The three worlds are, first, the physical world, second, the world of human beliefs and other 'objects' of individual consciousness and, finally, the world of objective knowledge ranging from mathematics and physics to urban geography and economics. Popper, in line with the long tradition of Platonic realism, argues that this third world, though man-made, is distinct from the second world of beliefs and other denizens of human consciousness or minds. We show how this Popperian, Platonic realism is crucial for his analysis of economic actions, his justification of the autonomy of economics, especially its independence from psychology and his situational analysis reading of neo-classical economics. To sum up, for Popper, realism in pure philosophy is far from idling in the philosophy of economics. On the contrary, it does indispensable work for him in his challenging reflections of economics and its philosophy.

Popper's realism in pure philosophy in turn informs his specific articulation of scientific realism. As Mäki points out, there are numerous versions of scientific realism. These range from Bhaskar to Putnam. We focus on Popper's unique development of scientific realism. Popper's scientific realism, like many other scientific realists, has a negative and positive component. Negatively it rejects descriptivist and instrumentalist readings of scientific theory. More generally it rejects empiricist readings of science ranging from Hume to Carnap to van Fraassen. Positively, it celebrates the indispensable role of theory in science, where theory is part of objective knowledge. Moreover, while emphasising that the aim of science is the elimination of false theories, he is equally emphatic that scientific theory is genuinely explanatory. In this fallibilist context, Popper develops a non-essentialist, realist theory of explanation. Popper uses this notion of explanation in his rejection of historicist explanation in the social sciences. This side of Popper is well known and well discussed. What has received less emphasis is the fact that Popper uses his non-essentialist thesis of explanation to draw our attention to the role of models in the physical and the human sciences. We demonstrate that, for Popper, the notion of model is absolutely indispensable to the notion of explanation in the full range of the social sciences. We suggest that the contemporary discussion of models in economics ranging from Mäki's realism to causal holism could benefit from re-engaging Popper's conception of the role of models in explanation (Boylan and O'Gorman 1995).

To conclude, the stand one takes on the induction/anti-induction and realism/anti-realism debates are crucial for one's evaluation of Popper. As we have just outlined, Popper favoured a realism cum anti-inductivist stand. Indeed, in view of his Platonic realist view of knowledge as non-justified, conjectural but critically objective, his leanings towards an anti-inductivist stand is not surprising.

This realist Popper not only casts a long shadow over the following chapters, he is a prevailing presence. Some, in sympathy with realism, explicate Popper's realism in challenging directions for philosophy of economics. Others, with a sympathy for the non-Popperian notion of knowledge as justified belief or at least requiring justification, sympathetically but critically, engage Popper's non-inductive methodology. Still others, in sympathy with varieties of anti-realism, vigorously interrogate this realist Popper. All of this is done in the Socratic spirit, so admired by Popper. Like the Socrates of the early dialogues, we hope that some light has been thrown on our quest to deepen our understanding of economics without, however, arriving at a final answer. Socratic dialogue must continue.

References

Boylan, T.A. and O'Gorman, P.F. (1995) *Beyond Rhetoric and Realism in Economics: Towards a Reformulation of Economic Methodology*, London: Routledge.

Mäki, U. (2002) 'Some nonreasons for nonrealism about economics', in U. Mäki (ed.) *Fact and Fiction in Economics: Models, Realism and Social Construction*, Cambridge: Cambridge University Press.

1 Popper, economic methodology and contemporary philosophy of science

Thomas A. Boylan and Paschal F. O'Gorman

Introduction

In this chapter our aim is, among other things, to examine Popper's standing in the literature on economic methodology, in particular, the work that has emerged from the revival of interest in methodology since the demise of logical positivism in which Popper played an important part in subverting from its dominant position of influence. The principal aspects of his philosophy that have preoccupied the attention of economic methodologists are centred arguably in three dimensions of his work, namely falsificationism, his writings on situational analysis, especially the rationality principle, and more recently the reassertion of the centrality of his critical rationalism. Each of these three areas has produced a voluminous corpus of work representing the vibrancy of the methodological debates that Popper's work has engendered within the economic methodology community. Therefore the first section of this chapter will rehearse, albeit within the constraints of a single chapter, a number of the major interpretations of Popper's doctrines, in particular, his falsificationism and critical rationalism, that have been discussed by economic methodologists.

Having engaged the central themes in Popperian economic methodology, in the remainder of this chapter we explore other dimensions of the Popperian landscape which are central to the chapters in this volume, namely Popper's engagement with major themes in twentieth-century philosophy and how this engagement has influenced his methodology of economics. In particular, we focus on the realism/anti-realism debate which was so influential in both pure or general philosophy on the one hand, and in philosophy of science on the other. We argue that Popper's specific realist stance, which in its own way was quite original, was a major influence on his reflections on economics and the other social sciences, an influence which has not been given sufficient attention in the extant literature. Moreover, we suggest how an anti-realist stance could provide, for both economics and economic methodology, a different development trajectory. But first we examine some of the major contributions to the interpretation of Popper's philosophy within economic methodology.

Popper and economic methodology

Popper's influence on methodological thinking in economics has been both significant and deeply challenging. It is almost seventy years since Popper's work was first invoked by Terence Hutchison in his seminal work on twentieth-century economic methodology (Hutchison 1938). Since then the interpretation of Popper's philosophy of science, and more specifically its implications for economics, has become an increasingly contested domain with respect to its relative emphasis, status and influence within economic methodology. There are now a number of different 'Poppers', or at least different aspects of his work, vying for the attention of economists. Each of them are vigorously defended by their respective advocates and each compete for the accolade of being considered the most suitable 'Popper' for adoption as the most appropriate for economics. There is the 'falsificationist Popper', the 'situational analysis Popper', and the 'critical rationalist Popper', all of whom have preoccupied the efforts of economic methodologists over the last thirty-five years.

It has recently been argued that Popper has 'had a greater impact on post-war economic methodology than any other single philosopher (or philosophical school)' (Hands 2001: 275–6). While opinions may differ on this particular assessment, there is no disputing the significance of what we elsewhere termed the 'Popperian Interlude' between the demise of logical positivism and the emergence of the 'growth of knowledge' tradition (Boylan and O'Gorman 1995). Popper has insisted on his role in contributing to the undermining of logical positivism, at least to the extent of sowing the seeds of its destruction (Popper 1976). The destruction of logical positivism was not his principal ambition he has claimed, but rather 'to point out what seemed to me a number of fundamental mistakes' (Popper 1976: 88), which supports Passmore's argument that the dissolution of logical positivism was due to the emergence of fundamental internal difficulties (Passmore 1967, 1968). What followed, which is generally referred to as 'the growth of knowledge' tradition, proved extremely attractive to economic methodologists and historians of economic thought. De Marchi has described what attracted economists and economic methodologists to Popper's philosophy of science:

> Quite apart from what he had to say viewed as matters of logical relations and of the properties of statements, he represented an *attitude* – to be critical. Neither fact nor theory is more than an element in the process of identifying error. This was liberating for economists in a special way. Popper's balanced insistence on empirical content *and* on the epistemological priority of theorizing might have been tailored to appeal to practitioners in a discipline where experimentation is difficult and inconclusive and theory seems more solid, yet where numbers are seen to be essential to adopting theory to yield advice for policy making. His stress on methodological conventions – rules of the game – was helpful to a group of social scientists anxious to be useful and to explain themselves to a somewhat reluctant public, yet conscious of the fallibility of their pronouncements. In short, in contrast to much writing in the

> philosophy of science, Popper's work was not only accessible to economists but seemed relevant.
>
> (De Marchi 1988: 4 italics in original)

The above account identifies, succinctly and perceptively, a number of the principal attributes that were 'liberating for economists in a special way', and economic methodologists and historians of economics were quick to enlist Popper's philosophy of science.

Among the economic methodologists one of the earliest and consistent advocates of the Popperian programme was Terence Hutchison, whose seminal work, *The Significance and Basic Postulates of Economic Theory* published in 1938, represented the first systematic introduction of the philosophical ideas of logical positivism and of Popper's ideas to economists and economic methodology (Coats 1983; Caldwell 1998). The main target of Hutchison's book was Mises's a priorism, which would later be extended to include Marx and Marxian economics, by virtue of their rejection of empirical testability and thereby their potential falsifiability. While the work represented in many ways a relatively sophisticated treatment of its topic, it was unambiguous in the central message it wished to convey – namely that economics should be a *science* and what distinguished science from non-science was the inclusion of propositions that were empirically testable. Demarcation was critical for Hutchison and in a forceful statement of his position he wrote:

> If there is any object in pursuing an activity one calls "scientific," and if the word "science' is not simply to be a comprehensive cloak for quackery, prejudice, and propaganda, then there must be a definite objective criterion for distinguishing propositions which may be material for science from those that are not, and there must be some effective barrier for excluding expressions of ethical or political passion, poetic emotion or metaphysical speculation from being mixed in with so-called "science."
>
> (Hutchison 1938: 10)

Throughout his later work Hutchison maintained his commitment to the Popperian programme and further refined his understanding of the Popperian doctrine of falsificationism (Hutchison, 1976, 1977, 1978, 1981). Hutchison was to be joined later by an influential group of writers on economic methodology, which included Blaug (1980a), Boland (1982), and Klant (1984), who adopted, albeit with different emphasis, the Popperian methodological framework to critically evaluate the practice of economists.

A number of the major schools of economics were subjected to a Popperian critique based on the criterion of falsifiability. Continuing the work initiated by Hutchison, the Austrian school, as represented in the work of Mises, and later Marxian political economy were both accused of infallibilism. In the case of Mises, the charge of infallibilism was based on the claim that the axioms of economics, though untestable, were deemed to be true a priori. This dogmatic claim to an a priori, infallibilist basis for economics, where *ipso facto* its axioms are unfalsifiable, excluded the Misesian system from admission to the domain of science (Blaug 1980a: 91–3). Marxism was also indicted of being guilty of infallibilism, with the difference that this system of ideas has been falsified in contrast to being in principle unfalsifiable (Blaug 1980b; Hutchison 1981). American institutionalists were also criticised for formulating theories that were too easy 'to verify and virtually impossible to falsify' (Blaug 1980a: 127). Equilibrium theorising was severely criticised by Hutchison, a critique he later extended to the excessive use of formalism, based on the fact that the empirical content is rendered vacuous by the use of assumptions such as perfect foresight (Hutchison 1938, 1977, 2000). Mainstream economics of the Marshallian partial equilibrium variety was admitted as scientific, but the use of immunising stratagems seriously undermined the project. The result was termed by Coddington 'innocuous falsificationism' (Coddington 1975: 542), which was more colourfully described by Blaug as 'playing tennis with the net down' (Blaug 1980a: 256). Blaug concluded his survey on economic methodology in 1980 by stating that for 'the most part, the battle for falsificationism has been won in modern economics', but that the problem 'now is to persuade economists to take falsificationism seriously' (Blaug 1980a: 260).

For those who took falsificationism seriously, problems quickly emerged with respect to the possibility of implementing the Popperian programme of falsificationism in economics. For Blaug and Hutchison, who must be counted as among the most committed advocates of falsificationism, the difficulties associated with pursuing Popper's prescriptivist methodology were acknowledged (Blaug 1980a; Hutchison 1981). This has given rise to a burgeoning literature which contains both a critical response to the Popperian programme of falsificationism and, more recently, a reinterpretation of the place of falsification within the Popperian tradition itself. The critical strand of this literature has produced a number of stringent interrogations of the falsificationist programme in economics. These included objections to the principle of testability of economic theories based on the impossibility of testing all the models that could conceivably be articulated to represent any particular theory (Papandreou 1958; Boland 1977). Additional objections were raised against the testability of assumptions in economics which included the problem of large numbers of initial conditions that are liable to change and in many cases are not independently observable, or the absence of truly general laws to be falsified (Machlup 1955; Melitz 1965; Robbins 1979). Further criticisms of the falsificationist programme were identified arising from the problems of attempting to falsify a single hypothesis due to the implications of the Duhem-Quine thesis (Cross 1982, 1984), while Salanti (1987) argued against the adoption of either Popperian fallibilism or falsificationism as providing a proper epistemological or methodological basis for economics.

In 1991 Caldwell undertook an extensive and penetrating examination of Popper's contribution to economic methodology (Caldwell 1991). Here we will concentrate on Caldwell's re-examination of the critique of falsification and its application to economics. Caldwell, as he described himself, was 'a frequent and persistent critic of falsificationism' (Caldwell 1981, 1982, 1984, 1985, 1986). However, at the outset of this important re-assessment of Popper's contribution to economic methodology, Caldwell conceded that one of his major arguments against falsificationism, if not wrong, was seriously incomplete. Caldwell's error, he conceded, was to argue that falsificationism was an inappropriate methodology for economics because most economic theories could not be conclusively falsified, and proceeded to buttress this line of criticism by invoking the various obstacles to achieving clear cut tests of theories in economics. But Popper had anticipated the central thrust of this objection, as noted by Blaug (1984) and Hausman (1985). The Popperian response was essentially that every science, because of the Duhem-Quine thesis and related problems, and not just economics, has difficulties with delivering unambiguous refutations. Notwithstanding these difficulties for Popperians, the principle of testing should be retained and when a refutation occurred, the response should not be recourse to the use of immunising stratagems in any subsequent theory modification. This explained for Caldwell the centrality of the analysis of ad hoc theory changes and immunising stratagems in Popper's methodology. If unambiguous tests of hypotheses cannot be achieved, the critical requirement must be to ensure that our hypotheses are not further protected by adjustments designed to immunise them from falsification. Given this Popperian response, Caldwell argued that it is not an effective argument against falsificationism to argue solely that unambiguous tests of hypotheses are difficult to achieve or that decisive refutations are rare. This is the norm rather than the exception. The argument, Caldwell now insists, must be redirected against 'Popper's insistence that *nevertheless* refutations should be taken seriously, and that when one occurs, certain theory adjustments are forbidden' (Caldwell 1991: 7, italics in original). On this interpretation the focus of attention for critics of falsificationism should be Popper's position on the role of immunising stratagems.

With the focus of analysis now directed to Popper's analysis of immunising stratagems, Caldwell identified three sets of objections, which provided a schematic and perceptive overview by an economic methodologist of the problems associated with Popper's doctrine of falsificationism. The first he termed the 'philosopher's objection', which contained a number of different lines of criticism. These included the argument that 'Popper never makes clear *why*, if tests results are always so ambiguous, scientists should adopt his prescriptions to avoid ad hoc theory adjustments' (Caldwell 1991: 8, italics in original). Popper's strident anti-inductivism was also seen as a problem. It implied that even in the case of recurring confirmations, these will not be allowed to carry any 'evidential weight'. The empirical data cannot be used to support theories, only to refute. For Caldwell the arguments emerging under the heading of the 'philosopher's objection' implied that the Popperian programme was inadequate as both an epistemological and methodological basis for a satisfactory philosophy of science. At the epistemological level, Popper's anti-inductivism ruled out any analysis of how evidence might support theories, while at the methodological level, Caldwell argued, pursuit of Popper's prescriptions could lead to very unsatisfactory results, including the rejection of true theories.

Caldwell's second category of critique he termed the 'historian's objection', which challenged the advocates of the Popperian position to provide examples of its successful application within a particular science. Popper's response to this challenge was contained in his later writings where he argued against the need to test his falsificationist methodology against the history of science, precisely because it is a prescriptivist doctrine. Notwithstanding his position on this issue, Popper provided an extended list of examples of refutations from the history of science, albeit exclusively from the realm of natural science, and argued for the superiority of refutability as a theory of science in explaining the historical evolution of science (Popper 1983a). With respect to the social sciences, however, it was argued that Popper offered no examples of historical refutability. Within economics, proponents of falsification have not observed Popper's dictum against the need to test falsificationism against the history of economics. This is hardly surprising, as noted by Caldwell, since two of the leading proponents of falsificationism, Hutchison and Blaug, are distinguished historians of economic thought. But Caldwell is not convinced by the specific examples produced by either Hutchison or Blaug. His comment on Hutchison's examples is that they 'do not accord well with the falsificationist image of a theory being subjected to a decisive refuting test', while Blaug in 'developing his examples' has moved away 'from Popper and into the camp of the erstwhile Popperian, Imre Lakatos' (Caldwell 1991: 9–10). The central issue in question here is the tension between the capacity of prescriptive methodologies to provide a descriptively adequate framework that will assist intellectual historians to interpret the historical development of the different disciplines. For the critics of falsificationism in economics, the issues identified by Caldwell under the rubric of the 'historian's objection' represent a challenging array of unresolved issues.

Caldwell's final category of critique he labelled the 'economic methodologist's objection'. The central issue here is that within economics there are 'good reasons' for rejecting Popper's arguments against immunising stratagems. Caldwell refers to the earlier work of Popper (1945, 1957, 1963), along with some later work (1976, 1983b), which he regards as the main corpus of Popper's writings on what he considered to be the most appropriate method for the social sciences, namely, the method of situational logic or situational analysis.[1] The basic tenet of this method is that the explanation of social behaviour must be sought in the 'situation' in which individuals find themselves. Given the objective situation there will be a unique response which follows from the 'logic' of the situation. The resulting observed action is then explained as a 'rational' or 'logical' response to the objective situational environment in which the individuals found themselves. This type of explanation is underlain by the rationality principle which states that people act in a way appropriate to their situation (Popper 1983b). What Caldwell argued as his central thesis against Popper's prohibitions on immunising stratagems was that 'the actual methodology followed in much of economics may best be described as one in which a particular immunising stratagem is elevated, and for good reasons, to the status of an inviolable methodological principle' (Caldwell 1991: 13). This immunising stratagem is none other than Popper's own analysis of situational logic. Caldwell goes on to identify the tensions that exist between the requirements of falsification and the logic of situational logic, but purports to find a solution to these tensions in another area of Popper's writings, namely that of critical rationalism (Caldwell 1991: 13–31).

The comprehensive review provided by Caldwell in 1991 of the arguments against Popperian falsificationism represented something of a progress report on what was a burgeoning literature on the topic. This included, in addition to Caldwell (1982, 1984, 1991, 1994), the work of Hands (1979, 1984, 1991a, 1991b, 1992, 1993). Hausman (1985, 1988, 1992, 1996), Latsis (1972, 1976, 1983), and Redman (1991), as a representative sample of where many of the issues pertaining to Popperian philosophy of science, and in particular falsificationism were discussed in relation to economic methodology. Over a decade after Caldwell's overview of this topic, Wade Hands in his masterly survey of economic methodology has commented that while 'it is clear that Popper had a significant impact on economic methodology, it is decidedly less clear just exactly what the nature of his contribution has been' (Hands 2001: 276). This assessment, taken in conjunction with Hands's earlier comment that Popper 'had a greater impact on post-war economic methodology than any other single philosopher (or philosophical school)', provides something of a perplexing challenge for economic methodologists.

In reflecting on the reasons for Popper's influence on post-war methodology, Hands noted that it seemed ironic that Popper's 'influence among economists is actually greater than his influence among philosophers of science in general' (ibid.: 276), and that for a number of reasons. One was the clarity of exposition and relative straightforwardness of Popper's philosophy of science and its application. It offered, as Hands put it, 'a relatively simple demarcation criterion as well as a set of easily implemented methodological rules for the proper conduct of scientific inquiry' (ibid.: 276). A second contributing factor was related to Popper's intellectual agenda. More specifically, this referred to Popper's hostility to both Freudian psychology and Marxist theory, especially his desire to use his falsificationist demarcation criterion to eliminate both these systems of ideas from the domain of legitimate scientific inquiry (Popper 1976). This agenda, combined with his commitment to classical political liberalism and his enlisting of conventional neoclassical economic theory as the appropriate method for social theorising, made Popper a figure of considerable attention for those interested in the methodology of economic science. Then there was his association, both personal and professional, with a number of very influential and methodologically sophisticated economists at the London School of Economics. These included Hayek, Lipsey, and in particular Blaug who has been a steadfast proponent of falsificationism in economics in both theory and practice. The association between Popper and these economists is well documented in the work of Caldwell (1992a, 1992b), Hutchison (1981, 1988), De Marchi (1988) and Blaug (1994a).

The more substantive and difficult task for Hands is to reconcile the fact that, notwithstanding Popper's very significant impact on economic methodology, why 'it is decidedly less clear just exactly what the nature of his contribution has been'. For Hands the difficulties encountered in evaluating Popper's contribution to economic methodology can be 'traced to various *problems and tensions within the Popperian philosophical tradition*' (Hands 2001: 276 italics in original). Three broad areas of 'problems and tensions' are identified. First, there are a series of tensions within Popper's philosophy of natural science itself; second, a critical fault line is identified between what is perceived to be Popper's philosophy of natural science and what he wrote about the social sciences, which in most cases was centred on economics; and finally, there are the tensions arising from the internal historiography of the 'Popperian school', more particularly, the differing views emerging from within this 'school' as to what is most fundamental in Popper's own work. The agendas identified within each of these broad areas of discussion represent an ongoing and challenging agenda in the process of what Caldwell had earlier termed 'clarifying Popper'.

Within the literature on economic methodology on falsificationism, the major issues identified, according to Hands, included the implications of the Duhem-Quine thesis, or the under-determination problem, which had been identified earlier by Caldwell. The issue here was the fact that no scientific theory could be tested in isolation. In the event of negative results for a particular theory, this indicated that at least one component of the system, interpreted as the theory in question in addition to any auxiliary hypotheses, was incompatible with the available evidence. This did not of necessity imply that the theory itself is the main problem. Popper himself was of course aware of this issue and suggested his own solution: assume all of the auxiliary hypotheses to be part of the background knowledge, the assumed tacit knowledge, with the result that the theory bore the responsibility for the refutation. It was argued that this effectively transformed falsificationism into a conventionalist philosophy, and in the context of particular instances of refutation was termed by Hausman a '*conventional* falsification' (Hausman 1996: 214). Lakatos had earlier used the phrase to describe Popper in this aspect of his work as a 'revolutionary conventionalist' (Lakatos 1970: 106), i.e. observation statements are accepted as given, and notwithstanding that these conventionally accepted statements are referred to as 'observational', this for Lakatos is 'only a manner of speech' (Lakatos 1970: 106–7). Popper's conventionalism is also invoked in response to the problem of theory-ladenness. The acceptance of empirical observations as unproblematic within the Popperian framework is in effect a conventionally accepted decision to embrace one particular category of theory, i.e. the theories pervasive within the data, while at the same time interrogating another theory, i.e. the theory being tested. But theories are ubiquitous and there is no place to stand that is free from the influence of the use of theories, in Quine's felicitous phrase, we cannot play 'the cosmic exile'. There are in other words no foundations, but Popper's conventionalism, it is argued, side steps this issue and does of course allow us to 'test' aspects of the theoretical system, while in Hands' words ' the whole ship remains afloat' (Hands 2001: 279).

Popper's conventionalism, even if accepted as an answer to the difficulties of underdetermination and theory-ladenness, still presents problems for his falsificationism. This aspect of the problem has been highlighted by Hausman (1992, 1996), who argues that the same conventionalist procedure that works for falsification will also work for the confirmation of theories, thus undermining the whole falsificationist project which was to replace verification with refutation. In Hausman's opinion:

> Regardless of the basis for the decision to rely on some propositions to falsify others, such decisions are unavoidable. But if it is permissible to include background knowledge among one's premises in order to make conventional *falsifications* possible, then one also makes conventional *verifications* possible. The conventional asymmetry thesis fails, and Popper has failed to defend his claim that scientists should seek falsification only.
>
> (Hausman 1992: 185 italics in original)

Other problems, to name but a few, that have received attention within the literature on Popperian falsificationism include the implications of underdetermination and theory-ladenness along with the difficulties for Popper's philosophy of the notion of truth that he worked with and the basis of his scientific realism. But perhaps the issue that is of most interest to economics is the perceived tension between Popper's falsificationism and his writings about the social sciences. These latter writings, which are dispersed within his large corpus of work and were written at different intervals in his career, centred on his concepts of 'situational analysis' and the 'rationality principle'. Neither of these concepts, it is argued, fit very comfortably with his doctrine of falsificationism (Caldwell 1991; Hands 2001). However, since these concepts are the subjects of Chapters 2 and 3 of this volume, we will not pursue them further at this juncture.

Falsificationism, the most common interpretation of Popper's philosophy, when subjected to the relentless interrogation both within the philosophy of science in general and in the literature on economic methodology, has been found not to be the methodological panacea that was originally claimed. If interpreted generously, falsificationism contains a useful set of general methodological guidelines for scientific practice. Both advocates and critics of falsificationism concede that it is difficult to achieve unambiguous tests of theory. Supporters of Popper's position insist on his prohibitions against the use of immunising stratagems, which are interpreted as essentially *ad hoc* theoretical adjustments aimed at saving theories from refutations. Critics of Popper, however, are sceptical of his hostility to the use of immunising stratagems, since their use according to the critics would lead quickly to the falsification of a great deal of what is considered to be science. This has proved to be a central stumbling bloc for Popper's philosophy of falsifying theories.

Falsificationism presents a set of additional problems within the social sciences. Popper proposed the method of situational analysis, in conjunction with the rationality principle, as the most appropriate method for the social sciences. In this context Popper claimed that situational analysis was in effect a generalisation of the methodology of conventional neoclassical economics. On critical examination, however, situational analysis appears to be incompatible with falsificationism. If one accepts the tenets of falsificationism, and depending on the interpretation of the rationality principle adopted, then it has been argued that either economics and the other social sciences are not sciences, or merely *ad hoc*, or else that they follow a method that is fundamentally different from the method that is claimed to be the basis of scientific method for the rest of science.

In the face of these developments, Popperians in general and those within economic methodology have regrouped to a large extent in a different domain of Popper's writings, what has come to be termed his critical rationalism. Though essentially a restatement of his fallibilism, Popper's later writings elaborated at some length his philosophy of critical rationalism, which may be viewed as a third pillar of his overall philosophy, following his falsificationism and situational analysis. In the Preface to the three-volume *Postscript to the Logic of Scientific Discovery* (Popper 1982) he denies that there is any easy method for either the discovery or verification of scientific hypotheses. In the same Preface he elaborates on what he means by 'the so-called method of science' in the following terms:

> The only things which partners in an argument must share are the wish to know, and the readiness to learn from the other fellow, by severely criticizing his views – in the strongest possible version that can be given to his views – and hearing what he has to say in reply.
>
> I believe that *the so-called method of science consists in this kind of criticism.* Scientific theories are distinguished from myths merely in being criticizable, and in being open to modification in the light of criticism.
>
> (Popper 1982: 7 italics in original)

The emphasis is on criticisability, a concept which for Popper has applicability not just to scientific theories, but also to metaphysical theory. But in addition to criticisability, Popper's critical rationalism also includes and valorises a critical *attitude* as an integral component. What distinguishes 'the attitude of rationality is simply openness to criticism' (Popper 1983a: 27). Popper's critical rationalism is not just a change of cognitive disposition towards the virtues of criticisability. While it is certainly a reorientation of focus within the Popperian framework, it represents an elaboration of his doctrine of fallibilism, along with being a replacement of the problem of justification with that of criticism. These developments imply that all knowledge is conjectural and that as a result a criterion of truth is not possible (Popper 1983a: xix). But while Popper argues that a criterion of truth is not possible, this does not prohibit him from believing in a theory of truth, a correspondence theory in the event, and that the search for truth is extremely important as a regulative principle for scientific practice. In his own words:

> My position is this. I assert that the search for truth – or for a true theory which can solve our problem – is all-important: *all rational criticism is criticism of the claim of a theory to be true, and to be able to solve the problem which it was designed to solve.*
>
> (Popper 1983a: 24 italics in original)

Popper further expands on this topic when he explained that:

> … in replacing the problem of justification by the problem of criticism we need give up neither the classical theory of truth as correspondence with the facts nor the acceptance of truth as one of our standards of criticism. (Other standards are relevance to our problems, and explanatory power.)
>
> Thus although I hold that more often than not we fail to find the truth, and do not know even when we have found it, I retain the classical idea of absolute or objective truth as a *regulative idea*; that is to say, *as a standard of which we may fall short.*
>
> (Popper 1983a: 26 italics in original)

Popper's advocacy of criticisability became central to his overall philosophy of science, and he passed an unambiguously severe judgement on theories that were not criticisable, and not directed at problem solving.

Critical rationalism was brought to the attention of economists and economic methodologists in an extraordinary insightful paper by Kurt Klappholz and Joseph Agassi in 1959 (Klappholz and Agassi 1959). Not that much notice was accorded to it by the economic community at the time. The paper was an extended book review of two books on economic methodology, but incorporated a searching critique, from a critical rationalist perspective, of all the contemporary leading writers on economic methodology, including, Hutchison, Robbins, Friedman and Samuelson. Their central message was stated clearly at the outset of their paper:

> The impatience appears to give rise to the belief that, if only economists adopted this or that methodological rule, the road ahead would be at least cleared (and possibly the traffic would move briskly along it). Our view, on the contrary, is that there is only one generally applicable methodological rule, and that is the exhortation to be critical and always ready to subject one's hypothesis to critical scrutiny.
>
> (Klappholz and Agassi 1959: 60)

The shift to criticisability is clear from this position, as is the underlying problem for many critical rationalists, as it is for Klappholz and Agassi, that falsificationism as a methodological rule is too restrictive and rules out many ideas, in particular metaphysical ideas, that Popper himself came to realise were essential for the growth of scientific knowledge. Klappholz and Agassi were quite insistent on the restrictiveness of privileging empirical testing to the exclusion of all other considerations. Empirical testing was of course important, but it was merely one particular mode of critical assessment. For Klappholz and Agassi it was 'a cardinal mistake to lay down the rule that empirical testing against observable phenomena should be the *only* acceptable method of criticism' (Klappholz and Agassi 1959: 66 italics in original). Criticism was, on the contrary, a complex and multi-dimensional concept, which could not and should not be reduced to a narrowly conceived set of rules, much less to a single-dimensional methodological rule.

The shift from methodological rule(s) to the adoption of criticisability was clearly reflected in Klappholz and Agassi's exhortation to 'guard against the illusion that there can exist in any science methodological rules the mere adoption of which will hasten its progress', and their declaration that the proper methodological disposition should be to 'advocate the critical attitude, by trying to demonstrate its fruitfulness or by arguing against different approaches' (Klappholz and Agassi 1959: 74).

The most influential advocate of critical rationalism in economic methodology has unquestionably been Lawrence Boland (1982, 1986, 1989, 1991, 1994, 1997). His work represents the most sustained and consistent elaboration and defence of Popper's critical rationalism. Boland locates Popper's critical rationalism within the framework of the Socratic tradition and defends a view of Popper that he describes as the 'Socratic Popper'. As Boland has articulated his position:

> There is a very different view of Popper's theory of science that is not well known in economics. In this alternative view, falsifiability plays a very minor role ... Briefly stated, science for Popper is a special case of Socratic dialogue, namely, one where we learn with the elimination of error in response to empirical criticism. Rationality is critical debate – with the emphasis on debate. Popper sometimes calls this Critical Rationalism. Given its emphasis on Socratic dialectics, I will call this view the Socratic Popper.
>
> (Boland 1997: 263)

In his writings over the last thirty years Boland has furrowed a unique path in his methodological trajectory centred on a stringent critique that, among other things, falsificationism as propounded by Popperian falsificationists was not a Popperian position at all. For Boland, the Popper who advocated criticisability cannot be circumscribed much less reduced to the methodological rules of falsificationism. The most recent interchange on the relationship between falsificationism and critical rationalism, which includes contributions from Boland, Blaug and Caldwell, is contained in Backhouse (1994). The task of 'clarifying' Popper, notwithstanding the attention it has received to-date, clearly remains an unsettled domain and continues to present a challenging set of issues for economic methodologists.

We now turn to our elaboration of Popper's philosophy and its implications for economic methodology in the light of major developments in twentieth-century philosophy, in particular the realist/anti-realist debate.

Economics – realism connections in Popper

Writing in *The London Review of Books* in January 2005, Richard Rorty stated that:

> to my mind, the story of 20th century analytic philosophy is best told by highlighting questions whether truth is a matter of correspondence, about

> which is or is not "out there" to be corresponded to, and about whether there is any sense in which thought makes "direct contact" with reality.
>
> (Rorty 2005: 12)

Whether or not this is the best way of telling the history of twentieth-century philosophy, there is little doubt that the so-called realism/anti-realism debate was one of its central issues. Indeed this debate is not confined to philosophy in general nor to the philosophy of the physical sciences. It has also cast its shadow over the philosophy of economics. One has only to read Mäki or Lawson to see the influence of realism on economic methodology. Moreover, the realism/anti-realism debate is also evident in the interpretation of economic models, with post-modernists, like McCloskey, taking an anti-realist stance.

As we already noted, much of the literature on Popper focuses on his anti-inductivist stance, his deductivism, his falsifiability and his situational analysis. Rather than directly evaluating these central themes, for the remainder of this chapter we propose to contextualise Popper's philosophy of economics and the social sciences *vis-à-vis* the realist/anti-realist debate. When this is achieved, we will be in a better position to appreciate how the various themes of realism inform Popper's reflections on economics and economic methodology, thereby gaining a deeper understanding of the sophistication of his philosophy of the social sciences.

In our view clarity can be served by distinguishing between the realism/anti-realism debates in 'pure' or general philosophy on the one hand and in philosophy of science on the other. In light of this distinction, we argue that Popper's realism in pure or general philosophy played a central role in his philosophy of economics and the social sciences. It is realism which saves us from irrationality. 'Denying realism amounts to megalomania' (Popper 1972: 41).

In looking at 'the economics-realism connections', one approach adopted by Mäki 'is to argue against positions that have been put forth for a non-realist view of economics' (Mäki 2002: 92). He correctly notes the vastness of the philosophical literature on realism and, in light of his own inability to find 'a single version of realist philosophy that would fit economics without major modification' (Mäki 2002: 91), he introduces what he calls a 'weak conception of realism' summed up in two themes:

> [R1] Entity X might exist
> [R2] Theory T might be true

'(where) "X" stands for an entity (thing, complex of properties, structure, process) purportedly referred to by an economic theory or its constituents'. and 'where "T" stands for an economic theory or model' (Mäki 2002: 92). Mäki concludes his intriguing discussion as follows: 'My fear is that giving up [R1] and [R2] would result in the worst kind of complacency. The resolution of the ultimate issue of whether economics is in touch with facts or whether it is a game of just playing with fictions would be biased towards the latter alternative' (Mäki 2002: 102).

Our thesis is that for Popper the realism-economics connection is embedded in the realism-methodology connection and that this latter connection is not merely one of complacency. Rather realism is an indispensable bulwark against any and every relativist interpretation of science. However, this was not Popper's own position prior to his reading of Tarski. As Popper points out in *Conjectures and Refutations*:

> so far I have spoken about science, its progress and its criterion of progress without ever mentioning *truth* … In fact before I became acquainted with Tarski's theory of truth, it appeared to me safer to discuss the criterion of progress without getting too deeply involved in the highly controversial problem connected with the use of the word 'true'.[2]
>
> (Popper 1963: 233 italics in original)

If we were to harden this Popperian position into the claim that it is possible to do philosophy of economics, without discussing the merits or otherwise of realism, perhaps we would be articulating a position which is implicitly held by many economists with an interest in economic methodology. In other words the highly abstract debate between realists and anti-realists conducted in 'pure' philosophy is irrelevant to the specific issues facing one in the methodology of economics. Alternatively, one may introduce 'a division of labour' into philosophy: philosophy in general is concerned with the various issues in the general realism/anti-realism debate, whereas these do not directly concern philosophers of economics, with their specific concerns. This alternative position, combined with some degree of pessimism of resolving the issues in philosophy in general, appears to have been Popper's position prior to reading Tarski. He says:

> My attitude at the time was this: although I accepted, as almost everybody does, the objective or absolute or correspondence theory of truth – truth as correspondence with the facts – I preferred to avoid the topic. For it appeared to me hopeless to try to understand clearly this strangely elusive idea of correspondence between a statement and a fact.
>
> (Popper 1963: 223)

Thus the early Popper envisages good arguments against realism and, second, acknowledges that the realism/anti-realism debate in philosophy is peripheral to our concerns in the methodology of the sciences, including the methodology of economics.

All of this changed with his reading of Tarski. According to Popper 'only with Tarski's work has the suspicion been removed that the objective theory of truth as correspondence to the facts may be either self-contradictory (because of the paradox of the liar) or empty and redundant (as Ramsey suggested) or barren, or at the very least redundant in the sense that we can do without it' (Popper 1963: 225–6).[3] Tarski enabled us to see the difference between the search for objective knowledge and the search for powerful instruments. Powerful instruments 'are, in many cases, quite well served by theories which are known to be false' (Popper 1963: 226). Popper compares 'the status of truth in the objective sense and its role as a regulative principle' to 'a mountain peak usually wrapped in clouds'. While a climber may have difficulty in getting to such a peak and indeed, because of the existence of clouds, may not know he has arrived there rather than at a subsidiary peak, these do not prohibit him from recognising the objective existence of the summit. 'The very idea of error, or of doubt (in the normal straightforward sense) implies the idea of an objective truth which we may fail to reach' (Popper 1963: 226).

In short, for Popper, Tarski enables him to claim that 'our main concern in science and in philosophy is, or ought to be, the search for truth by way of bold conjectures and the critical search for what is false in our varying competing theories' (Popper 1972: 319). Indeed he directs us to an 'improved formulation' for the methodology of the physical sciences namely:

> But some of us … have reason to conjecture that Einstein's theory of gravity is *not true*, but that it is a *better approximation to truth* than Newton's. To be able to say such a thing with a good conscience seems to me a major desideratum of the methodology of the natural sciences.
>
> (Popper 1972: 335 italics in original)

Be that as it may, our present concern is with the centrality of the objective theory of truth to the methodology of any science, including the methodology of economics. This is a central pillar of Popper's realist reflection on the realism-economics nexus which he constructed from his reading of Tarski. Prior to this reading his position seems to have been one of a pragmatic division of labour between those concerned with realism on the one hand and those concerned with issues in methodology on the other.

Economics and Popper's logical realism

Thus far we have characterised Popper's realism in contrast with Mäki's version by reference to his reading of Tarski as a correspondence theorist of truth and how he maintains that realism saves us from irrationality. The question arises: how else does Popper characterise his realism? There are at least two other dimensions which are crucially relevant to Popperian methodology of economics, namely his 'realist view of logic' (Popper 1972: 304) and his 'thesis of the three worlds' (Popper 1972: 153). In *Objective Knowledge*, he explicitly states that his Three World Thesis is an integral part of his common sense realism (Popper 1972: 323, footnote 7). We will discuss his Three World Thesis in the next section, but here we turn to his realism in logic and how it affects the mathematical modelling of an economy.

If we look at the mathematical model of an economy used by Arrow, Debreu and others in developing general equilibrium theory, we see that their model is based on Cantorian, infinitist, set theory. They use the full resources of infinitist

Cantorian set theory in establishing their theorems of general equilibrium theory. Our thesis is that, if one accepts what Popper calls realism in logic then, in principle, there are no difficulties in using the full and powerful resources of Cantorian set theory in modelling an economy. However, if, contrary to Popper, one is an anti-realist in logic then one is in principle excluded from any such recourse to Cantorian infinitist set theory in modelling an economy. In other words the powerful mathematical tools of Cantorian infinitist set theory are not at the disposal of an anti-realist in logic in modelling an economy. Anti-realism limits recourse in mathematical modelling to what is called finitist, or more precisely, constructivist mathematics. In this way, a Popperian realist view of logic has implications for both economic methodology and economics. For a Popperian realist in logic, the use of Cantorian infinite set theory is in principle justifiable in mathematically modelling an economy and hence there is in principle no objection to the development of general equilibrium theory, whereas an anti-realist in logic is in principle opposed to any such development. Anti-realists will limit their mathematical modelling to finitist, constructivist mathematics.

The mathematisation of economics in the course of the twentieth century was initially dominated by recourse to calculus and later by recourse to Cantorian infinite set theory. However, mathematics in the course of the twentieth century also took a finitist or constructivist turn summed up in the work of Church, Post and Turing to mention but a few. This finitist development grew out of the failure of the Hilbert programme to consolidate Cantorian infinity. 'No one will drive us out of the paradise Cantor has created for us' (Hilbert 1926: 191). The finitist, constructivist programme, which developed as a result of the collapse of the Hilbert programme could be summed up by saying that it has removed any and every temptation to ever enter into Cantor's paradise. Why then has theoretical economics ignored these finitist developments in mathematics?[4] In particular, why didn't Popper, as it were, see the potential for such a development? We maintained above that Popper's logical realism is the reason why he did not envisage the exploration of the resources of finitist mathematics in the construction of economic theory. Though fully aware of the developments of Brouwer, Church and Turing, Popper still retained his commitment to Cantorian infinitist mathematics and the basic reason for this is his realist reading of logic in light of his realist reading of Tarski.

Popper outlined his realist reading of logic in Chapter 8 of his *Objective Knowledge*. There he distinguished between 'two main uses of logic': (1) in mathematics and (2) in the empirical sciences. In the case of the empirical sciences, 'we want our criticism to be *severe*' and to attain this aim we should use 'the strongest logic', i.e. classical logic (Popper 1972: 305). If we were to use 'some weaker logic – say intuitionist logic, or some three-valued logic … then I assert we are not critical enough; it is a sign that there is something rotten in the state of Denmark' (Popper 1972: 305–6).

How are we to decipher this sign of rottenness? Popper clearly acknowledges the mathematical value of intuitionist logic. Its first advantage is 'it tries to prove as many mathematical theorems as possible with reduced logical means' (Popper

1972: 307), i.e. it can prove theorems with methods weaker than the full battery of classical logic. Second, although one can show that the law of the excluded middle is a well-formed formula in intuitionist logic, it is not demonstrable within the system. Third, intuitionist logic is 'an attempt to make more certain that our arguments are consistent and that we do not get into hidden inconsistencies or paradoxes or antinomies' (Popper 1972: 307). Thus Popper sums up his sympathies with intuitionist logic by saying 'if you wish to prove … you should use weak means'. However, our interests, especially in the sciences, are concerned with criticising, not proof. Moreover, and this is the crucial point for the (Popperian) rationalist, '*any* criticism is welcome' and 'this rationalist view is a realist view of logic' (Popper 1972: 307), which *ipso facto* includes classical, non-intuitionist logic.

In his homage to Brouwer, delivered at the Third International Congress for Logic, Methodology and Philosophy of Science in 1967, Popper suggested that we 'naively distinguish two main ways of being interested in mathematics' (Popper 1972: 133). The first puts the emphasis on theorems, – 'in the truth or falsity of mathematical propositions', which leads to a preoccupation with Platonistic objects – the things of which mathematical propositions are true. This approach culminates in Cantorian infinities of infinite sets. In the second approach, that advocated by Brouwer, the emphasis is on *proving* a theorem. In this approach 'to assert a theorem was to assert the existence of a (finite) proof for it' (Popper 1972: 133). This in turn leads to Brouwer's rejection of the principle of the excluded middle, to his rejection of *reductio ad absurdum* proofs for mathematical existence and its replacement by 'the demand that existence can only be proved by the actual construction' (Popper 1972: 133–4). In short, Brouwer, as a key intuitionist thinker, rejects Platonism in general and Cantorian, non-constructivist, infinities in particular.

Popper raises a number of objections to Brouwer. He rejects Brouwer's grounding of arithmetic in the (Kantian) intuition of time. Second, Popper espouses a Platonism *vis-à-vis* mathematics, where mathematics is autonomous and goes beyond Brouwerian constructivism. Moreover, intuitionism cannot adequately distinguish between a thesis and the evidence for a thesis: intuitionist logic 'results from *the conflation of evidence, or proof and the assertion to be proved*' (Popper 1972: 139 italics in original). Finally for Popper deduction involves '*the transmission of truth and the retransmission of falsity*: in a valid inference truth is transmitted from the premisses to the conclusion' and 'falsity is also retransmitted from the conclusion to (at least) one of the premisses' (Popper 1972: 304 italics in original). This realist reading of deduction implies or presupposes classical, two-valued logic, i.e. the realist bivalence assumption of just two truth values, namely the true and the false, which is core to Popper's reading of Tarski.

Certainly Popper has some good reasons for committing himself to classical logic and its corresponding realism. However, in line with the early Popper, let us suppose that the anti-realist can come up with good counter arguments. For instance, Dummett claims to have convincing reasons for anti-realism, especially the espousal of an intuitionist logic without the Brouwerian–Kantian overtones noted by Popper. How would such an anti-realist view the mathematical modelling of an economy along the lines of Arrow and Debreu? Because it is grounded in Cantorian infinitist set theory, the anti-realist will reject it. One could say that, while for Popper the realist theory of truth is a key regulative idea, i.e. 'the standard of which we fall short', a non-realist would reject this regulative idea and replace it with the Church-Turing thesis, which would limit mathematical modelling to the parameters of a Universal Turing machine and other finitist, constructivist means. In particular, a non-realist in logic would have to reconstruct theoretical economics without the notions of equilibrium and rationality as characterised in general equilibrium theory. Logical realism, as articulated by Popper, is indispensable to the correct understanding of equilibrium and rationality in the general equilibrium theory of Arrow and Debreu and others. If one rejects this realism, one moves into computable economics under the shadow of a Universal Turing machine where the notions of rationality and equilibrium as understood by Arrow and Debreu are no longer operational. In this non-realist economics, *homo economicus* is like Simon's bounded rational agent, with the Universal Turing machine as the limiting concept of such bounded rationality. In short, 'the realism-economics connection' does crucial, indispensable work for general equilibrium in its explication of rationality and equilibrium in terms of Cantor's set theory. If one is an anti-realist in the domain of logic, such mathematical models are excluded on philosophical, non-realist grounds. Cantor's paradise of infinite set theory grounded in what Popper calls logical realism is not at the disposal of anti-realists in constructing mathematical models of an economy. Thus what Popper calls logical realism is presupposed by general equilibrium theorists.

To sum up this section, we suggest, in line with the early Popper, that there are some good reasons for anti-realism in general. In particular, in adopting what Popper calls an anti-realist stance in logic, one is not a relativist and neither is one committed to 'the worst kind of complacency' (Mäki 2002: 102). Moreover, this kind of anti-realism, contrary to the early Popper, has crucial implications for economic practice, especially general equilibrium theory. This anti-realism prohibits the economist from recourse to Cantorian, infinite set theory in modelling a complex economic system: the methods used to prove the existence of an equilibrium by Debreu and others are not acceptable. On the contrary, the economist, on anti-realist grounds, will exploit the resources of finitist, computable economics in mathematically modelling a complex economic system. Far from being irrelevant, the realist/anti-realist debate in pure philosophy is crucial to the issue of how to mathematically model an economy.

Popper's realism, his Three Worlds and economics

As we already noted, Popper's realism is not confined to his reading of Tarski. It also includes his 'Thesis of the Three Worlds'. He introduces this thesis as follows:

> …without taking the words 'world' or 'universe' too seriously, we may distinguish the following three worlds or universes: first, the world of physical objects or of physical states; secondly, the world of states of consciousness or of mental states, or perhaps of behavioural dispositions to act; and thirdly the world of *objective contents of thought*, especially of scientific and poetic thoughts and of works of art.
>
> (Popper 1972: 106 italics in original)

He proceeds to inform us that among the constituents of the third world we find, 'theoretical systems', 'problems', 'problem situations', 'critical arguments', 'the contents of journals, books and libraries' (Popper 1972: 107). Popper is emphatic that this third world is distinct from the second world, the world of beliefs and other elements of human consciousness. In this respect Popper stands in a long line of realist philosophers ranging from Plato to Frege. Thus he sees himself in the line of those interpreters of Plato who hold that Plato's Forms or Ideas are different from bodies on the one hand and from ideas in the mind on the other. In this reading, Platonic Forms constituted 'an objective, autonomous third world which existed in addition to the physical world and the world of mind' (Popper 1972: 154). In this vein he also notes that his 'third world resembles most closely the universe of Frege's objective contents of thought' (Popper 1972: 106).

The relationship between these worlds is crucial for Popper. The second world, the world of subjective or personal experiences directly interacts with the first world; for instance, the human mind can see a physical body. Moreover, the second world also interacts with the third world; for instance it grasps arithmetical truths or theoretical statements. In this way the human mind is 'an organ for interacting with the objects of the third world; for understanding them, contributing to them, participating in them' (Popper 1972: 156). Finally, the second world brings the contents of the third world to bear on the first world. 'The first and the third world cannot interact save through the interaction of the second world' (Popper 1972: 155). In this way the third world of mathematics and scientific theories exerts an extraordinary influence on the physical world, i.e. the first world. This is a key to Popper's philosophy of technology. Technologists integrate the mathematics and science of the third world into their own individual minds and thereby effect dramatic change in the physical world.

For Popper the mistake of confusing world three with world two has a long history culminating in the erroneous view of knowledge as justified true belief. Rather for Popper scientific knowledge exists in the third world and this conjectural knowledge is centrally conveyed by language. Popper points out that language belongs to the three worlds. In so far as it consists of physical symbols or actions it belongs to the first world. In so far as it expresses a subjective or psychological state it belongs to the second world. In so far as it contains information or statements which either entail others or conflicts with others, it pertains to the third world. Thus Popper concludes, '*Theories, or propositions, or statements are the most important third-world linguistic entities*' (Popper 1972: 157 italics in original).

The third world is objective: its objects are open to critical scrutiny. Moreover, it is 'man-made' but it is also 'autonomous'. Popper sees his own originality in holding '*that it is possible to accept the reality or (as it may be called) the autonomy of the third world and at the same time to admit that the third world originates as a product of human activity*'(Popper 1972: 159 italics in original). For instance, if we look at developments in mathematics and the sciences, these developments are produced by different mathematicians and scientists over thousands of years. Yet this knowledge, presented through language and stored in books, libraries, computer banks, etc., has grown far beyond the grasp of any individual mind and each individual's contribution to this vast store of autonomous knowledge is 'vanishingly small' (Popper 1972: 161).

We now come to the realism-economics connection. Popper locates economics in his third world. It is a product of human individual minds, but it also transcends these minds: it is autonomous. From here it has 'tremendous effects' on the first world, mediated through the second. Popper takes this for granted and does not systematically develop this thesis. Having insisted on the impact of the third world on the first via the second, he asks us to think of the impact of electrical power transmission 'or the impact of economic theories on the decision whether to build a boat or an aeroplane' (Popper 1972: 159).

In the third world economics is not static: it exists in the dynamic Popperian quadruple of problem – tentative solution – error elimination – problem. However, Popper is well aware that frequently in the social sciences 'we know that we have to work with theories which are *at best* approximations – that is to say theories of which we actually know they cannot be true' (Popper 1963: 235 italics in original). Clearly the Rationality Principle falls into this category. It belongs to the autonomous third world and in this sense it is objective. Moreover, the Rationality Principle is an integral component in his modelling of the social sciences on the neo-classical theory of rationality. Once again, the neo-classical theory is objective, autonomous but 'we know that it cannot be true'. What then is its role? In the third world it plays the role of a regulative principle, i.e. an ideal from which we fall short in actual decision-making. In this sense, it is an objective, autonomous benchmark. Thus in his *Poverty of Historicism* he characterises his 'zero method' as 'the method of constructing a model on the assumption of complete rationality (and perhaps also on the assumption of the possession of complete information) on the part of all the individuals concerned, and of estimating the deviation of the actual behaviour of people from the model behaviour using the latter as a kind of zero co-ordinate' (Popper 1957: 141). In this way Popper's zero method can be recontextualised in his Three Worlds Thesis.

Our hypothesis is that Popper's Three Worlds Thesis is integral to his realism and the three worlds become for him an indispensable framework in which to locate the social sciences in general and economics in particular. To conclude, Mäki is correct to draw economic methodologists' attention to the realism-economics connection. Thus far we have attempted to re-engage Popper's reflections on economics in his own working out of his rich, but controversial, realist framework.

Popper's scientific realism and economics: from D-N explanation to models

Popper was not just concerned with realist debates in pure philosophy. He also developed his own specific and unique realist philosophy of science. We now turn to this realism, with a view to exploring the scientific realism – social sciences – economics connections. Popper developed his own version of scientific realism in the context of his famous demarcation criterion of science, namely falsifiability and his analysis of scientific methodology in terms of the deductive theory of testing. The realist themes evident in Popper's sophisticated, methodological falsificationism are both negative and positive. Like many scientific realists, he dissociates himself from any instrumentalist reading of science. Theoretical sentences for him are either true or false, though we may never know that they are true. Theories are not simply heuristic devices or inference tickets with no truth-value, so loved by instrumentalists. More particularly, Popper rejects the anti-metaphysical stance advocated by the logical positivists. As Popper puts it: 'The repeated attempts made by Rudolf Carnap to show that the demarcation between science and metaphysics coincides between sense and nonsense have failed' (Popper 1963: 253). In short, for Popper, 'non-testable (i.e. irrefutable) metaphysical theories may be rationally arguable' (Popper 1972: 40, footnote 9).

The version of scientific realism developed by Popper is anti-essentialist. In his *Logic of Scientific Discovery*, he portrays the aim of science as the elimination of false theories. Given that we can never know that we have attained the truth, one might imagine that Popper's realism would interrogate the realist notion of explanation. Indeed he does do this and his conclusion is to reject the realist notion of ultimate explanation by recourse to essences. Popper's fallibilism, especially his conjectural account of human knowledge, prohibits us from knowing the essences. Nevertheless, he retains the view that '*the scientist aims at finding a true theory or description of the world* (and especially of its regularities or 'laws'), *which shall also be an explanation of the observable facts*' (Popper 1963: 103 italics in original). What he calls essentialism he sums up as follows:

> *The best, the truly scientific theories, describe the 'essences' or the 'essential natures' of things – the realities which lie behind the appearances.* Such theories are neither in need nor susceptible of further explanation: they are ultimate explanations and to find them is the ultimate aim of the scientist.
>
> (Popper 1963: 104 italics in original)

Like instrumentalism, Popper rejects essentialism. However, unlike instrumentalism, he subscribes to the view that theories are either true or false and that they explain. Like the logical positivists, he rejects essentialism but, unlike the logical positivists, he does not banish explanation from science into the territory of meaningless metaphysics. Similarly, like van Fraassen's constructive empiricism, he rejects essentialism, but, unlike van Fraassen, he does not relegate explanation to the domain of pragmatics (van Fraassen 1980).

Popper wants to retain the notion of a 'hidden' mechanism without accepting the realist thesis that science can discover the ultimate, unobservable essences. Like the essentialist, Popper agrees that 'much is hidden from us and that much of what is hidden may be discovered' (Popper 1963: 105). However, the hidden which science discovers cannot be identified with the hidden essences. Thus the aim of science for Popper is not 'ultimate explanation'. In short, as Popper himself puts it, 'whether essences exist or not, the belief in them does not help us in any way and indeed is likely to hamper us; so that there is no reason why the scientist should *assume* their existence' (Popper 1963: 105 italics in original).

We are all aware of how Popper applies this anti-essentialism in his philosophy of the social sciences. It is not inaccurate to describe his *Poverty of Historicism* and his *Open Society* as his anti-essentialist reflections on the social sciences. Once again we see that Popper closely intertwines his scientific realism with his philosophy of the social sciences. In particular, Popper's position implies that the aim of economics as a science cannot be to unearth the ultimate hidden essences of an economy. Nonetheless, economics, as a science, can explain.

We have seen how Popper tells us what scientific explanation is not: it is not concerned with essences. In what sense then does science explain? For Popper science explains 'one or a small number of singular events' (Popper 1994: 162). For instance, in physics one wants to explain the lunar eclipse which occurred last month, or, in the social sciences, 'the rise in unemployment in the Midlands at a specific time'. Also in science we explain 'a certain *kind* or *type* of event' (Popper 1994: 163 italics in original). For instance, why do lunar eclipses occur again and again and only when there is a full moon? In economics one may ask 'why is there a seasonal increase and decrease of unemployment in the building industry?' (Popper 1994: 163). Despite this overlap of explanatory endeavours between the physical and the social sciences, 'the fundamental problem of both the theoretical and the historical social sciences is *to explain and understand events in terms of human actions and social situation*' (Popper 1994: 166 italics in original). Our thesis is that the realist context in which Popper locates human actions and social situations is his 'three worlds thesis'. Without the three worlds thesis we fail to fully understand Popper's analysis of human action. In this way Popper's scientific realism in the social sciences is inextricably linked to this three world thesis, and thereby to his general realism.

In connection with the explanation of individual events in physics, Popper is basically adopting what has come to be known as the D-N model of explanation. In this view, the event to be explained is deduced from a set of law-like statements and initial conditions. Thus we explain a particular lunar eclipse by recourse to Newton's Laws and a set of initial conditions specifying the masses, velocities, positions and diameters of the sun, earth and the moon together with the fact that the sun is the relevant source of light. However, in connection with the explanation of types or kinds of events, the history of the physical sciences draws our attention to the use of models. For instance, in response to the question why lunar eclipses occur again and again only when there is a full moon, we may construct a rough mechanical model. The model used may be a lamp (representing the sun) a small ball (representing the earth) moving in a circle around the lamp and a smaller ball (representing the moon) circulating the 'earth' ball. Despite the fact that the model may obtain its motion from a battery or human hand, rather than from Newton's Laws, 'it serves its purpose very well, since it solves the problem of explanation which has been posed' (Popper 1994: 163). In other words, it complies with the Popperian quadruple framework of problem – tentative solution – error elimination – problem. However, the 'lamp' model, by solving our first problem of explanation, still leaves us with another problem, 'how are the earth and the moon propelled in the real world?' (Popper 1994: 163). However, in light of his anti-essentialism, the explanatory quadruple framework will continue indefinitely. Nonetheless, we have succeeded in explaining in the sense of offering a (problem-laden) answer to the original 'why' question. Be that as it may, to return to the query of how are the earth and the moon in motion? We come again to Newton's Laws, but this time there is no reference to initial conditions. Popper's next move here is crucial. He maintains that in the case of the explanation of types of events 'initial conditions may be completely replaced by the construction of a model: this, one might say, incorporates *typical* initial conditions' (Popper 1994: 163–4). In short, in contrast to the explanation of a specific event where one must have recourse to laws and to initial or boundary conditions, the explanation of types or kinds of events uses 'models which represent something like *typical* initial conditions' (Popper 1994: 164, italics ours). However, as is clear from the example just discussed, the model on its own requires recourse to some 'animating laws' to show how the model works. In other words, in explaining a type of event, we don't have to focus on specific initial conditions. Rather we take, as it were, a typical situation and partially explain this by recourse to a model. However, to complete the explanation we must also introduce some animating principle or laws to show how the model works. In physics these animating principles are the laws or theories of physics. Moreover, in physics recourse to models 'ends and the purely abstract animating laws come in which govern the various parts or structures that constitute the model' (Popper 1994: 165).

This Popperian account of models in the physical sciences is rather incomplete. One can ask the question posed and answered by Black and others namely, are models 'props for feeble minds' in that they help us imagine the explanatory principles but may be eliminated and replaced by, in Popperian terms, 'the abstract animating laws?' Alternatively, are they indispensable ways of gaining scientific knowledge which cannot in principle be eliminated? Whatever Popper's answer may be to these questions, his thesis is that 'models are more important in the social sciences because the Newtonian method of explaining and predicting singular events by universal laws and initial conditions is hardly ever applicable in the theoretical social sciences' (Popper 1994: 165–6). Unlike the physical sciences, the theoretical social sciences 'almost always' have recourse to the construction of models. In other words in the social sciences we almost always turn the specific event into a typical or representative situation.

This thesis of the centrality of models to the social sciences is *prima facie* plausible, especially given Popper's general characterisation of the explanation of events in the social sciences, namely one explains an event 'in terms of human actions and social situations' (Popper 1994: 166). It is impossible to describe in a complete way a specific social situation. Rather we 'reconstruct' it in terms of a typical social situation and our social scientific models are descriptions of this reconstruction. Whether or not models are indispensable in the physical sciences, they are, for the most part, indispensable for the social sciences. In this unique way Popper works out his realist notion of explanation for the social sciences. Moreover, in our opinion, much of the contemporary discussion of models in economics, ranging from Mäki to McCloskey, could benefit from re-engaging Popper's stimulating account of models in the social sciences.

We have seen that models on their own are not sufficient. They must be complemented by some 'animating principle'. In the case of physics these animating principles will come from Newtonian, Einsteinian or Quantum physics. In the case of the social sciences, the animating principle is the famous 'rationality principle'. In other words explanation in the social sciences has two indispensable elements, namely models and the rationality principle. As we have already noted, much has been written about the rationality principle and indeed it is re-engaged in some of the other chapters in this volume. Our point here is that it is combined with a model, in the Popperian analysis of social explanation. He calls this explanatory process situational analysis.

We have seen that Popper qualifies his account of situational analysis with terms like 'almost always' or 'for the most part'. This seems to imply that there could be some notable exceptions. Indeed there are. For instance, Historicist explanations do not adhere to the methodology of situational analysis. However, such Historicist explanations are rejected by Popper. Rather our question is: are there, in Popper's eyes, genuine explanations in the social sciences, which fall outside the scope of situational analysis? If so, perhaps economics could be one such exception?

Popper, however, though brief, does not think that economics is such an exception:

> To take a familiar example, the most important part of classical economic theory is the theory of perfect competition. It may be developed as the situational logic of an idealised or over-simplified social situation – the situation of people acting within the institutional framework of a perfectly free market in which buyers and sellers are equally informed of the physical qualities of the goods that are bought or sold.
>
> (Popper 1994: 170)

Clearly Popper is here defending neo-classical economics as an authentic piece of situational logic. In terms of his three worlds thesis, neo-classical economics, as an idealised account of rational agents operating in a perfectly free market, is firmly located in the objective, autonomous third world. What needs to be explored is its role in the third world. As we have already seen, it is an ideal benchmark against which specific actions can be measured to see how far they deviate from this ideal. In short, Popper locates neo-classical economics as an idealised, autonomous account of rational action in his objective, autonomous third world where it is understood as a central piece of situational analysis which acts as a benchmark against which we can measure how far the economic actions of second world economic agents acting in the first world (already effected by other actions by other second-world agents) deviate from this ideal of rationality.

To conclude, one is surely struck by the extended view of realism in general, and scientific realism in particular, developed by Popper in contrast to 'the weak conception' of realism used by Mäki to engage the realism-economics nexus. In the course of this chapter we have given a brief, schematic, view of the complex and engaging way Popper has merged his realism both general and scientific with his philosophy of the social sciences, including economics. We are not claiming that this Popperian synthesis is without difficulties. Rather we are attempting to give the reader a deeper appreciation of how Popper's realist philosophy coloured his philosophy of the social sciences, including economics.

These Popperian themes are further analysed, explicated, evaluated and criticised in the following chapters from both realist and anti-realist perspectives. In this chapter our aim was to elucidate, not to evaluate. The remaining chapters are principally concerned with the task of evaluating. As pointed out in the introduction, the evaluations here are carried out in the non-dogmatic spirit of Socrates so much appreciated by Popper.

Notes

1 These writings are examined in Chapter 3 of this volume.
2 In an address to a Symposium in Honour of Alfred Tarki on the occasion of his seventieth birthday, held at the University of California, June 1971, and subsequently published as Chapter 9 of his *Objective Knowledge*, Popper gives a slightly different account. Nonetheless he admits his 'uneasiness' with the notion of truth as correspondence which 'had been for some time attacked by some philosophers, and with good arguments', and especially the view 'that if we wish to speak of truth, we should be able to give a criterion of truth' (Popper 1972: 320).
3 Popper correctly points out that this is his own reading of Tarski in the context of his own (Popper's) commitment to 'common sense realism' (Popper 1972: 323). Popper acknowledges 'I never found out precisely what Tarski's attitude to realism was' (ibid.: 323).
4 This was the perceptive and searching comment made by Vela Velupillai at the Symposium on Popper in Galway, in September 2002. This section of the chapter was motivated by our attempt to engage this intriguing and fundamental issue. Velupillai's pioneering work in mathematical economics, in particular his work on computable mathematics and economics represents one of the most innovative and creative applications of constructivist mathematics to theoretical economics (Velupillai 2000).

References

Backhouse, R. (ed.) (1994) *New Directions in Economic Methodology*, London: Routledge.

Benacerraf, P. and Putnam, H. (eds) (1983) *Philosophy of Mathematics*, 2nd edn, Cambridge: Cambridge University Press.

Blaug, M. (1980a) *The Methodology of Economics* (2nd edn 1992), Cambridge: Cambridge University Press.

—— (1980b) *A Methodological Appraisal of Marxian Economics*, Amsterdam: North-Holland.

—— (1984) 'Comment on Hutchison: our methodological crisis', in P. Wiles and G. Routh (eds) *Economics in Disarray*, Oxford: Basil Blackwell.

—— (1994a) 'Not only an economist – autobiographical reflections of a historian of economic thought', *The American Economist*, 38: 12–27.

Boland, L. (1977) 'Testability in economic science', *South African Journal of Economics* 45: 93–105.

—— (1982) *The Foundations of Economic Method*, London: Allen and Unwin.

—— (1986) *Methodology for a New Microeconomics*, London: Allen and Unwin.

—— (1989) *Methodology of Economic Model Building*, London: Routledge.

—— (1991) 'The theory and practice of economic methodology', *Methodus*, 3: 6–17.

—— (1994) 'Scientific thinking without scientific method: two views of Popper', in R. Backhouse (ed.) *New Directions in Economic Methodology*, London: Routledge.

—— (1997) *Critical Economic Methodology: A Personal Odyssey*, London: Routledge.

Boylan, T.A. and O'Gorman, P.F. (1995) *Beyond Rhetoric and Realism in Economics: Towards a Reformulation of Economic Methodology*, London: Routledge.

Caldwell, B.J. (1981) 'Book review: Blaug's *The Methodology of Economics*', *Southern Economic Journal*, 14: 489–95.

—— (1982) *Beyond Positivism: Economic Methodology in the Twentieth Century* (2nd edn 1994), London: Allen and Unwin.

—— (1984) 'Some problems with falsification in economics', *Philosophy of the Social Sciences*, 14: 489–95.

—— (1985) 'Some reflections on *Beyond Positivism*', *Journal of Economic Issues*, 19: 187–94.

—— (1986) 'Towards a broader conception of criticism', *History of Political Economy*, 18: 675–81.

—— (1991) 'Clarifying Popper', *Journal of Economic Literature*, 24: 1–33.

—— (1992a) 'Hayek and falsificationist?: a refutation', *Research in the History of Economic Thought and Methodology*, 10: 1–15.

—— (1992b) 'Hayek the falsificationist: reply to Hutchison', *Research in the History of Economic Thought and Methodology*, 10: 33–42.

—— (1994) 'Two proposals for the recovery of economic practice', in R. Backhouse (ed.) *New Directions in Economic Methodology*, London: Routledge.

—— (1998) 'Hutchison, Terence W.', in J.B. Davis, D.W. Hands and W. Mäki (eds) *The Handbook of Economic Methodology*, Cheltenham: Edward Elgar.

Coats, A.W. (1983) 'Half a century of methodological controversy in economics as reflected in the writings of T.W. Hutchison', in A.W. Coats (ed.) *Methodological Controversy in Economics: Historical Essays in Honour of T.W. Hutchison*, Greenwich, CT: JAI Press.

Coddington, A. (1975) 'The rationale of general equilibrium economics', *Economic Inquiry*, 13: 539–58.

Cross, R. (1982) 'The Duhem-Quine thesis, Lakatos and the appraisal of theories in macroeconomics', *Economic Journal*, 92: 320–40.

—— (1984) 'Monetarism and Duhem's thesis', in P. Wiles and G. Routh (eds) *Economics in Disarray*, Oxford: Basil Blackwell.

De Marchi, N. (ed.) (1988) *The Popperian Legacy in Economics*, Cambridge: Cambridge University Press.

Hands, D. Wade (1979) 'The methodology of economic research programmes', *Philosophy of the Social Sciences*, 9: 293–303. Reprinted in Hands (1993).

—— (1984) 'Blaug's economic methodology', *Philosophy of the Social Sciences*, 14: 115–25. Reprinted in Hands (1993).

—— (1991a) 'Popper, the rationality principle and economic explanation', in G.K. Shaw (ed.) *Economics, Culture and Education: Essays in Honour of Mark Blaug*, Aldershot: Edward Elgar.

—— (1991b) 'The problem of excess content: economics, novelty, and a long Popperian tale', in M. Blaug and N. de Marchi (eds) *Appraising Economic Theories: Studies in the Methodology of Scientific Research Programmes*, Aldershot: Edward Elgar.

—— (1992) 'Falsification, situational analysis, and scientific research programmes: the Popperian tradition in economic methodology', in N. De Marchi (ed.) *Post-Popperian Methodology of Economics*, Boston: Kluwer. Reprinted in Hands (1993).

—— (1993) *Testing, Rationality, and Progress: Essays on the Popperian Tradition in Economic Methodology*, Lanham, MD: Rowman and Littlefield.

—— (2001) *Reflections without Rules: Economic Methodology and Contemporary Science Theory,* Cambridge: Cambridge University Press.

Hausman, D.M. (1985) 'Is falsification unpractised or unpractisable?', *Philosophy of the Social Sciences*, 15: 313–19.

—— (1988) 'An appraisal of Popperian economic methodology', in N. De Marchi (ed.) *The Popperian Legacy in Economics*, Cambridge: Cambridge University Press.

—— (1992) *The Inexact and Separate Science of Economics*, Cambridge: Cambridge University Press.

—— (1996) 'Economics as separate and inexact', *Economics and Philosophy*, 12: 207–20.

Hilbert, D. (1926) 'Uber das Unendliche', *Mathematische Annalen*, 95: 161–90. Reprinted as 'On the Infinite', in Benacerraf and Putnam (1983).

Hutchison, T.W. (1938) *The Significance and Basic Postulates of Economic Theory*, London: Macmillan.

—— (1976) 'On the history and philosophy of science and economics', in S. Latsis (ed.) *Method and Appraisal in Economics*, Cambridge: Cambridge University Press.

—— (1977) *Knowledge and Ignorance in Economics*, Oxford: Basil Blackwell.

—— (1978) *On Revolution and Progress in Economic Knowledge*, Cambridge: Cambridge University Press.

—— (1981) *The Politics and Philosophy of Economics: Marxians, Keynesians, and Austrians*, Oxford: Basil Blackwell.

—— (1988) 'The case for falsificationism', in N. de Marchi (ed.) *The Popperian Legacy in Economics*, Cambridge: Cambridge University Press.

—— (2000) *On the Methodology of Economics and the Formalist Revolution*, Cheltenham: Edward Elgar.

Klant, J. (1984) *The Rules of the Game: The Logical Structure of Economic Theories*, trans. I. Swart, Cambridge: Cambridge University Press.

Klappholz, K. and Agassi, K. (1959) 'Methodological Prescription in Economics', *Economica*, 26: 60–74.

Lakatos, I. (1970) 'Falsification and the methodology of scientific research programmes', in I. Lakatos and A. Musgrave (eds) *Criticism and the Growth of Knowledge*, Cambridge: Cambridge University Press.

Latsis, S.J. (1972) 'Situational determinism in economics', *British Journal for the Philosophy of Science*, 23: 207–45.

—— (ed.) (1976) *Method and Appraisal in Economics*, Cambridge: Cambridge University Press.

—— (1983) 'The role and status of the rationality principle in the social sciences', in R.S. Cohen and M.M. Wartofsky (eds) *Epistemology, Methodology, and the Social Science*, Dordrecht: D. Reidel.

Machlup, F. (1955) 'The problem of verification in economics', *Southern Economic Journal*, 22: 1–21.

Mäki, U. (ed.) (2002) *Fact and Fiction in Economics*, Cambridge: Cambridge University Press.

Melitz, J. (1965) 'Friedman and Machlup on the significance of testing economic assumptions', *Journal of Political Economy*, 73: 37–60.

Papandeou, A.G. (1958) *Economics as a Science*, Chicago, IL: Lippincott.

Passmore, J. (1967) 'Logical positivism', in *The Encyclopaedia of Philosophy*, 5: 52–7, London and New York: The Macmillan Company and the Free Press.

—— (1968) *A Hundred Years of Philosophy*, Harmondsworth: Penguin Books.

Popper, K. (1945) *The Open Society and its Enemies*, 2 vols, London: Routledge and Kegan Paul.

—— (1957) *The Poverty of Historicism*, London: Routledge and Kegan Paul.

—— (1959) *The Logic of Scientific Discovery*, London: Hutchison.

—— (1963) *Conjectures and Refutations*, London: Routledge and Kegan Paul.

—— (1972) *Objective Knowledge: An Evolutionary Approach*, Oxford: Clarendon Press.

—— (1976) *Unended Quest: An Intellectual Biography*, London: Fontana.

—— (1982) *Quantum Theory and the Schism in Physics*, vol. 3 of the postscript to *The Logic of Scientific Discovery*, W.W. Bartley III (ed.), Totowa, NJ: Ronman and Littlefield.

—— (1983a) *Realism and the Aim of Science*, London: Routledge.

—— (1983b) 'The Rationality Principle', in D. Millar (ed.) *A Pocket Popper*, Oxford: Fontana Paperbacks.

—— (1994) *The Myth of the Framework: In Defence of Science and Rationality*, London: Routledge.

Redman, D. (1991) *Economics and the Philosophy of Science*, Cambridge, MA: MIT Press.

Robbins, L. (1979) 'On Latsis' *Method and Appraisal in Economics:* A Review Essay', *Journal of Economic Literature*, 17: 996–1004.

Rorty, R. (2005) 'How many gains make a heap?', *London Review of Books*, 20 January 12–13.

Salanti, A. (1987) 'Falsificationism and fallibilism as epistemic foundations of economics: a critical view', *Kyklos*, 40: 368–92.

Van Fraassen, B. (1980) *The Scientific Image*, Oxford: Clarendon Press.

Velupillai, K. (2000) *Computable Economics*, Oxford: Oxford University Press.

2 Situational analysis and Popper's Three World Thesis

The quest for understanding

Paschal F. O'Gorman

Introduction

When we look at Popper's writings, which extend over six decades of the twentieth century, we see a vast, complex and engaging tapestry. His reflections on the physical sciences, ranging from the pre-Socratics to relativity theory and quantum physics is integrally and extensively woven through this philosophical tapestry. In this connection, whether we agree or not, we can all admire his elaborate, coherent, well developed philosophy of the physical sciences centred on problem solving and the deductive testing of theories conceived as bold conjectures which must be falsifiable. Also woven through this tapestry we see his later reflections on metaphysics, with the emphasis on non-provable, non-falsifiable but arguable positions. However, these reflections on metaphysics are neither as extensively nor as systematically elaborated as his reflections on physics. Nonetheless his case for the arguability of a metaphysical position is evident in his own metaphysical commitment to realism in the context of his presentation of the realism–idealism debate.[1]

Our concern is this chapter is with Popper's reflections on the methodology of the social sciences, which are also not as extensive/systematic as his reflections on physics, and how these reflections are woven into his philosophical framework. According to Popper, the social sciences, which include anthropology, economics, history and sociology, in so far as they practise situational analysis, are woven into the scientific, rather than the metaphysical, sector of his framework. In other words, in so far as social disciplines use situational analysis, which is the only legitimate method for any social science, they are genuine sciences.

However, according to some commentators, Popper's weaving of situational analysis (SA) into science is seriously flawed. As Wade Hands recently puts it:

> One obvious difficulty with SA explanations is that they are extremely hard to reconcile with falsificationism; social science based on SA … does not seem to be "science" at all on the basis of Popper's own (falsificationist) demarcation criterion.
>
> (Hands 2001: 284)

Our thesis is that, while it may be difficult to reconcile Popper's SA with his falsificationsim, when we see how Popper responded to the so-called Duhem-Quine thesis, in conjunction with his notion of a model, a reconciliation is possible.

Having placed models at the core of Popperian situational analysis, we proceed to re-engage his situational analysis in light of what he himself identified as a significant development in his later philosophical reflections, namely his Three Worlds Thesis. In this connection Popperian models are third world entities which, in comparison with physics, have low degrees of testability. We argue that this development has no adverse effects for the Popperian thesis of piecemeal engineering. However, the same is not the case for his thesis of methodological individualism. Our hypothesis is that a Popperian third world analysis implies a qualified methodological individualism which is opposed to individualistic reductionism, i.e. to the thesis that any and every reference to social structures must be eliminated and replaced by statements about the actions of individuals. Social structures, compatible with Popperian qualified methodological individualism, are real and subsist in Popper's third world.

The shift to Popper's Three Worlds Thesis, with his emphasis on the third world, also has major implications for those advocating a hermeneutical approach to economic methodology.[2] Popper and hermeneutics share a colonial expansionist policy *vis-à-vis* the social sciences, namely there is one and only one method to be used. They differ, however, in the specification of the method to be used. According to Popper the only method is that of situational analysis whereas, for hermeneutics, the only method is one of achieving understanding, based on the model of the interpretation of a foreign text, as found in the hermeneutical tradition from Dilthey to Gadamer.

In this connection we show how Popper's situational analysis, when located in his third world, rejected some of the central tenets of classical hermeneutics. Despite this, it has much in common with those advocating a contemporary hermeneutical approach to the methodology of the social sciences in general and economic methodology in particular. We identify a number of common themes to Popperian situational analysis and contemporary hermeneutics, including a shared antipathy to both a positivist approach to methodology and to foundational epistemologies used in justifying spurious methodologies. We suggest that those advocating a hermeneutical approach to economic methodology do not appreciate Popper's anti-positivist approach. In particular, we distinguish between economic methodology and the history of economic thought. We attempt to show how situational analysis, when separated from its colonial expansionist moorings, could fruitfully complement a hermeneutical approach to the history of economic thought, especially the study of canonical texts (provided hermeneutics too severs its own connections to its colonialist expansionist moorings). In the domain of economic methodology in some respects situational analysis has advantages over hermeneutics – for instance, it is not impressed with the core methodological thesis that an economy is a text. In other respects hermeneutics, especially as articulated by Ricoeur, has advantages over situational analysis – for instance the issue of ideology is re-engaged in a way which avoids the Popperian polemic against Marx, while simultaneously avoiding a pro-Marxist polemic.

Problem solving as the generic core of all science

The Popperian legacy in economic methodology is far from being uniform. Broadly speaking it can be divided along three dimensions. First there exists the Popperian falsificationist approach which prescribes that economics as a science must be falsifiable. Next, arising out the first, there is the Lakatosian research programme approach which views economics as having a hard core surrounded by a protective belt, where the research programme can either progress or degenerate. Third, and more recently, an extensive literature exists on Popperian situational analysis, where the Popperian rationality principle is of central concern. As we already noted much attention has focused on the tension which allegedly exists between the first and third approach. As Caldwell puts it:

> Depending on how one defines the rationality principle, if one accepts the tenets of falsificationism, then economics and other social sciences are either not sciences or ad hoc or follow a method radically different from the method alleged to be followed in all the sciences.
>
> (Caldwell 1991: 27–8)

Caldwell's solution to this 'dilemma' is to posit, in line with Popper's own writings, a 'broader conception of scientific practice' than that of falsificationism, namely critical rationalism (Caldwell 1991: 22). The advantage of this solution is that critical rationalism, with it focus on 'being criticizable' (Popper 1983: 7), allows one to move from falsificationism to situational analysis and vice versa depending on the context. The generic scientific commitment is to criticisability and after that the context deems whether falsificationism or situational analysis is the most appropriate.

Our thesis is in the spirit, rather than the letter, of Caldwell's solution. Our starting point is with Popper's anti-inductivism, which is central to his philosophy of the physical sciences. According to Popper the physical sciences, contrary to the inductivists, do not start with observations. Rather the physical sciences start with problems. This gives rise to Popper's famous quadruple, namely P_1 – TS – EE – P_2.[3] Given a specific problem, the scientist constructs a tentative solution (TS). This tentative solution if successful, leads to error elimination (EE). However, because our knowledge is conjectural, the tentative solution invariably gives rise to novel problems, P_2, and now the quadruple process is once again reiterated.

This according to Popper holds also for the social sciences. Moreover, Popper is correct in pointing out that this is central to his early views on the social sciences. Thus in the *Poverty of Historicism,* when discussing pre-scientific and scientific experimental approaches, we read:

> Both approaches may be described, fundamentally, as utilizing the method of trial and error. We try; that is we do not merely register an observation but make active attempts to solve some more or less practical and definite problems. And we make progress if, and only if, we are prepared to *learn from our mistakes*: to recognise our errors and to utilise them critically instead of persevering in them dogmatically. Though this analysis may sound trivial, it describes, I believe, the method of all empirical sciences … And this formula covers not only the method of experiment, but also the relationship between theory and experiment.
>
> (Popper 1957: 87 italics in original)

In our reading the quadruple $P_1 - TS - EE - P_2$ may be seen as articulating the method of trial and error and this quadruple is an indispensable part of the core of Popper's critical rationalism. Moreover, according to Popper, the quadruple applies right across living organisms. In his own words it applies to an amoeba and to Einstein. The difference between an amoeba and Einstein, according to Popper, lies 'in their attitudes towards error. Einstein, unlike the amoeba, consciously tries his best, whenever a new solution occurred to him, to fault it and detect an error in it: he approached his own solutions *critically*' (Popper 1972: 247, italics in original). Finally, as seen from the *Poverty of Historicism*, a crucial contrast is between being consciously critical rather than being dogmatic.[4] All science is characterised by being prepared to learn from mistakes. In this view all scientific knowledge is conjectural and is open to the recognition of errors and efforts at eliminating these errors.

Critical problem solving we take to be the generic core of Caldwell's interpretation of critical rationalism. Caldwell, however, goes further. He insists that, depending on the context, the quadruple can go in divergent directions, namely in the case of the physical sciences down the road of falsificationism based on the deductive testing of theories and, in the case of the social sciences, down the different road of situational analysis.[5] We now turn to this controversial claim.

Models and situational analysis

In our reading of Caldwell, many economic methodologists mistakenly identified the generic core of scientific method with falsificationism.[6] Rather the generic core of scientific methodology is conveyed by his critical problem-solving quadruple. This quadruple takes on the specific form of falsificationism when problems emerge in the physical sciences. $P_1 - TS - EE - P_2$ in physics means the construction of bold conjectural theories to solve the initial problem. These theories are, in conjunction with given initial conditions, logically exploited by deducing a range of consequences. Finally these consequences are experimentally tested. If the theory passes the test it is corroborated and in turn the theory gives rise to new problems. If the theory is falsified we must try a different tentative solution to the original problem. In short the spirit of falsificationism dominates or should dominate in the physical sciences.[7]

In the social sciences the situation is different. According to Popper:

> The fundamental problem of both the theoretical and historical social sciences is *to explain and understand events in terms of human actions and social situations*. The key term here is '*social situation*'.
>
> The description of a concrete historical *social situation* is what corresponds in the *social sciences* to a statement of *initial conditions* in the natural sciences. And the 'models' of the theoretical social sciences are essentially descriptions or reconstructions of *typical social situations*.
>
> (Popper 1994: 166 italics in original)

Thus in the social sciences models are crucially important.[8] However, one must distinguish explanation via models, from the D-N account of explanation used in connection with the explanation of a specific event in the physical sciences. The D-N account consists of the specification of the relevant laws and the initial conditions. In the social sciences, models do not specify laws. Neither do they describe initial conditions. Rather a model is a description of 'a typical case rather than a singular case' (Popper 1994: 168). The model as it were turns the individual 'into "anybody" who may share the relevant situation', with specific relevant aims, and focuses on the typical agent's knowledge which is also relevant to the situation (ibid.). The model will also make reference to those physical things and their properties which are relevant to the situation. Finally, it will also make reference to the relevant social institutions.

A model on its own, however, does not give us the full explanation. Just as mechanical models in physics require the indispensable use of Newtonian or some other laws to satisfy our explanatory requirements, in the social sciences there is an analogous 'animating' principle. This is the famous Popperian rationality principle. This principle is 'the assumption that the various persons or agents involved act *adequately* or *appropriately* that is to say, in accordance with the situation' (Popper 1994: 169).[9] Thus explanation in the social sciences has two indispensable elements, namely models of the typical, representative situation and the rationality principle.

Popper's 'standard example' of situational analysis is Richard, a pedestrian, who wants to catch a train and is in a hurry to cross a crowded road with moving vehicles and also cars parked along the kerb. The task is to explain Richard's rather erratic movements while crossing the road. To explain his movements we construct a model of the situation. The model will include the relevant physical objects and their properties, e.g. the parked cars, which impose some limits on Richard's movements. Here we choose the relevant factors, e.g. the make of engine in a parked car is not relevant. The model will also identify the social institutions relevant to the situation, such as the relevant rules of the road, traffic signals and so on. To complete the model we attribute a specific aim to Richard, i.e. to cross the road, not catch a train, and we also attribute to him the relevant knowledge, such as his capacity to understand traffic signals. In this connection Popper is at pains to be consistent with his anti-psychologism. The model is not concerned with what

Richard actually had in mind while crossing the road: he may have been thinking about Fermat's last theorem! Rather in the model we 'replaced Richard's concrete conscious or unconscious psychological experiences by some abstract and typical situational elements, such as those we dubbed "aims" and "knowledge"' (Popper 1994: 169). In short the model transforms the singular case of Richard into a typical case: it turns Richard into 'anybody' who shares the relevant situation. To complete the explanation we now add the rationality principle, namely the pedestrian acted adequately to the situation, i.e. in accordance with the situation.

Much of the debate on situational analysis has focused on Popper's claim that the rationality principle is not falsifiable.[10] Our concern here is with the degree to which situational analysis is compatible with Popper's falsificationism. According to Popper there is no incompatibility. To show this we identify Popper's response to what we today call the Duhem-Quine thesis:

> Now if a theory is tested and found faulty, then we have always to decide which of its various constituent parts we shall make accountable for its failure. My thesis is that is it a *sound methodological policy* to decide not to make the rationality principle but, the rest of the theory – that is, the model – accountable.
>
> (Popper 1994: 177 italics in original)

In other words, according to Popper, situational models are in principle testable. Their testability, in our view, concerns at least three factors. First, testability concerns the accuracy of the model's description of the relevant physical factors: this will include the justification of the relevancy of the physical factors chosen. Second, testability concerns the accuracy of the model's description of the relevant institutional factors. Finally, testability will concern the accuracy of the description of the knowledge base attributed to the representative agent. In light of these parameters one can in principle specify which of two (or more) competing models is the better.

In this fashion Popper renders situational analysis compatible with falsificationism, without falling into inconsistency. Contrary to Caldwell, situational analysis, according to Popper, does not in principle bring the quadruple P_1 – TS – EE – P_2 down an alternative route to falsificationism. In short any explanation in the social sciences consists of a model and the rationality principle, and this whole is in principle testable. However, since the rationality principle will be common to competing explanations in the social sciences, it is a sound methodological policy to let the competing models take the brunt of the testing.

In our view there is yet another dimension to Popperian situational analysis, namely what he calls 'the zero method'. This concerns the evaluation of the rationality of the actions of the specific agent. This basically consists of two steps. First, we describe the specific agents' actions in the given situation and we compare this to the best model chosen in light of the parameters outlined above. Second, the degree to which the agent's actions conform to the model is the degree of rationality of the agent's actions.

Popper's narrative, however, does not stop here. He concedes that in the social sciences the tests of a model 'are not easily obtainable and are usually not very clear-cut' (Popper 1994: 170).[11] Social science models 'are always and necessarily rough and schematic over-simplifications' which leaves us with 'a comparatively low degree of testability' (ibid.).[12] In short the degree of testability in the physical sciences is, on the whole, much higher than the low degree which pertains in the social sciences, whereas testability does not apply at all in metaphysics. However, Popper is optimistic that within the social sciences we can still rank order, according to the criteria outlined above (in the third last paragraph), the better explanations, despite the fact that these, relative to the standards of physics, have low testability. We address some implications of this low degree of testability in the next section.

Practical problems, piecemeal engineering and Popper's three worlds

According to Popper some problems in the social sciences have their origins in practical problems. He gives the example of the practical problem of combating poverty. This problem leads on to:

> the purely theoretical problem 'Why are people poor?' and from there to the theory of wages and prices, and so on – in other words to pure economic theory, which of course constantly creates its own new theoretical problems. In the development of the theory, the problems dealt with – and especially the unsolved problems – multiply, and they become differentiated, as they always do when our knowledge grows.
>
> (Popper 1994: 176–7)

Clearly the focus here has quickly shifted to theoretical problems. Nonetheless, agents still also have to act in the social world . In light of Popper's own example, policies must be drawn up on a rational basis and implemented to combat poverty. In this section we will explicate Popper's account of rational action in the practical sphere in terms of his Three World Thesis which, according to Popper, 'plays such a role in the philosophy of my old age' (Popper 1976: 60). This explication will illuminate the Popperian limitation of social action to piecemeal social engineering.

As is well known, Popper distinguishes between the first world, which is the physical world or the world of physical states; the second world, i.e. the world of mental states; and the third world, which:

> is the world of intelligibles or of *ideas in the objective sense*; it is the world of possible objects of thought: the world of theories in themselves and their logical relations; of arguments in themselves; and of problem situations in themselves.[13]
>
> (Popper 1972: 154)

What is of crucial importance to Popper is that World 3 , though manmade, is both objective and autonomous. Moreover, while World 2 can interact with both World 1 and World 3, World 3 and World 1 can only interact through the intervention of World 2.

According to Popper the third world of mathematics and scientific theories 'exerts an immense influence upon the first world' especially through technology (Popper 1972: 155). This influence is always mediated through the second world. Moreover, Popper's 'main thesis' about the second world is that 'almost all our subjective knowledge (World 2 knowledge) depends upon World 3, that is to say on (at least virtually) *linguistically formulated* theories … I propose the thesis that *full consciousness of self* depends upon all these (World 3) theories' (Popper 1972: 74, italics in original). Contrary to numerous philosophical traditions which give priority to subjective accounts of World 2 in terms of private mental entities, Popper views World 2 through the *linguistically* enunciated parameters of the appropriate theories of World 3. In short, for Popper, World 3, though manmade, is autonomous and the relevant psychological parameters of World 2 depend upon World 3 theories.

How does this apply to the rationality of the actions of those agents in the social world directed at immediate, demanding, practical problems? First, a number of approaches are ruled out by Popper as irrational. In particular, any approach based on dogmatism is irrational. Here, dogmatism includes that form of essentialism which postulates that humans can know the essence of anything either physical or social. Rather all relevant third world knowledge is conjectural and fallible. This anti-essentialism rules out holistic solutions on the one hand and dictatorial ones on the other. Holisitic and dictatorial solutions share an erroneous commitment to dogmatic essentialism.

Second, a theory of practical rationality must be compatible with the Popperian principle of rationality, i.e. the agent must act appropriate to her/his position. In terms of his Three Worlds, we take this to mean that agents, governed by World 2, engage their pressing, practical problems by recourse to the relevant scientific theories, physical or social, which have an autonomous existence in World 3. According to Popper this is clearly evident in the success of the major technological advances of the twentieth century. Technologists solve their practical problems from World 1 by recourse to contemporary, fallible but testable theories of World 3. Moreover, these practical solutions are not ideal: they are subject to the limitations of Popper's problem solving quadruple.

When dealing with the urgent practical problems in the social realm, much the same applies to rational agents. They will engage these problems in light of relevant third world models which, like technology in the physical, biological and informational systems, are conjectural and fallible. However, unlike physics, the theories or models used will frequently have a low degree of testability. Thus social engineering, unlike physical engineering, is based on knowledge which has on the whole a low degree of testability. In light of this we might say that, for Popper, it is better to act on theories with low testability rather than acting on dogmatic positions which are not at all testable. The best the World 2 agents can do in the social realm is to act on these conjectural, fallible theories with low testability. This, as it were, is the human predicament of the rational social agent. Once agents realise this, they will rationally avoid large scale, holistic solutions or, if they do not, given our knowledge limitations in the social realm, their holistic solutions will inevitably collapse into piecemeal engineering ones which in turn are indispensably embedded in the 'logic' of Popper's problem-solving quadruple. In short, in the language of neoclassical economics, rational action directed at pressing social problems is, on Popperian analysis, limited to marginal adjustments. In this fashion we maintain that Popper's Three World Thesis has no adverse effects on his thesis of social engineering. On the contrary it buttresses his earlier articulation of this position.

Methodological individualism in Popper's three worlds

As Wade Hands points out methodological individualism is a common position in philosophy of economics. It is frequently associated with J.S. Mill, Robbins, von Mises, Hayek and Popper. Moreover, Hands is also correct in pointing out that philosophy 'is replete with numerous specific versions of methodological individualism' (Hands 2001: 43). Nonetheless, in our opinion, Giddens is correct in maintaining that methodological individualism is frequently seen as 'a natural enemy' to any recourse to social structures in the social sciences (Giddens 1984: 213). Giddens, following Lukes, identifies four theses usually associated with methodological individualism. In the same spirit we initially identify five theses: three ontological and two methodological. We divide the ontological theses into the weak, the stronger and the strongest. The strongest ontological thesis states that only individuals are real. As Stokes argues, 'what really exists are not societies or governments, for example, but the individuals that comprise them' (Stokes 1998: 78). The weak ontological thesis states that there could be no society without individuals. The weak thesis is frequently seen as being trivially true. As such it has nothing to say about the legitimacy or otherwise of recourse to social structures, institutions or large-scale phenomena. The stronger ontological thesis, unlike the strongest, does not necessarily rule out all reference to social structures, institutions or large-scale phenomena. All that it requires is that we avoid the fallacy of conceiving these as if they subsisted as physical objects or planetary systems. Rather social structures and institutions are conceived as *real* outcomes of combinations of intended and unintended consequences of individual actions. In Giddens' terminology they 'are always nothing more and nothing less than mixes of intended and unintended consequences of (individual) actions undertaken in specifiable contexts' (Giddens 1984: 220). Clearly the strongest and stronger theses are incompatible. We now turn to the two methodological theses, i.e. the individualistic reductionist thesis and the psychological reductionist thesis. The individualistic reductionist thesis claims that all statements about social phenomena can be reduced without remainder to descriptions about individuals. As Watkins puts it:

> There may be unfinished or half-way explanations of large-scale phenomena (say inflation) in terms of other large-scale phenomena (say full employment); but we shall not have arrived at rock-bottom explanations of such large-scale phenomena until we have deduced an account of them from statements about ... individuals.[14]
>
> (Watkins 1959: 6, as quoted in Nagel 1961: 541)

The psychological reductionist thesis claims that all our rock-bottom explanations must be in terms of *psychological* statements about individuals. In this view, as Popper puts it, psychology is 'the basis of all social sciences' (Popper 1957: 142).

In his early work Popper emphatically rejected the psychological reductionist thesis.[15] In the *Poverty of Historicism* he tells us 'the social sciences are comparatively independent of psychological assumptions and that psychology can be treated, not as the basis of all social sciences, but as one social science among others' (Popper 1957: 142). Later he emphatically repeats this rejection of 'methodological psychologism'. The doctrine, he declares:

> which teaches the reduction of social theories to psychology, in the same way as we try to reduce chemistry to physics, is, I believe, based on a misunderstanding. It arises from the false belief that this 'methodological psychologism' is a necessary corollary of a methodological individualism – of the quite unassailable doctrine that we must try to understand all collective phenomena as due to the actions, interactions, aims, hopes and thought of individual men and as due to traditions created and preserved by individual men. But we can be individualists without accepting psychologism.
>
> (Popper 1957: 157–8)

Before addressing Popper's attitude to the individualistic reductionist thesis, let us first look at his attitude towards the ontological theses. As we already noted the weak ontological thesis, namely there could be no society without individuals, is trivially true and is obviously espoused by Popper. In the *Poverty of Historicism* Popper appears to endorse the stronger ontological thesis. He claims that:

> the social sciences are largely concerned with the unintended consequences or repercussions of human actions. And 'unintended' in this context does not perhaps mean 'not *consciously* intended'; rather it characterizes repercussions which may violate *all* interests of the social agent whether conscious or unconscious.
>
> (Popper 1957: 158)

Clearly this claim on its own does not imply a commitment on Popper's part to the stronger thesis. However, when this is combined with his explicit reference to the legitimate recourse to 'traditions created and preserved by men' in his endorsement of methodological individualism as opposed to methodological psychologism, Popper appears to be espousing the stronger thesis. This is so if we read his reference to traditions to include real structures and institutions which are the outcomes of combinations of intended and unintended consequences of individual actions. These structural outcomes, subsist in some fashion as yet to be specified. For the moment all we are told is that these are not to be conceptualised as subsisting *à la* physical objects or planetary systems.

Where does Popper stand *vis-à-vis* the strongest ontological thesis? This strongest thesis is completely hostile to any use of social structures, institutions or large-scale phenomena in explanations in the human sciences. Social structures are fictions which must be eliminated from any genuine social science. Moreover, this strongest ontological thesis appears to be the *raison d'être* of the methodological individualistic reductionist thesis. If one asks why should one accept the individualistic reductionist thesis at the methodological level, one plausible answer is the strongest ontological thesis. If one accepts that the strongest ontological thesis is the raison d'être of the methodological reductionist thesis, we could say that, in this scenario, the individualistic reductionist thesis corresponds at the methodological level to the strongest thesis at the ontological level. However, as we already pointed out, the stronger ontological thesis is incompatible with the strongest ontological thesis: the stronger thesis is not completely hostile to the use of social structures in our social explanations. What it is completely hostile to is any understanding of the modus operandi of these in terms of the relevant parameters operable in the physical sciences. In short, if Popper espouses the stronger ontological thesis then logically he must reject the strongest ontological thesis and its corresponding individualistic reductionist thesis at the methodological level.

Before deciding on Popper's position *vis-à-vis* the strongest ontological thesis and its corresponding individualistic reductionist thesis, we introduce, corresponding to the stronger ontological thesis, a *qualified* individualistic reductionist thesis at the *methodological* level. This qualified methodological individualistic reductionist thesis states that *where possible* eliminate in terms of individualistic parameters our social sciences' references to social structures, institutions, etc. In this qualified methodological individualistic reductionist scenario, methodologists would treat social scientists' references to social structures, etc., with suspicion and do their best to eliminate these in terms of individualistic parameters.[16] Some social structures, however, will resist elimination and these, as it were, remain on the scientific books. The *raison d'être* of this qualified individualistic reductionist thesis is not the strongest ontological thesis. On the contrary, it would be grounded in methodological suspicion: in their historical development the social sciences contain a number of explanations in terms of social structures which are spurious, in the sense that better explanations may be constructed in terms of acceptable social structures combined with individualistic parameters. Moreover these better explanations are subject to Popper's problem-solving quadruple.

We are now in a position to interpret Popper's methodological individualism.[17] We suggest two hypotheses. First, it is arguable that the early Popper oscillates between the qualified and unqualified individualistic reductionist theses, but that, on the whole, his commitment to the unqualified individualistic reductionist thesis predominates. We have already outlined how one could interpret Popper in his *Poverty of Historicism* as accepting the stronger ontological theses which at the methodological level, would endorse the qualified individualistic reductionist position. However, on the other hand he also insists in this work that 'the task of social theory is to construct and to analyse our sociological models carefully in descriptive or nominalist terms, that is to say *in terms of individuals*' (Popper 1957: 136 italics in original).[18] This suggests the acceptance of the unqualified methodological individualistic reductionist thesis.

Our second hypothesis, which for us is the principal one, is that the later Popper, i.e. the Popper of the Three Worlds, unequivocally accepts the qualified methodological individualistic reductionist thesis. More precisely the logic of Popper's Three Worlds implies the stronger, as opposed to the strongest, ontological thesis. In order to legitimate this hypothesis, we explicate Popper's methodological individualism in terms of Popper's Three Worlds. This explication has at least five central theses.

1 World 1 (the world of physical bodies) is effected through World 2 agents (intentional agents).
2 World 2 individual agents, in engaging World 1, use theories and models which pertain to the *real* and *autonomous* World 3.
3 Both individual and social actions in World 1 and social interaction of all kinds presuppose a range of institutions which subsist in World 3, such as language, rules, regulations, conventions.[19]
4 These World 3 institutions are real, autonomous and are the unintended outcomes of human actions. As World 3 entities, their subsistence and modus operandi are not like those of World 1.
5 The intentionality of World 2 agents is largely parasitic on World 3, especially language and our psychological theories expressed in language.

In connection with thesis 5, we see how Popper continues to reject psychological individualism. For the later Popper, psychology is not the basis of the social sciences. Rather psychology is one among many social sciences in the sense that it is parasitic upon language, which is an indispensable social institution. As we noted above, Popper insists that we look on World 2, not through the eyes of nineteenth-century psychology, where the primacy is given to private mental states, but through the public, linguistic constituents of our theoretical constructs which subsist in the autonomous World 3.[20]

Popper in his later writings is emphatic about the reality and autonomy of World 3. Though man-made, World 3 has a genuine autonomy. By reinterpreting Frege, Kronecker and others, he explains 'why the third world which, in its origin, is our product, is *autonomous* in what may be called its ontological status' (Popper 1972: 161). He frequently draws our attention to language to illustrate this autonomy. 'The world of language, of conjectures, theories and arguments, in brief the universe of objective knowledge – is one of the most important of these man-created, yet at the same time largely autonomous, universes' (Popper 1972: 118). Moreover, a large part of this objective World 3 is the unintended consequence of human actions. In this connection what is of crucial importance to Popper is that, like an animal path through a jungle,[21] this large segment of World 3 is not planned. Finally it is in this context useful social *institutions* emerge.

> This is how a path is originally made – perhaps even by men – and how language and any other institutions which are useful may arise ... They are not planned or intended, and there was perhaps no need for them before they came into existence.
>
> (Popper 1972: 117)

Thus the mode of existence of institutions is that of the third, not the first, world. Institutions do not subsist like planetary systems in the first world.[22] To conclude: the strongest ontological thesis with its complementary unqualified methodological individualistic reductionist thesis is the 'natural enemy' of social institutions. These are not part of Popper's Three Worlds philosophy. Rather, as outlined above, the later Popper adopts the stronger ontological thesis with its complementary qualified individualistic reductionist thesis. Situational analysis in the context of Popper's Three Worlds does not encompass the total rejection of social institutions. Rather, while being suspicious of holistic and historicist structural explanations, and indeed rejecting these, it does not reject a judicious recourse to relevant institutions properly understood in its construction of situational analysis.

Popper's situational analysis and classical hermeneutics: the centrality of Popper's third world

As we already noted, according to Popper, situational analysis ought to be the core common method practised across the spectrum of the humanities ranging from economics to history. This we call Popper's universalisation thesis for the social sciences. Another major tradition, namely hermeneutics, also postulates a universalisation thesis for the humanities including the social sciences, but its universalisation thesis is not that of Popper's. Hermeneutics was traditionally concerned with the very limited task of interpreting classical texts as well as exegetical studies of the Old and New Testaments. In exceptional cases some passages proved difficult to understand and hermeneutics served as a pedagogical aid in deciphering these exceptional passages. The tacit assumption was that correct understanding is natural and normal or, alternatively, misunderstanding is exceptional or abnormal. In this context hermeneutics was a series of techniques which enabled classical scholars to avoid misunderstanding these exceptional passages. Schleiermacher, who was influenced by the Romantic movement, questioned this tacit assumption. According to Schleiermacher, the correct understanding of a traditional text is not evident: on the contrary, it is hidden. The correct understanding mirrors or reveals what the author of the text had in mind – her or his intentions, for instance – when writing the text. A central task for hermeneutics is to reconstruct the mind of the author from the written work. In order to accomplish this, hermeneutical scholars must transcend their own prejudices and conceptions and become immersed in the mind of the author.

Dilthey broadened the scope of hermeneutics from the narrow domain of the interpretation of texts to that of the human sciences or, more precisely, *Geisteswissenschaften*. Thus hermeneutics is extended to any situation in which we encounter meanings that are not immediately understood and thereby require interpretation. In this fashion, hermeneutics is extended to the interpretation of works of art, the actions of historical figures, direct conversation and self-understanding. Like Schleiermacher, the true meaning of a piece of historical writing is obtained by reconstructing the subjective intention or mind of its author and the same holds for the other domains. In short, Dilthey emphasises the *opposition* between *understanding* and *scientific explanation*. Historical understanding, for instance, is not achievable by any method modelled on the physical sciences. Empiricism fails to grasp that understanding is much closer to interpreting a foreign text than to the construction of a scientific theory *à la physics*. The latter is concerned with the purposes of science, the former with deepening or enriching our understanding of human actions which have both an exterior, i.e. behavioural, and an interior, i.e. mind-dependent, dimension. In general, correct understanding is achieved in proportion to the interpreter's ability to abstract from or set aside her or his own ideas and cultural influences and to penetrate or become immersed in the stream of consciousness of the relevant author.

Popper takes issue with this classical hermeneutical position on a number of grounds. First, Popper's anti-psychologism comes into play. Traditional hermeneutics places undue emphasis on subjective understanding which prioritises the private subjective mind of the agent to the detriment of the Popperian, objective third world. According to Popper:

> Here I will start from the assumption that it is *the understanding of objects belonging to the third world* which constitute the central problem of the humanities. This, it appears, is a radical departure from the fundamental dogma … that the objects of our understanding belong mainly to the second world, or that they are at any rate to be explained in psychological terms.
>
> (Popper 1972: 162, italics in original)

Once again his anti-psychologism is spelled out in terms of his third world. While acknowledging a subjective dimension to understanding, Popper specifies three theses concerning the subjective act of understanding:

(1) That every subjective act of understanding is largely anchored in the third world;
(2) that almost all important remarks which can be made about such an act consist in pointing out its relations to third-world objects, and

(3) that such an act consists in the main of operations with third-world objects: we operate with these objects almost as if they were physical objects.

(Popper 1972: 163)

Classical hermeneutics either ignores, misrepresents or does not give sufficient credence to these Popperian theses.

Second, while acknowledging that the aim of the humanities is understanding, he rejects the hermeneutical thesis that this aim is distinct from that of the physical sciences. The physical sciences also aim at understanding. Popper is both explicit and emphatic on this. Concretely he points out that Einstein's efforts are 'attempts to understand' in a sense of understanding which has a number of significant similarities with understanding in the humanities (Popper 1972: 184). In general he says 'Thus I oppose the attempt to proclaim the method of understanding as the characteristic of the humanities, the mark by which we may distinguish them from the natural sciences' (Popper 1972: 185). Clearly Popper does not wish to concede the concept of understanding to hermeneutics – the physical and the human sciences are both striving for understanding, with minor differences between the understanding achieved in both.[23] In short, for Popper:

> Labouring the difference between science and the humanities has long been a fashion and has become a bore. The method of problem solving, the method of conjecture and refutation, is practised in both. It is practised in reconstructing a damaged text as well as in constructing a theory of radioactivity.[24]
>
> (Popper 1972: 185)

It should be noted that the concept of understanding which Popper is using has not got a subjectivist ring to it. For him 'the activity of understanding is essentially the same as that of all problem solving' (Popper 1972: 184). In particular, understanding is achieved in the humanities by the method of situational analysis. Moreover understanding is centrally situated in his third, not his second, world: it is thoroughly linguistic-laden and consequently public. In addition it is subject to the Popperian problem-solving quadruple, which entails that we can never have a definitive or complete understanding.

Popper's situational analysis and contemporary hermeneutics: a possible colonisation

The hermeneutical tradition is not a static one: it was revolutionised by Gadamer and this challenging rearticulation has been extended and reshaped by other contemporary philosophers, such as Ricoeur. It is largely the impact of these developments for economics which is explored in Lavoie's *Economics and Hermeneutics*. Our thesis is that these contemporary hermeneutical developments have much in common with Popper. We will note six significant overlapping themes. First, Gadamer and Ricoeur prioritise language as public and social over private subjective minds, a theme which is absolutely indispensable to Popper's World 3.[25] Second, Popper and contemporary hermeneutics share a deep-seated antipathy to empiricism/logical positivism.[26] Thus Popper and hermeneutics endorse the task of liberating economics and the other social sciences 'from the inhibitions of positivism' (Lavoie 1991: 6). Third, Popper and contemporary hermeneutics abandon Enlightenment foundational concerns. Popper's philosophical reflections are not aimed at a search for solid foundations – a search which, according to contemporary hermeneutics was central to both Cartesian rationalism and Humean empiricism. Fourth, they share the view that the quest for understanding is a task to be accomplished: there is no final, definitive overarching understanding available to fallible human beings. Fifth, for both, history matters. Contemporary hermeneutics is post-existentialist; human historicity is ontological. According to Popper, 'the field of history' and especially 'the history of human opinion, of human knowledge, which comprises the history of religion, of philosophy and of science' is indispensable (Popper 1972: 185).[27] Finally contemporary hermeneutics, especially that of Gadamer, has imperialistic tendencies. As Madison notes, for Gadamer hermeneutics is an 'all inclusive discipline' covering the whole range of human studies (Madison 1991: 36), whereas Popper's methodological imperialism is that of situational analysis.

Moreover despite the fact that Gadamer retains the classical hermeneutical distinction between understanding achieved in the humanities and explanation achieved by the laws of physics, Ricoeur explicitly synergises scientific explanation and understanding, a merger which may be welcomed by Popper.[28] In view of these similarities, where does Popper differ from contemporary hermeneutics? Do the imperialistic tendencies of hermeneutics and of Popper converge? In some senses they clearly merge. Let us briefly look at some general points of convergence. For Gadamar the issue of the interpretation of a text, economic or otherwise, is a question of 'the fusion of horizons': the horizon of the text, which includes the records of the author's intentions and socio-cultural context of the text, is fused with the horizon of the interpreter, which includes the interpreter's 'prejudices' in the sense of his or her pre-judgements which are publicly accessible and located in historical time. One could argue that this is a metaphorical presentation of Popperian situational analysis. For Popper the situational analyst, in developing his or her hypothesis about some problem related to a text, is duty bound, in the name of objectivity, to properly recognise the historical context of the text. More precisely, relative to the problem which is of concern to the text's interpreter, in formulating a hypothetical solution to that problem, one must identify the relevant historical factors. In this sense one cannot escape the objective demands of the horizon of the text. Also the horizon of the interpreter comes into play in a number of crucial respects. The choice of problem is specific to the interpreter, especially to his or her beliefs about the relevant contents of the Popperian third world of objective knowledge. Moreover, once a tentative solution is offered, it is engaged within the critical parameters of Popper's third world: its strengths and weaknesses are articulated under the rubric of Popper's problem-solving quadruple. This third world critique will inevitably lead to new problems and thus, *à la* Gadamer, no definitive interpretation will emerge.

On this reading, Gadamer's metaphorical account of understanding as a 'fusion of horizons' is methodologically explicated in terms of Popperian situational analysis. Moreover, it could be argued that this explication is methodologically more specific and detailed than Gadamer's metaphorical account. In this fashion, situational analysis effects Popper's colonial expansionist policy for the humanities by colonising Gadamerian hermeneutics within its imperial remit.[29]

This Popperian colonisation, however, like socio-political colonisation, entails substantial change in the sense of the abandonment of some key constituent elements of the pre-colonised domain. One key element of contemporary hermeneutics rejected by Popperian situational analysis is the centrality of the text. As Lavoie correctly points out, hermeneutics not only applies to the interpretation of canonical and contemporary economic texts; it also claims to clarify 'the 'text' of the economy' (Lavoie 1991: 2). A hermeneutical approach to economics entails recognising the truth that the concept of the economy as a text is a powerful, emphatic, resonant and indispensable metaphor, a truth not appreciated by the economic methodologists of orthodox economics. One version of this hermeneutical approach to economics culminates in rhetoric as expounded by, for instance, Deirdre McCloskey and Arjo Klamer.[30]

Popperian situational analysis does not confuse an economic text with an economy. The history of and the current workings of an economy ranging over interconnected markets with hosts of suppliers and consumers of vast numbers of goods and services is not like a text. In light of Popper's Three Worlds, an economy is a vast, historically contingent, highly complex, unintended outcome of the economic actions and reactions of numerous agents past and present. This unintended outcome is a dynamic complex of innumerable first, second and third world entities. By comparison, a text is static, limited and mostly a third world entity. The hermeneutical metaphor of the economy as a text is consequently a gross oversimplification and not as cognitively illuminating as claimed by those methodologists who wish to adopt a hermeneutical approach to the study of economies.

Freedom, equality and language: Popperian limitations

The narrative thus far has by and large favoured Popper. Hermeneutical economic methodologists do not recognise the sophistication of Popper's situational analysis in his rejection of both positivism and foundationalism. It is now time to redress the situation by pointing to limitations of this Popperian approach. In this connection we will focus on three issues close to the core of contemporary hermeneutics: metaphysics, language and ideology. In this section we will look at metaphysics and language.

Popper, unlike the members of the Vienna Circle was not hostile to metaphysics. He emphatically rejects the logical positivist thesis that metaphysics is meaningless. In his robust defence of metaphysics, one could sum up by saying that it is the hand-maiden of science. Popper emphasises the heuristic role of metaphysics as a pre-scientific source of fruitful scientific concepts. Contemporary hermeneutics, like Popper, reject the logical positivist thesis that metaphysics is meaningless. However, they also reject Popper's analysis of metaphysics as the hand-maiden of science. For instance, if one looks at Ricoeur's vast output, one is struck by the range of metaphysical issues engaged in a spirit of openness, of dialectical analysis of historical richness and of humanity, which is not serving the interest of any science. Popper is certainly correct in locating metaphysical traditions from the ancient Greeks to contemporary metaphysicians in his World 3. Moreover, just as Popper concedes that 'there is too much specialization and too much professionalism in contemporary science' (Popper 1972: 185), one could say the same of a number of metaphysical traditions. Nevertheless, the spirit of many non-dogmatic metaphysical traditions is not that of science. In Wittgensteinian terminology these metaphysical language-games are not to be confused with those of science and neither are non-dogmatic metaphysicians scientific underlabourers. For Popper 'working on science is a human activity like building a cathedral' (Popper 1972: 185), whereas working on non-dogmatic metaphysics is like a Socratic dialogue, with all the richness, nuances, and humanity evident in Plato's early works.[31] There are different fields of human endeavour, all occupying Popper's World 3, but their modus operandi and modes of rationality differ. Contemporary hermeneutics is much more appreciative of the ethos, sophistication, richness, distinctness and humanity of non-dogmatic metaphysics, in comparison with the Popperian narrow, under labourer approach.[32]

We now turn to the centrality of language for Popper. As we already noted, contemporary hermeneutics celebrates the centrality of language. However, once again hermeneutics will draw attention to the narrow conception of language in the Popperian literature. Hermeneutics would not disagree with Popper that language 'is the most important of human creations' (Popper 1972: 119). Popper, however, quickly limits his focus to 'the two most important higher functions of human languages' (Popper 1972: 120), namely their descriptive and argumentative functions. Contemporary hermeneutics would be much more sympathetic to a Wittgensteinian approach to language, where language is a vast, motley combination of language-games or forms of life, where scientific description and argumentation are not privileged. Popper with his sincere passion for the world of science and his deep-seated opposition to Wittgenstein's and other philosophies of language, is blinded to the full richness, diversity, complexity and dynamism of human languages and mistakenly locks these into the service of science. Thus Popper is mistaken in maintaining that 'it is to this development of the higher functions of language that we owe our humanity and our reason' (Popper 1972: 120–1). Our humanity and our reason are intimately bound to our languages but these transcend the narrow parameters set by Popper. This can be seen from the reflections of non-hermeneutical philosophers such as Wittgenstein, and hermeneutical philosophers such as Ricoeur.

Moreover, and this is our central thesis, this difference over language is not insignificant for the evaluation of Popperian social science. The social sciences, for Popper, are or should be dominated by situational analysis. Moreover this Popperian approach is totally opposed to Marxism. In his autobiography Popper tells us that by the time he was seventeen he had become an anti-Marxist. 'I realized the dogmatic character of its creed and its incredible intellectual arrogance … Once I looked at it critically, the gaps and loop holes and inconsistencies in the Marxist theory became obvious' (Popper 1976: 34). Despite his rejection of Marxism, he admits that he remained a socialist for a number of years and maintains that, if socialism could be combined with individual liberty, he would still be a socialist:

> For nothing could be better than living a modest, simple and free life in an egalitarian society. It took some time before I recognized this as no more than a beautiful dream; that freedom is more important than equality; that the attempt to realize equality endangers freedom; and that if freedom is lost there will not even be equality among the unfree.
>
> (Popper 1976: 36)

How are we to evaluate this sincere Popperian vision? A Popperian could argue that this is the outcome of a critical reflection on the social sciences, including economics, practised according to the prescriptions of situational analysis. Our thesis, however, is that this Popperian vision does not follow from a philosophical analysis of language, which for Popper is indispensable to all science, provided we take language in its full richness and diversity. Philosophical analyses of the richer conceptions of language appreciated by numerous philosophers as divergent as Habermas, Ricoeur, Searle and Wittgenstein, lead to different, more balanced, dynamic, tension-ridden relationships between the values of freedom and equality than that of Popper. Without endorsing all the element of Habermas' universal pragmatics, it clearly suggests how a different, more optimistic balance can be drawn between the values of freedom and equality than that acknowledged by Popper. The same moral emerges from reflecting on the ways we learn and use ordinary language in Wittgenstein's forms of life. In particular, an analysis of different forms of life show that freedom is prioritised in some whereas in others equality is prioritised. The rich diversity of human values such as freedom, equality, respect, trust, etc., are embedded in the ways we learn and use ordinary language in our forms of life. Our hypothesis is that the Popperian programme is an attempt to colonise all forms of life into one where freedom is prioritised, under the guise of a unified theory of rationality. We, in the spirit of Wittgenstein, acknowledge the diversity of forms of life, the complex web of relationships between freedom and equality in these forms of life where neither at rock bottom is prioritised and where a unified Popperian theory of rationality does not operate.[33]

Situational analysis and hermeneutics: the search for a Marxist neutral social science

In this section we attempt to show how a contemporary hermeneutical approach to the human sciences, in certain respects and with certain modifications, is more enabling and less constraining than situational analysis. Our thesis is that when situational analysis is duly modified it constitutes an important dimension of social studies; but that the social sciences is not reducible to situational analysis. We illustrate this by reference to Ricoeur's hermeneutical analysis of the Marxist notion of ideology.

Ricoeur explicitly strives for an analysis of ideology which is neutral *vis-à-vis* Marx. He wishes to avoid a sterile polemic for or against Marx. Thus he does not start his reflections with the standard Marxist stereotypes of ideology, such as the thesis that ideology is a case of false consciousness; is used by one class to dominate another and that genuine social science provides an ideologically free perspective on social reality. This Ricoeurian open approach is in marked contrast with Popper's anti-Marxist stand. In developing his analysis of ideology, Ricoeur starts from a Weberian perspective in which social action is interpersonal, i.e. directed towards other persons and is meaning-laden i.e. embedded in meaning frames. In this context he develops his reflections on ideology. According to Ricoeur a social group has an image of itself and it acquires this image by looking back at its founding events, e.g. Bastille Day in France or American Independence Day. Ideology is linked to this image and its formation. Ideology serves two purposes here: it diffuses into the contemporary social group the convictions of the original founders; their creed must become our creed. It also perpetuates the initial energy and enthusiasm beyond its first appearance. In this way ideology is intellectually and socially mobilising. Ideology is also justificatory. It gives a degree of justification or legitimation to the institutions of the group, in that the institutionalised actions are deemed to be acceptable in light of its ideology. For instance, innovation is, as it were, checked against the ideological presentation of the founders' ideals. In this way many groups display traits of orthodoxy; intolerance begins when novelty threatens orthodoxy.

Ideology also has the dimension of a project to be accomplished. The ideals of the founders must be realised in our contemporary institutions. Moreover, ideology tends to be rather schematic and simplifying, as it may frequently be expressed in slogans. Furthermore, ideology pertains to tacit or practical knowledge rather than explicit, theoretical knowledge; we think *from* ideology rather than *about it*. Epistemologically it belongs to the domain of doxa or opinion rather than to (Platonic) true knowledge. It is closely related to Aristotelian rhetoric as the art of the probable and the persuasive.

This is the rich, historically thick, non-Popperian setting in which Ricoeur addresses the Marxist issues of ideology and domination; ideology and distortion and the possibility of an ideology-free social science. *Vis-à-vis* the issue of domination, the upshot of Ricoeur's hermeneutical analysis is that ideology, by legitimating authorities, is *ipso facto* legitimating domination. In any social group with a system of authority, ideology serves to justify this authority and this is a question of power of one person/group over others. The challenge is to distinguish just from unjust authority; to specify criteria for identifying abuses of authority and so on. Clearly the issues of authority, power, domination are integral to the social sciences in this hermeneutical perspective – issues which with Popper's anti-Marxist commitments are off the agenda of his limited situational analyses.

In connection with the issue of distortion, given that ideology is schematic, located in the domain of doxa, and that it is tacit, clearly there is the possibility of distortion. However, the issue of distortion is not the crucial element. An ideology, whether a distortion or not, can serve the interests of one group over another. A system does not have to be a distortion to be ideological in the sense of illegitimately justifying the interests of one group over another. Thus the possibility emerges that science which in one socio-historical context is liberating may in another socio-historical context be ideological in the sense that it is illegitimately used by one group to dominate another. Once again possibilities not entertained by Popperian situational analysis arise for the social sciences.

Finally, *vis-à-vis* the issue of an ideological-free social science, Ricoeur argues that there is no such discipline. Ricoeur points out that a positivist approach to the social sciences implies this possibility. Hence by *modus tollens*, so loved by Popper, positivism is to be rejected or at least must be revised. The same applies to Popperian situational analysis as presented by Popper. For Popper situational analysis is the ideological-free social science. A hermeneutical reflection on the human social condition suggests that this is a Popperian dream. Ideology, for a hermeneutical social science is not a fiction – the theoretical social scientist must critically engage it – another crucial issue which fails to get on the agenda of Popperian social science limited to situational analysis. In short, for contemporary hermeneutics the social sciences engage a rich and varied diversity of issues at the theoretical level which situational analysis cannot adequately address.

Conclusion

In economic methodology, Popper is frequently associated with falsificationism and methodological individualism. In this chapter we have re-engaged these themes in light of Popper's insistence on situational analysis as the method of the social sciences and his unequivocal commitment to his Three Worlds Thesis. We have argued that, when his conception of a model in the social sciences is fully appreciated and clearly distinguished from the D-N model of explanation in physics, Popper is consistent in holding that these models are weakly falsifiable. Like physics, these models must come before the bar of experience but, unlike physics, the outcome of this testing is, on the whole, less certain than in physics. Metaphysics for Popper is not testable at all, physics is strongly testable and situational analysis models are weakly testable.

In his later writings Popper insists that his Three Worlds Thesis is crucial. In light of this, we re-engaged his earlier commitments to piecemeal social engineering and to methodological individualism. We attempted to show that Popperian piecemeal engineering remains largely unscathed in Popper's three worlds. Economic actions directed at solving pressing, practical, economic problems are limited to marginal adjustments. However, at the level of economic methodology, we argued that, while the early Popper is, on the whole, committed to the wholescale reductionist programme of eliminating any and every reference to social structures or aggregates, etc., in terms of the actions of individual agents, this radical reductionist programme of methodological individualism is inconsistent with his Three Worlds Thesis. In opposition to this radical reductionist programme, we suggest that Popper is operating with a qualified methodological individualism, where some institutions resist the reduction to individual actions.

Moreover in light of his Three Worlds Thesis, we investigated where Popper stands *vis-à-vis* those advocating a hermeneutical approach to economic methodology. In this connection we addressed the possibility that Popperian situational analysis in the context of his problem-solving quadruple could make a significant contribution to the history of economic thought, especially to the historical study of canonical, economic texts. This situational analysis approach complements other approaches to the study of canonical economic texts explored by contemporary, as distinct from classical, hermeneutics. The price to be paid for this complementarity thesis between Popperian situational analysis and Gadamarian hermeneutics is that both should abandon their respective colonial expansionist policies for understanding canonical texts and recognise the rich motley of methods available to the historians of economic thought.

Finally, we concur with Popper that economic methodology should not be confused with the history of economic thought in the sense that the metaphor of an economy as a text is not as insightful as that claimed by those advocating a hermeneutical approach to economic methodology. Nonetheless, those advocating a hermeneutical approach to the social sciences, raise interesting possibilities, totally precluded by Popperian situational analysis. One such possibility is that the best economic science available may, nonetheless, be used ideologically in some social settings by one group to illegitimately dominate another. There is more to the social sciences than that prescribed by Popperian situational analysis.

Notes

1 In the 1980s Popper qualified his position on the similarities between science and metaphysics by acknowledging that both 'claim to be considered tentatively as true' (Popper 1983: 199). In this crucial respect a metaphysical theory is similar to a scientific theory. However, and this is crucial to our separation of science from metaphysics, according to Popper, metaphysics is not science: 'it is vaguer no doubt, and inferior in many respects; and its irrefutability, or lack of testability, is its greatest vice' (ibid.).

2 In this connection we use Lavoie's *Economics and Hermeneutics* (1991) as a *locus classicus* for the various efforts at introducing hermeneutics into economic methodology.

3 Popper tends to use TT rather than TS. However, he reads TT as either tentative solution or tentative theory.

4 Popper, throughout his life, was hostile to all substantive forms of dogmatism.

5 The above quadruple is oversimplified according to Popper. It does not include 'the multiplicity of tentative solutions, the multiplicity of trials' (Popper 1972: 243). For our present purposes we need not address Popper's complexification of the quadruple. Whatever the complexification, the resultant outcome is still critical problem solving which is integral to Popperian critical rationalism.

6 The reasons for this mistake are many, ranging from Popper's own solution to the problem of demarcation to the ways Popper has been interpreted in the secondary literature and university courses. In Caldwell's eyes falsificationism is the 'alleged' method of science whereas it is merely a part of the method.

7 This is an oversimplification. For Caldwell the physical sciences are predominantly falsificationist, while the social sciences may frequently use situational analysis.

8 Models according to Popper also occur in physics. However, physics can explain individual events, whereas in the social sciences we always explain typical events by recourse to models.

9 This is just one Popperian formulation of the rationality principle. Others can be found throughout the literature.

10 See T.A. Boylan's piece in this volume for a discussion of this.

11 This difference is, according to Popper, one of degree rather than of kind. Sometimes in the physical sciences testing is also not so clear cut. However, the problem is more pervasive in the social sciences.

12 Popper points out that, despite this difficulty, we can at least sometimes test which of two competing models is better.

13 Popper, in his publications, gives us different characterisations of World 3 which include 'the world of the logical *contents* of books, libraries, computer memories and such like' (Popper 1972: 74) or 'the world of *objective contents of thoughts* especially of scientific and poetic thoughts and works of art' (Popper 1972: 106).

14 In order to distinguish individualistic reductionism from psychological reductionism we omitted Watkins reference to 'dispositions and beliefs' of individuals. This reference runs the danger of conflating individualistic reductionism and psychological reductionism. Popper clearly rejects psychological reductionism.

15 Popper adheres to this rejection throughout his life.

16 In his *Poverty of Historicism* Popper claims that we 'must *try* to understand' collective phenomena in individualistic terms. It is this which suggested the qualified thesis to us.

17 In Popperian terminology, this is a legitimate problem located in Popper's own World 3, and is subject to critical scrutiny.

18 The same idiom is found in his *Open Society*, Vol. II (Popper 1945: 91, 98).

19 All of these World 3 institutions have some basis in World 1, e.g. language presupposes sound but is not reducible to sound. For Popper physical entities like traffic lights have a World 3 component in their use.

20 See Popper's main thesis about World 2 quoted in the previous section.

21 This is Popper's own example (cf. Popper 1972: 117).

22 Talking of 'the mode of existence' of World 3 is a gross oversimplification. In view of the motley array of entities in Popper's third world, talking as if there were a common mode of existence shared by these is misleading. While acknowledging this, all that is being conveyed is the Popperian thesis that institutions are manmade, unintended, real and autonomous.

23 In Wittgensteinian terms, the concept understanding is a multiple-criteria, family resemblance one, which has appropriate and acceptable usages in both the physical sciences and the humanities. However, this way of putting the matter may be acceptable to neither Popper nor classical hermeneutical scholars. For Popper there is a common core running through both, namely problem solving cum conjecture and refutation which takes on the form of situational analysis in the humanities, whereas a Wittgensteinian would be sceptical about this essentialist core.

24 Popper's own reflections on the pre-Socratics constitute a beautiful example of what Popper means by reconstructing a damaged text. This is core to the paradigm of classical hermeneutics, i.e. the interpretation of texts.

25 This position needs qualification. For Gadamer language is the house of being and the task of interpretation is one of a fusion of horizons. Similarly this is true for

Ricoeur. However, when one reads Ricoeur's *Oneself as Another*, one is struck by the sophisticated position of Ricoeur on the self – an original fusion of the public and private. However, for Popper all of this is in his third world – it is open to public scrutiny.

26 Popper is clearly offended by hermeneutical philosophers' failure to appreciate his deep-seated and explicit opposition to the empiricist analysis of the physical sciences.

27 It is clear from Popper's writings that this list is incomplete. For instance it does not include the history of music, painting, etc. all which are explicitly noted by Popper.

28 I surmise that Ricoeur's merger is much richer than what Popper would admit.

29 In our opinion Popperian situational analysis is an important methodological tool for historians of economic thought in dealing with their canonical texts. Situational analyses of these texts are in a position to enhance our scholarship in this field. However in our view historical scholarship is not confined to situational analyses: historical scholarship in the field of the history of economic thought consists of a diversified family of methods. To use a phrase of Wittgenstein, we would want to restore 'the motley' to historical scholarship, in opposition to both Popperian and hermeneutical essentialist approaches.

30 It is no accident that Lavoie included papers by these two creative methodologists of economics in his book *Hermeneutics and Economics* (1991).

31 Popper sees himself as 'a disciple of Socrates' (Popper 1976: 6). While this is so, it is very much an impoverished Socratic approach adopted by Popper.

32 For a different analysis of Popperian metaphysics see Giorello and Motterlini's piece in this volume.

33 For a more detailed account of this see Boylan and O'Gorman (2003).

References

Backhouse, R.E. (ed.) (1994) *New Directions in Economic Methodology*, London: Routledge.

Boland, L.A. (1994) 'Scientific thinking without scientific method: two views of Popper' in R.E. Backhouse (ed.) *New Directions in Economic Methodology*, London: Routledge, pp. 154–71.

Boylan, T.A. and O'Gorman, F.P. (2003) 'Economic theory and rationality: a Wittgensteinian interpretation', *Review of Political Economy*, 15: 231–44.

Caldwell, B.J. (1991) 'Clarifying Popper', *Journal of Economic Literature*, 29: 1–33.

De Marchi, N. (ed.) (1988) *The Popperian Legacy in Economics*, Cambridge: Cambridge University Press.

Gadamer, H.G. (1909) *Truth and Method*, 2nd edn, trans. J. Weinsheimer and D.G. Marshall, London: Shead and Ward.

Giddens, A. (1984) *The Constitution of Society*, Cambridge: Polity Press.

Hands, W.D. (2001) *Reflection without Rules: Economic Methodology and Contemporary Science Theory*, Cambridge: Cambridge University Press.

Habermas, J. (1987) *The Philosophical Discourse of Modernity*, trans. by F. Lawrence, Cambridge: Polity Press.

Koertge, N. (1979) 'The methodological status of Popper's Rationality Principle', *Theory and Decision*, 10: 83–95.

Lavoie, D. (ed.) (1991) *Economics and Hermeneutics*, London: Routledge.

Madison, G.B. (1991) 'Getting beyond objectivism: the philosophical hermeneutics of Gadamer and Ricoeur', in D. Lavoie (ed.) *Economics and Hermeneutics*, London: Routledge.

Nagel, E. (1961), *The Structure of Science*, London: Routledge and Kegan Paul.
Popper, K.R. (1945) *The Open Society and its Enemies*, Vol. I and II, London: Routledge and Kegan Paul.
—— (1957) *The Poverty of Historicism*, London: Routledge and Kegan Paul.
—— (1959) *The Logic of Scientific Discovery*, London: Hutchinson and Co.
—— (1963) *Conjectures and Refutations*, London: Routledge and Kegan Paul.
—— (1972) *Objective Knowledge*, Oxford: Clarendon Press.
—— (1976) *Unended Quest, An Intellectual Autobiography*, London: Fontana.
—— (1983) *Realism and the Aim of Science*, London: Routledge.
—— (1994) 'Models, instruments and truth': the status of the rationality principle in the social sciences', in *The Myth of the Framework*, London: Routledge.
Ricoeur, P. (1983) *Hermeneutics and the Human Sciences*, trans. by J.B. Thomson, Cambridge: Cambridge University Press.
—— (1994) *Oneself as Another*, trans. by K. Blaney, Chicago, IL: The University of Chicago Press.
Stokes, G. (1998) *Popper, Philosophy, Politics and Scientific Method*, Cambridge: Polity Press.
Watkins, J.W.N. (1959) 'Historical explanation in the social sciences', in P. Gardiner (ed.) *Theories of History*, Glencoe, IL: Free Press.

3 Challenging Popperian rationality

Wittgenstein and Quine reconsidered

Thomas A. Boylan

Introduction

The rationality principle has long been considered one of the core concepts of economics and has been privileged as a pivotal methodological tenet of economic theorising (Hogarth and Reder 1986; Sugden 1991; Foley 1998; Vanberg 2004). In addition to its centrality in economics the rationality principle has successfully colonised the theoretical heartland of a number of cognate social sciences, including political science and sociology (Friedman 1996; Hechter and Kanazawa 1997). This intellectual colonisation has now been upgraded to the status of 'economic imperialism', a term first used by William Souter in 1933 (Souter 1933),[1] and firmly established by a number of pioneering studies in the 1950s in which the conceptual framework of mainstream economics was applied to a number of different non-economic topics including discrimination, democracy and the economics of slavery (Becker 1957; Downs 1957; Conrad and Meyer 1958). This process of intellectual expansionism continued through the 1960s and arguably culminated in 1976 with the publication of Becker's *The Economic Approach to Human Behaviour*, which in tone and methodological approach unambiguously conveyed the imperial superiority of the economic approach centred on the theory of rational choice.

Notwithstanding its standing within economics and its 'imperialist' successes outside of economics, the rationality principle has been and continues to be the target of sustained criticism from a variety of sources within economics in addition to those from other social and behavioural sciences (Green and Shapiro 1994; Laville 2000). Despite the paradigmatic centrality of the rationality principle, ambiguities abound with respect to its methodological status and its specific empirical content on the part of both its adherents and critics alike. While economists largely agree that rationality lies at the centre of their discipline, they disagree about its nature, limits and what should be assumed about economic agents for the purposes of economic modelling. Some of the adherents of the rationality principle view it as part of the metaphysical hard-core of economics which represents a non-refutable axiomatic doctrine (Boland 1981). Others regard it as containing empirical content and therefore represents an empirically testable hypothesis, while still others hold the view that it is primarily a normative principle that indicates how we ought to act and choose as rational agents (Harsanyi 1977; Sugden 1991). For those who criticise or reject the rational choice model, their critiques reflect a number of different motivating factors. Some reject it on the basis of its patent conflict with reality; others accuse it of being empirically vacuous, while others contend that it is normatively unsatisfactory if not totally inadequate.[2] These conflicting views have arisen, in part at least, from comparatively recent developments in such diverse areas as decision and game theory, experimental psychology, and philosophy. As a result there now exists an extremely voluminous literature on rationality in economics, including different generalisations of expected utility theory, theories of bounded rationality and satisfying behaviour, quasi rationality, particular versions of rationality developed for game theoretic applications in addition to various accounts drawn from a broader array of disciplines such as moral and social theory.[3]

Popper's contribution to the methodology of the social sciences was centred on the rationality principle and its role within the framework of his situational analysis. This was critically influenced by what Popper perceived as the method of the most advanced theoretical social science, economics. Hayek was clearly a pivotal presence in this, since Popper, on his own admission, 'was particularly impressed by Hayek's formulation that economics is the "logic of choice"'. This led Popper to his formulation of the 'logic of the situation' (Popper 1994: 181 fn. 1).[4] Interestingly Popper viewed the 'logic of the situation' as embracing both the 'logic of choice' and the 'logic of historical problem situations', and indicates that the 'origin of this idea may explain why I rarely stressed the fact that I did not look at the logic of the situation as a deterministic theory: I had in mind the logic of situational choices' (ibid.: 181 fn. 1). Mention of the 'historical problem situation' by Popper is instructive in reminding us of his major methodological concern at this time, namely his emerging critique of historicism, which would be joined by his corresponding hostility to psychologism. Popper was 'particularly impressed' by the formulation of Hayek's paper 'Economics and Knowledge', first published in *Economica* in 1937, a year after Popper's first presentation of his critique of historicism in a paper entitled 'The Poverty of Historicism' in a private session in the house of his friend Alfred Braunthal in Brussels. Shortly afterwards he presented a similar paper at Hayek's seminar at the London School of Economics.[5] This was the beginning of Popper's major contribution to the methodology of the social sciences, though on his own admission 'the social sciences never had for me the same attraction as the theoretical natural sciences. In fact, the only theoretical social science which appealed to me was economics' (Popper 2002: 139).

The appeal of economics to Popper was in fact clearly limited to methodological concerns. Popper had arguably no real interest in the substantive or technical contents of economics. He had however an abiding and highly motivated interest in the methodological approach of economics, which would serve his larger agenda of providing him with a framework to provide a critique of historicism and psychologism. In his own words, his interest was 'to compare the natural and social sciences from the point of view of their methods' (ibid.: 139), a project that had clearly begun in *The Poverty of Historicism*. An informing principle of this chapter is that Popper's methodological interest in economics was dominated by methodological considerations arising from his critical engagement with both historicism and psychologism. A corollary of this position is that criticisms of Popper's knowledge of economics or of any of the social sciences, while perhaps perfectly valid, are misplaced and throw little light on his substantive methodological engagement with the social sciences.

The main aim of this chapter, however, is to focus on the concept of rationality that Popper was prepared to work with within the framework of his situational analysis, and more specifically to critically examine why this concept of rationality is, and remains, methodologically privileged in orthodox economic theorising. We will suggest that if Popper had been prepared to engage the work of some of his contemporaries, in this case Quine and Wittgenstein, very considerable modifications to his concept of rationality could have resulted. Their work would have given him very considerable food for thought and in our estimation could have greatly enriched his very considerable contribution to the methodology of the social sciences. Before considering the work of Quine and Wittgenstein, we will examine Popper's formulation and development of the principle of rationality within the framework of his situational analysis.

Popperian rationality and the quest for objectivity

Popper's writings on the philosophy of the social sciences emerged from two distinct periods of his career: an early period from the mid-1930s to the mid-1940s and a later period which extended through the 1960s. In the intervening period he was preoccupied with his principal area of interest, the philosophy of the physical sciences, and in the latter part of his career with what a recent study of his philosophy refers to as 'Metaphysics' (Keuth 2005). The earlier period of his work on the methodology of the social sciences is dominated by the production of two of his major works, *The Poverty of Historicism* and *The Open Society and Its Enemies*, respectively, which he referred to as his 'war effort' (Popper 2002: 131). He has described them as 'books on the philosophy of politics', born out of his concern that 'freedom might become a problem again ... and so these books were meant as a defence of freedom against totalitarian and authoritarian ideas, and as a warning against the dangers of historicist superstitions' (ibid.: 131).[6] While this represented his political agenda, subverting the 'historicist superstitions' was his methodological objective. Pursuing this latter objective involved developing a non-historicist model of historical explanation. It was at this juncture that Popper invoked the method of economic theory to provide him with the building blocks that would become his 'method of situational analysis'.

Popper has remained astonishingly faithful to his method of situational analysis and the role played by economics in its formation. He recounts that a voluminous literature arose from misguided criticism of his ideas on historical explanation (Popper 2002: 134). But this analysis, which went under the rubric of 'the deductive model', was not particularly important in his estimation. What was important 'needed some further years to mature, and this was the 'rationality principle' or 'the zero method' or 'the logic of the situation'. One of the earliest formulations of the 'zero method' was contained in *The Poverty of Historicism* in the context of his defence of the unity of method thesis. While conceding that there were some differences 'between the theoretical science of nature and of society' (Popper 1957: 130), for instance the specific difficulties in conducting experiments and in applying quantitative methods, these were 'differences of degree rather than of kind' (ibid.: 141). However, there was a more substantive difference for Popper, which indicated to him 'a considerable difference between the natural and social sciences – perhaps *the most important difference in their methods* (ibid.: 141 italics in original). For Popper, most social situations, if not all, possessed an element of rationality in which people acted more or less rationally. This makes possible the construction of comparatively simple models of human action and their interactions and these models can be used as approximations. The abiding presence of rationality for Popper provided the possibility of adopting in the social sciences the method of 'logical or rational constructions, or perhaps the "zero method"' (ibid.: 141).[7] Popper defined the zero method as:

> the method of constructing a model on the assumption of complete rationality (and perhaps also on the assumption of the possession of complete information) on the part of all the individuals concerned, and of estimating the deviation of the actual behaviour of people from the model behaviour, using the latter as a kind of zero co-ordinate.
>
> (Popper 1957: 141)

Popper immediately adds that neither the principle of methodological individualism nor that of the zero method of constructing rational models implied or required the adoption of a psychological method. On the contrary he believed that these principles (methodological individualism and the zero method) are compatible with the view that the social sciences 'are comparatively independent of psychological assumptions, and that psychology can be treated, not as the basis of all social sciences, but as one social science among others' (Popper 1957: 142). The privileging of psychology as the foundational bedrock of social science was at the core of Comte's and J.S. Mill's theory of social progress. These are Popper's main targets in this domain against which he was implacably opposed.[8]

Popper's criticism of psychologism, along with the development of his overall 'critical or rational attitude', were elaborated more fully in *The Open Society*, his second major contribution in this initial phase of his work on the philosophy of the social sciences.[9] Popper had argued that both *The Poverty of Historicism* and *The Open Society* 'grew out of the theory of knowledge of *Logic der Forschung*' and from his firm conviction 'that our unconscious views on the theory of knowledge and its central problems … are decisive for our attitude towards ourselves and towards politics' (Popper 2002: 131). This is clearly evident in *The Open Society* in that Popper generalises his critical approach and extends its applications 'as far as possible'. This extension was to include the clashes of values in society and the conflict that may arise between moral principles. This arises for Popper from the realisation 'that we shall always have to live in an imperfect society' and that there 'can be no human society without conflict' (Popper 2002: 133). One of the main arguments in *The Open Society* is directed against what he terms *moral relativism*. The fact that moral values or principles may clash does not, he argues, invalidate them. Such values or principles may be discovered, even invented, and may be deemed relevant or irrelevant, depending on the situation. Conflict in this domain is not the problem for Popper, though every effort should be pursued to reduce it. In fact for Popper the 'clashes of values and principles may be valuable, and indeed essential or an open society' (ibid.: 133).

The Open Society was a major contribution to political philosophy and the philosophy of the social sciences, which addressed a number of pivotal areas, including Popper's first exposition of his anti-essentialist position, issues in the history of philosophy and the philosophy of history.[10] Our interest in it, however, arises from the fact that in Chapter 14 Popper expanded on his method of situational analysis building on what he had earlier called the 'zero method'. The main point here was that he also perceived himself as attempting '*to generalize the method of economic theory (marginal utility theory) so as to become applicable to the other theoretical social sciences*' (Popper 2002: 135 italics in original). In his intellectual autobiography he states that in 'my later formulations this method consists of constructing a *model of the social situation*, including especially the institutional situation, in which an agent is acting, in such a manner as to explain the rationality (the zero character) of his action' (Popper 2002: 135 italics in original). His 'later formulations' belong to the second phase of his work on the philosophy of the social sciences and are contained in a series of publications during the course of the 1960s. In the remainder of this section, we will examine, albeit briefly, the principal contents of these contributions.

Following the publication of 'The Poverty of Historicism' in journal form and *The Open Society*, Popper re-engaged his work on the philosophy of the physical sciences, and during the course of the 1950s one of his principal tasks was the preparation of an English edition of *Logik der Forschung*. The event that was instrumental in his return to work on the methodology of the social sciences was the invitation in 1960 to deliver the opening contribution to a conference of the German Sociological Association in Tübingen in 1961 on 'The Logic of the Social Sciences'. Popper was asked by the organisers to present his paper in the form of a number of definite theses in order to facilitate critical discussion, since the second speaker was Adorno, the leading exponent of critical theory developed at the Frankfurt School. It was expected that the confrontation between Popper and Adorno would produce both heat and light in the course of expounding their respective positions. In the event the intellectual confrontation did not materialise, but the contents of Popper's contribution is of interest in the development of his thinking on situational analysis.

Most of Popper's 1961 presentation deals with his general philosophy of science common to both the physical and social sciences. Of the twenty-seven tightly formulated theses in which Popper presented his paper only the last six theses referred to the social sciences specifically. Popper again rejected psychologism as the basis of social science by arguing that 'psychology presupposes social ideas; which shows that it is impossible to explain society exclusively in psychological terms, or to reduce it to psychology' (Popper 1976: 101). The fundamental task of the social sciences for Popper is to describe the social environment since this is the framework within which 'every psychological explanation' will occur. This task is best allocated to sociology as being the most appropriate discipline for the task. From this the autonomy of sociology is defended by Popper. Sociology 'can and must make itself independent of psychology' given the dependence of psychology on social ideas, which is 'due to the important fact that sociology is constantly faced with the task of 'explaining unintended and often undesired consequences of human action', a task which psychology is unable to deliver (Popper 1976: 102). In addition Popper offered a second reason for the autonomy of sociology. In the most succinctly formulated of all his twenty-seven theses, he simply states that 'we cannot reduce to psychology what has often been termed 'verstehende Soziologie' (the sociology of [objective] understanding)' (ibid.: 102).[11]

In the following thesis, the twenty-fifth, Popper elaborates on what he means by objective and will invoke economics as the exemplar of his approach. His situational logic is now equated with a 'method of *objective* understanding', which emanates from the 'logical investigation of economics', which culminates 'in a result which can be applied to all social sciences'. For Popper this result delivers '*a purely objective method* in the social sciences' (ibid.: 102 italics in original). Central to Popper's objective is that a social science oriented towards 'objective understanding or situational logic' can be developed independently of all subjective or psychological ideas. This will entail the analysis of the social situation which will provide an explanation of human action without any help from psychology. Objective understanding 'consists in realizing that the action was objectively *appropriate to the situation*'. This entails that the situation 'is analyzed far enough for the elements which initially appeared to be psychological (such as wishes, motives, memories, and associations) to be transformed into elements of the situations' (ibid.: 102 italics in original). What Popper achieves here is a mapping or transformation of the psychological elements of the individual into 'elements of the situation'. The nexus of psychological characteristics, such as wishes, motives, memories and associations, are transformed or reduced into aims and information. In Popper's account:

> The man with certain wishes therefore becomes a man whose situation may be characterized by the fact that he pursues certain objective *aims*; and a man with certain memories or associations becomes a man whose situation can be characterized by the fact that he is equipped objectively with certain theories or with certain information.
>
> (Popper 1976: 102–3 italics in original)

Popper later juxtaposes the terms goals and knowledge for aims and information in his account of situational logic.

Following this reconfiguration of the individual and their incorporation into 'elements of the situation', Popper is at pains to emphasise that the 'method of situational analysis is certainly an individualistic method and yet it is certainly not a psychological one', since it 'excludes, in principle, all psychological elements and replaces them with objective situational elements' (Popper 1976: 103).[12] In the final thesis he identifies a new dimension of situational logic, the role of social institutions. Integral to the situational logic is, in addition to the physical world, the site of both physical resources and physical barriers, there is the social world. This social world is populated by people 'about whose goals we know something (often not very much), and, furthermore, *social institutions*' (ibid.: 103 italics in original). The social institutions consist, for Popper, of all the social realities of the social world, corresponding 'to some extent' to the things of the physical world. He cites an array of entities extending from a grocer's shop, a university institute, a police force, a law, along with churches, state and marriage as examples of social institutions. The social institutions determine the peculiarly social character of the social environment. Popper does not elaborate beyond this in his final thesis. He does, however, end his paper with a 'suggestion' which is addressed to sociology. He identifies what he considers, at least provisionally, what he considers to be the fundamental 'problems of a purely theoretical sociology'. This would consist for him of elaborating and developing 'the general situational logic of and the theory of institutions and traditions' (ibid.: 103). More specifically this would include such problems as theorising how individuals act in or for or through institutions, since for Popper institutions can never act. Working out the general situational logic of these institutionally mediated actions would constitute 'the theory of the quasi-actions of institutions'.[13] A second problem identified by Popper was the construction of a theory of the intended or unintended institutional consequences of purposive action, which he felt could lead to a theory of the creation and development of institutions.

Popper's return to work on the methodology of the social sciences, as reflected in his 1961 contribution, provided an important elaboration of his thinking on situational analysis. The 1961 paper, reiterating the pivotal positions of the economic framework, intensified the search for an objective approach to social theorising which would render psychology redundant. If the earlier work of the 1930s and 1940s was more focused on historicism, his work in the 1960s was directed against psychologism through a dependency and extension of the conceptual coherence of situational analysis. This is well reflected in two later contributions of the 1960s which we will examine in the remainder of this section. In 1963 Popper was invited to lecture on the methodology of the social sciences in the Department of Economics at Harvard University.[14] Addressing mainly an audience of economists, Popper opened with a fulsome, but oft repeated, accolade to the method of economics. 'My views on the methodology of the social sciences', he states, 'are the result of my admiration for economic theory: I began to develop them, some twenty-five years ago, by trying to generalize the method of theoretical economics' (Popper 1994: 154).[15] This lecture represents the most complete exposition provided by Popper on the role of situational analysis as an explanatory theory of human action in the social sciences. About a third of the lecture is devoted to an exposition of Popper's views on the 'methodology of science' in general, followed by his analysis of the problems peculiar to the social sciences. The final sections of the original lecture ends with a critique of instrumentalism, 'that still fashionable philosophical theory of pragmatism which tells us that our theories are nothing but instruments' (ibid.: 154).[16] While a great deal of the material of this lecture could not be said to be new, its novel features are to be found in Popper's elaboration of the role of models and his clarification of the status of the rationality principle within these models.

Popper is emphatic on the centrality of models to the social sciences. The fundamental problem for Popper in both the theoretical and the historical social sciences is *'to explain and understand events in terms of human actions and social situations'* (Popper 1994: 166 italics in original), and the key term is 'social situation'. In fact, he argues, 'the idea of a *social situation* is the fundamental category of the methodology of the social sciences' (ibid.: 166 italics in original). Within the framework of his argument, however, the concept of *typical social situations* is arguably even more fundamental, which links directly to the need for models, since he argues that 'the "*models*" of the theoretical social sciences are essentially descriptions or reconstructions of *typical social situations*' (ibid.: 166 italics in original). Typical social situations can only be analysed through the construction of models. Invoking his distinction between attempting to explain or predict *singular events* as distinct from a *kind of type* of event, Popper argues that the former category of event can be solved '*without constructing a model*', while the latter is 'most easily solved *by means of constructing a model*' (ibid.: 163 italics in original). Solving the first problem is illustrated by Popper by reference to the Newtonian method of explaining and predicting singular events through the use of universal laws and relevant initial conditions. But for Popper the Newtonian method of universal laws and initial conditions are 'hardly ever applicable in the theoretical social sciences'. Hence they operate 'almost always by the method of constructing *typical* situations or conditions – that is, by the method of constructing models' (ibid.: 166 italics in original). Engaging a modicum of linguistic joined up thinking, Popper combines his conceptual analysis of depicting typical situations through the use of models into the linguistic term, *typical situational model*, which finally transmogrifies into his *situational analysis*.[17]

Popper has now established the role of models at the centre of his situational analysis. But he is left with a question, how is the model of a social situation to be animated? This is analogous for Popper to asking the question in a different context: what corresponds in the social situation to Newton's universal law of motion which animates the model of the solar system? The usual mistake, according to Popper, is to reach for 'the laws of human psychology in general' or to the 'laws of individual psychology' (ibid.: 169). But these have been rendered redundant within the logic of his situational analysis as demonstrated in his earlier work. There is only one animating law involved, namely the principle of 'acting appropriately to the situation' which is of course his celebrated rationality principle, a concept which he described as 'an *almost empty* principle' and one that 'has led to countless misunderstandings' (ibid.: 169 italics in original). In attempting to redress these 'countless misunderstandings' we get Popper's clearest account of the status and role of the rationality principle.

The rationality principle follows from the adoption of a more fundamental methodological postulate which dictates that our whole theoretical or explanatory efforts should be directed into the analysis of the situation, i.e. into our models. The rationality principle in this context has little or nothing to do with the empirical, much less the psychological, claim that people always, or in general, act rationally. If the methodological postulate is adopted, then the rationality principle as the animating law becomes as a consequence 'a kind of zero-principle'. The principle is formulated by Popper as follows:

> Once we have constructed our model of the situation, we assume no more than that the actors act within the terms of the model, or that they 'work out' what was *implicit* in the situation. That incidentally, is what the term 'situational logic' is meant to allude to.
>
> (Popper 1994: 169 italics in original)

The rationality principle, following as a consequence or 'by-product' of Popper's methodological postulate, has no role as an empirical explanatory theory or a testable hypothesis. The only empirical explanatory theories or hypotheses are the models of the situational analyses. Only the models will be deemed to be empirically adequate or inadequate following from the testing procedures implemented.

Following discussion after the lecture at Harvard, Popper added a short section in which he provided further elucidation of his thinking on the status of the rationality principle.[18] Popper was challenged with respect to what he called his 'own version' of the rationality principle as a 'principle of adequacy of action'. The accusation of confusion on Popper's part with respect to his position on the status of the rationality principle was whether it represented a methodological principle or an empirical conjecture. If the former, then empirical testing was not an issue, and it formed part of a successful or unsuccessful methodological strategy to be evaluated by criteria other than direct testing. If the latter then it would become part of some empirical theory and would be subject to testing along with the rest of the theory, subject to rejection if found inadequate. Popper indicates that it is the second option identified, i.e. as an empirical conjecture, 'that corresponds better to my own view of the status of the rationality principle' (Popper 1994: 177). The rationality principle is, for Popper, an integral part of every, or nearly every testable social theory. If a theory is then tested and found wanting, there is the issue of deciding which of the constituent components of the model are accountable for its failure. Here he introduces his important thesis 'that it is *sound methodological policy* to decide not to make the rationality principle, but the rest of the theory – that is, the model – accountable' (ibid.: 177 italics in original). Popper is quick to point out that this thesis would appear to confer on the rationality principle the status of a 'logical or a metaphysical principle exempt from refutation: as unfalsifiable or, as *a priori* valid' (ibid.: 177). This is rejected by Popper since he holds that the rationality principle may be actually false, though perhaps a good approximation to the truth. Consequently he does not hold it as a principle to be *a priori* valid. For Popper then it is 'good policy, a good methodological device' to avoid blaming the rationality for the inadequacy of our theories. We learn more, he argues, if we blame the contents and analysis of our situational models. His policy on the role of the rationality principle as a crucial component of our methodological strategy is defended by Popper on the following grounds. First, the situational model is more interesting, informative and testable than the rationality principle. We know already that as a principle it may not be strictly true, and may be even false, so little is learned from establishing this result. In the event of our models being empirically refutable, the falsity of the rationality principle may well be a contributing factor, but the main responsibility will rest with the model. Second, any attempt to replace the rationality principle by an alternative one runs the risk of introducing 'complete arbitrariness in our model building' (ibid.: 178). And finally, it involves finding the better of two or more competing theories which may have a good deal in common, including of course for most of them the principle of adequacy, or the rationality principle, since he had argued in his earlier work that 'in most social situations, if not in all, there is an element of *rationality*' (Popper 1957: 140 italics in original).

This was arguably the most complete exposition that Popper provided of his thinking on the rationality principle and situational analysis.[19] And it is clear that his preoccupation with forging his overarching philosophy of critical rationalism and more specifically his contribution to the methodology of social science was, by the early 1960s, essentially well delineated. His concern to refute and provide alternatives to historicism and psychologism in social philosophy dominated his efforts in both the early and later periods of his work on social philosophy. His formulation of situational analysis and the role of the rationality principle represented one of the major contributions to the philosophy of the social sciences. And along the way economics provided him with the exemplar of rational choice theory as a method which supplied him with the requisite methodological framework in the pursuit of his subversion of historicism and psychology. If the 1963 Harvard lecture was the most comprehensive exposé on the rationality principle and situational analysis, it was not his final contribution. In 1968 Popper delivered an extremely significant contribution for both his overall philosophical position and for the philosophy of the social sciences. This was his lecture 'On the Theory of the Objective Mind', delivered in Vienna in September 1968.[20]

In this lecture Popper developed his 'Three World Theses', with the first world identified with physical objects, while the second world contained the mental world of beliefs and subjective experiences. Distinguished from the second world is the third world, which contains the contents of such entities as scientific theories, mathematics, logical relationships, arguments and problem situations. This third world is autonomous from the second world, and Popper notes that its autonomy and objectivity have a long philosophical lineage extending from Plato to Frege. To appreciate what is informing Popper, Frege is a good place to start. In the Introduction to his *Foundations of Arithmetic*, Frege stated the following principle: 'always to separate sharply the psychological from the logical, the subjective from the objective' (Frege 1968: ix). For instance, the socio-psychological origins of the concept of number is completely distinct from the autonomous logical problem of furnishing the correct definition of a number. Thus the Fregean attempt at furnishing the correct definition belongs to Popper's third world. To take a different example, the actual psychological influences on Cantor when he introduced transfinite numbers into mathematics would belong to Popper's second world. However, the analysis of the problem situation in mathematics and Cantor's response to it in terms of infinite sets has nothing to do with psychology. The issues here belong to Popper's third world. In Wittgensteinian terminology, which Popper would probably not appreciate, the third world pertains to an entirely different language-game to the language-game of psychology.

Popper, however, explicitly locates his situational analysis in the third and not in the second world. In the course of his analysis of the problems of historical understanding and of illustrating 'the superiority of the third-world method of critically reconstructing problem situations over the second-world method of intuitively re-living some personal experience', he draws a number of important lessons. For Popper perhaps the 'most important point concerns what I have sometimes described as *situational logic* or *situational analysis*' (Popper 1972: 170 fn. 18, 178 italics in original). He now tells us:

> By a situational analysis I mean a certain kind of tentative or conjectural explanation of some human action which appeals to the situation in which the agent finds himself … we can try, conjecturally, to give an idealized reconstruction of the problem situation in which the agent found himself, and to that extent make the action 'understandable' (or 'rationally understandable'), that is to say, adequate to his situation as he saw it. This method of situational analysis may be described as an application of the rationality principle.
>
> (Popper 1972: 179 italics in original)

Clearly this location of situational analysis to the third world is very useful for Popperian scholars. It helps, for instance, to clarify Popper's famous distinction between 'methodological individualism; and 'methodological psychologism'. In the three world division methodological psychologism is certainly not 'a necessary corollary of a methodological individualism' since 'psychology cannot be the basis of social science' (Popper 1957: 157, 158).[21]

However, it also poses a number of challenging problems for Popperian scholars ranging from subtle movements in Popper's understanding of methodological individualism to the compatibility of his mature position with his criterion of demarcation.[22]

Our methodological concerns are different. We wish to critically interrogate the orthodox economic theory which clearly, as referred to earlier in this chapter, informed Popper's situational analysis. Among the central notions of orthodox economics are equilibrium and rationality. In connection with the concept of equilibrium, Popper makes an interesting comment in the context of rejecting Comte's doctrine of the laws of succession which the latter claimed corresponded to dynamics.[23] Popper reinterprets Comte's concept of dynamic 'in a reasonable way' by distinguishing between 'laws that do not involve the concept of *time*, and laws into whose formulation *time* enters' (Popper 1972: 116). For equilibrium economics, however, Popper pointed out that:

> It may be worth mentioning that equilibrium economics is undoubtedly *dynamic* (in the 'reasonable' as opposed to the 'Comtean' sense of this term), even though time does not occur in its equation. For this theory does not assert that the equilibrium is anywhere realized; it merely asserts that every disturbance (and disturbances occur all the time) is followed by an adjustment – by a 'movement' towards equilibrium.
>
> (Popper 1957: 116 fn. 2 italics in original)

In the context of Popper's third world, one could argue that orthodox economics, with its idealised notion of equilibrium is providing economists with an indispensable parameter for economic explanation. The challenge for economists as empirical scientists is to form conjectures about the disturbances and adjustments and then to test them.

Following up on these suggestions, one could adopt a Lakatosian-type framework to interpret Popper's position on equilibrium economics.[24] In this Lakatosian approach, orthodox economics has a hard core which includes equilibrium along with a protective belt which includes conjectural adjustments. The protective belt takes the brunt of the testing. However, if one is faithful to the spirit of Lakatos, one must envisage the possibility of this orthodox research programme running into serious trouble, to such an extent that it can become degenerate. In short, a scientific research programme, as understood by Lakatos, would not privilege the equilibrium core of orthodox economics. In the long run it is subjected to serious critique and could falter (Lakatos 1970).

However, when we pass to the other major parameter of the core of orthodox economics, namely rationality, the situation is different. The concept of rationality in this core is that of a maximiser operating under given constraints. Rationality in this orthodox conception is absolutely privileged in the sense that in the long run it is not open to faltering and is therefore not vulnerable to Lakatosian degeneration. Popper arguably recognised this explicitly in his Harvard lecture, as we saw earlier, when he insisted that 'the attempt to replace the rationality principle by another one seems to lead to complete arbitrariness in our model-building' (Popper 1994: 78).

Why is the concept of rationality absolutely privileged? There is a complex network of interrelated reasons. First, the concept of rationality is analogous to the concept of consistency in formal logic in that it has a prescriptive dimension to it. In the prescriptive discipline of logic, from Aristotle to Frege and Hilbert, the notion of consistency is absolutely indispensable. Logicians must ascertain whether or not a particular deductive system is consistent. If it is found to be inconsistent, it is dismissed as being seriously flawed. Similarly with the prescriptive notion of rationality: it is absolutely indispensable to any critical evaluation of our behaviour or actions. Like logic, we should be in a position to ascertain whether or not a specific action or range of actions, is rational or not. If an action is found to be irrational, is it dismissed as being flawed. Both consistency and rationality are prescriptive and evaluative concepts. Second, thanks to the astonishing developments in logic in the early twentieth century, accomplished by Frege, Russell, Hilbert and others, logicians developed objective standards for systematically evaluating the consistency of deductive systems. Have we any similar objective criterion or benchmark against which we can evaluate the rationality of our actions? The benchmark emerges as *homo economicus*, the utility maximiser of orthodox neoclassical economic theory, who will play the pivotal role in evaluating schematically the consistency of our deductive thinking. Finally, in classical logic the issue of consistency is subject to the law of the excluded middle; a deductive system is either consistent or not. There are no gradations. The situation is not the same with rationality, which was understood and explicitly acknowledged by Popper. We do not attain the ideal of rationality, rather we act in a more or less rational way. This was precisely Popper's definition of his 'zero method', which entailed, as we saw earlier, the construction of models on the assumption of complex rationality and then estimating the deviation of actual behaviour from the model behaviour, with the latter serving as a kind of zero co-ordinate.

Clearly Popper's assumption of complete rationality, the *homo economicus* of orthodox economic theory, is an idealisation which functions as a fundamental, indispensable benchmark. It is the ideal against which, or in light of which, social scientists estimate the deviation of actual behaviour. In this sense rationality is similar in nature and function to the concept of equilibrium. Popper is not claiming that an idealised rational agent actually exists in social reality. It does however exist in Popper's third world. In this Popperian third world, orthodox theorising has spelled out in clear terms what precisely is involved in being completely rational, i.e. in being a maximising rational agent. The Popperian 'zero method' to be used in any third world social science is to estimate the deviation of actual behaviour from this ideal.

Popperian scholars are concerned with examining how Popper developed this conception of the 'zero method' and its implications, strengths and weaknesses for the methodology of the social sciences. Our purpose in this chapter is not concerned with this particular aspect of Popperian scholarship. Rather, we wish to address the substantive Popperian claim that any rejection of the orthodox conception of an idealised rational agent would render our model building completely arbitrary. Our aim, in short, is to critically interrogate the privileging of the core of rationality, a position which retains its centrality and pivotal methodological role in orthodox economic theorising and model building. In the following sections we will examine the contributions of two of the leading philosophers of the twentieth century, Quine and Wittgenstein, whose works included the most powerful insights into the conceptual and pragmatic dimensions of rationality provided in contemporary philosophical thinking.

The rationality principle and the Duhem-Quine thesis

As noted in the previous section, one of the central constituents of Popper's third world is the problem situation. One may legitimately ask what the problem situations are in contemporary economic methodology. In a recent major survey of the field, the following issues were identified; 'under-determination, theory-ladenness, the social nature of science, relativism, antifoundationalism, and naturalism' (Hands 2001: 5),[25] to name but a few. In economic methodology the Duhem-Quine thesis is frequently addressed in the context of the testing of individual hypotheses (Cross 1982; Heijdra and Lowenberg 1986; Sawyer *et al.* 1997). According to the Duhem-Quine thesis, no hypothesis comes before the 'bar of experience' in total isolation. Rather what comes before the bar of experience is a specific hypothesis and its background context, what Popper calls 'background knowledge'. Hence if the logical consequence of a hypothesis is shown to be false, one in principle has a choice of where to lay the fault. The fault could lie with the hypothesis in question or with the background knowledge.

As early as the *Poverty of Historicism*, Popper was aware of this thesis, as elaborated by Duhem. Popper described Duhem as one of 'the greatest modern deductivists', and praised him for his anti-inductivist stand. Popper reads Duhem as an instrumentalist. However, even here he admits that 'Duhem is right when he says that we can test only huge and complex theoretical systems rather than isolated hypotheses' (Popper 1957: 131 fn. 2). He suggests, however, that the testing of an individual hypothesis is not completely ruled out by this Duhem thesis. He maintains that:

> If we test two such systems which differ in one hypothesis only, and if we can design experiments which refute the first system while leaving the second very well corroborated, then we may be on reasonably safe grounds if we attribute the failure of the first system to that hypothesis in which it differs from the other.
>
> (Popper 1957: 131 fn. 2)

This Popperian response to the Duhem-Quine thesis is compatible with his falsifiability principle.

Over the last decade, Hausman also uses the Duhem-Quine thesis to legitimise the rational core of orthodox economics, or, if one prefers, Popper's rationality principle. This claim is, to say the least, rather interesting. Hausman insists that he 'has serious objections to Popper's philosophy of science (Hausman 1992a: 74). Hausman's objections pertain to Popper's falsifiability criterion and do not address Popper's philosophy of the social sciences. According to Hausman, 'economics is built around a normative theory of rationality' (ibid.: 2). 'This normative theory is not open to falsification because of the Duhem-Quine thesis

(Hausman 1992b: 207). To justify this conclusion, Hausman adds what he terms 'the weak-link principle' to the Duhem-Quine thesis. This weak-link principle is *prima facie* unobjectionable. It states that 'when a false conclusion depends on a number of uncertain premises, attribute the mistake to the most uncertain of the premises' (ibid.: 207). When this weak-link principle is applied to orthodox economics, its normative theory of rationality is absolutely privileged and is not open to rejection. Rather orthodox economists believe that their simplifications and *ceteris paribus* assumptions are the weak links. In other words, when a prediction of orthodox economics is falsified by empirical data, the blame lies at the door of economists' weak-link assumptions and not at the door of their theory of rationality. In short, according to Hausman, 'mistaken predictions *never* wind up disconfirming the theory' (Hausman 1992b: 208). Thus Hausman concurs with Popper's thesis that 'the attempt to replace the rationality principle by another one seems to lead to complete arbitrariness in our model building' (Popper 1994: 178). In our opinion this defence of the rationality principle is not justifiable. In order to show this we revisit the Duhem-Quine thesis.

An important dimension of the Duhem-Quine under-determination thesis is focused on the theory of testing. Three versions of this thesis can be distinguished. As noted above, the underdetermination thesis holds that single descriptive propositions or hypotheses are never tested in isolation. Empirical testing presupposes complexes or systems of sentences. We call this formulation of the thesis the weak version of the Duhem-Quine under-determination thesis. This weak version of the thesis at the level of testing follows from the meaning dimension of Quine's holism. Since, for Quine, meaning is characterised as existing within a system of sentences, it follows that at the level of testing a single descriptive sentence cannot be tested on its own. Consequently, the assertion of Quine's holism at the level of meaning and the denial of the weak Duhem-Quine under-determination thesis at the level of testing is inconsistent.

A second and stronger version of the under-determination thesis is discernible in Quine's work. Hesse articulates this stronger thesis as follows: 'no *descriptive* statement can be individually falsified by evidence, whatever the evidence may be, since adjustments in the rest of the system can always be devised to prevent its *falsification*' (Hesse 1970: 195 our italics). The weak thesis refers only to the fact that single propositions are not tested individually. It makes no reference to the issue of adjusting the system for the purposes of preventing the falsification of some preferred proposition or belief. This latter issue is identified and resolved by the formulation of the stronger version of the under-determination thesis. It asserts that science can dramatically adjust its system in order to prevent the falsification of any descriptive statement taken on its own.

The stronger version of the Duhem-Quine underdetermination thesis explicitly allows for the bar of experience at a holistic level. It is a scientific system as a whole, rather than individual propositions, which comes before the tribunal of experience. Allowing for this, Popperians are arguably correct in pointing out that actual science can and does refute definite portions of a theory and the stronger version of the underdetermination thesis cannot coherently account for this fact

(Popper 1963: 243). Popperians are drawing our attention to the scientific practice of empirically testing individual propositions which is as old as science itself. While the stronger version of the Duhem-Quine thesis challenges this practice, we argue that the weak version of the thesis does not. Rather, the latter version retains the scientific practice but fully acknowledges its fragility and fallibility.

We can examine, albeit briefly, by way of illustration two of the usual ways in which it has been suggested that an isolated proposition may be refuted. The first involves the Popperian notion of testing *vis-à-vis* background knowledge. According to some Popperians we can hold the background knowledge stable and thereby refute an isolated hypothesis. In principle, what we can call weak Duhem-Quine theorists, have no objection to this pragmatic approach. On the contrary, they quickly draw our attention to the fact that such an acceptance or retention of the background knowledge is, even by Popperian standards, provisional. Consequently, this Popperian strategy is not incompatible with the weak Duhem-Quine thesis. There is nothing in the latter approach which rules out this kind of pragmatic strategy. The weak Duhem-Quine thesis underlines both the vulnerability of this strategy and its pragmatic character. In the second approach, practising scientists tend to divide their theories into high-level and low-level parts and they frequently hold that the lower-level is better corroborated or confirmed than the higher level. Consequently, if a scientific theory is falsified by empirical evidence, the scientists, quite correctly, tend to locate the responsibility in the less confirmed parts of the theory. Without prejudice to the complexities of confirmation theory, weak Duhem-Quine theorists do not make a fundamental or epistemological distinction between the theoretical and observational aspects of science. This does not mean that they do not accept the wisdom of various pragmatic procedures developed during the course of the history of science. Their point is that these pragmatic approaches have no grounding in some absolutist foundational epistemology. The fifth milestone of Quine's naturalism, namely, the abandonment of a first philosophy, comes into play at this point. Our epistemological endeavours are much more modest and fragile than those warranted by the reconstruction of the whole edifice of knowledge from unassailable foundations.

The third and strongest version of the Duhem-Quine underdetermination thesis is succinctly summarised in Quine's own words: 'Any statement can be held true come what may, if we make drastic enough adjustments elsewhere in the system' (Quine 1953: 43). This strongest version of the thesis is very radical in both content and implications. It applies to every kind of statement – descriptive, theoretical, law-like, a priori, analytical, logical laws – whereas the stronger version merely applies to descriptive statements. Quine's famous rejection of the analytic/synthetic dichotomy is a pivotal influence in this extension to every kind of statement. Since the whole of our knowledge is a man-made web which touches reality only along the edges, there is no foundational epistemological way of dividing this web into purely analytical and synthetic dimensions or, alternatively stated, into logical and empirical dimensions. Consequently, this version of the thesis is extended to every category of statement. Unlike the second or stronger version of the under-determination thesis, this third version goes well beyond the issue of the falsifiability of an individual descriptive statement or scientific hypothesis. The focus is on the truth of these and other statements or hypotheses, rather than their falsifiability. The strongest thesis maintains that any statement can be held true by adding sufficiently drastic adjustments to the rest of the system. Clearly, this strongest version of the thesis is very close to relativism in tone and content.

Quine endorsed all three theses as identified here. More often than not the three theses are not distinguished from each other, particularly since the weak and stronger theses are implied by the strongest underdetermination version of the thesis. For our purposes, however, the distinction is vital. We do not subscribe to the Duhem-Quine thesis in its strongest version. We start with Quine's holism at the level of meaning, in particular the thesis that all scientific descriptions are theory-laden. From this the issue that is of interest to us is, what price must be paid at the level of testing for accepting this holistic thesis at the level of meaning. Quine himself, as commonly interpreted, wants to extract the highest price, i.e. the strongest underdetermination thesis. There is, however, no need to pay such a high price. The weak underdetermination thesis is necessarily implied by Quine's holism at the level of meaning, but this in turn does not necessarily imply either the stronger or the strongest thesis. In particular, and in view of Quine's fifth milestone of naturalism, that there is no prior philosophy, the weak Duhem-Quine underdetermination theorist holds that the well established scientific strategy of testing statements in isolation is not grounded in any absolutist foundational epistemology. For Quine, according to this fifth milestone, there is no such epistemological vantage point. However, this does not imply that the established scientific strategy of testing statements in isolation, when properly used, is not a wise practice. The weak Duhem-Quine underdetermination theorist retains it as such and thereby draws our attention to its sheer contingency and fallibility. In principle, science has the option of questioning the results of the empirical testing of individual sentences.

In general past experience teaches science not to exercise this principle except in exceptional circumstances. But is this not the point of Hausman's weak-link principle? Exceptional circumstances arise in economics. The weakness of the orthodox simplifications are such that it is reasonable to divert the impact of negative evidence onto these and away from the privileged core. However, in applying the Duhem-Quine thesis to orthodox economics, Hausman is assuming that the core of orthodoxy is guaranteed as being for the most part true. In a Quinean perspective the core of orthodoxy, like the core of any other science, is theory-laden. And from an economic point of view the core of orthodoxy, as specified by Hausman, is argued to be so restrictive as to be inhibiting in enabling the full potential of theory-laden research within orthodoxy itself to be carried out.[26] The core itself is not privileged, it is in a Quinean framework open to the bar of experience.

Why is the core of orthodox economics so blessed for Hausman? A principal reason is his acceptance of common-sense realism, which became evident in his work in the late 1990s (Hausman 1998). Common-sense realism makes economics a unique science, according to Hausman, quite distinct from physics.

'Physics postulates new unobservables', Hausman argues, ' to whose existence common-sense realism does not commit us. Although economics refers to unobservables, it does not, in contrast to physics, postulate new ones'. Rather economic unobservables 'have been part of common-sense understanding of the world for millennia' (Hausman 1998: 197–8). The core of orthodox economics is guaranteed by common-sense realism, and the orthodox understanding of rationality is guaranteed by our common-sense notion of a rational person which has been central to a long tradition of western thought.

In our view it is certainly true to say that the orthodox economic notion of rationality is linked to our common-sense networks of rational decision-making. The link, however, is not one of defining rationality in a realist sense, i.e. specifying the essence of rationality. Rather the orthodox theory of rationality is, in Quinean terminology, an explication of our so-called common-sense usages of the term 'rational' in our language-games. This Quinean explication works in the following way. Orthodox economists are aware of how the term 'rational' is used in our language-games, ranging from law to investment decisions. They are also aware that its usage in specific language-games can be troublesome. For instance, inconsistency in some legal decision-making over time or across different legal jurisdictions is well acknowledged. This troublesome aspect, however, is not insurmountable. Orthodox economists have focused on particular functions of our common-sense usages of rationality that they consider fruitful and they then 'devised a substitute, clear and couched in terms to their liking that fills those functions. Beyond these conditions of partial agreements dictated by their interests and purposes', their theory introduced 'all manner of novel connotations never associated' with the ordinary usages of rationality (Quine 1960: 258–9). In this way the orthodox notion of rationality is certainly linked to our so-called common-sense usages, but it neither sums it up nor defines it. Rather it is a novel reconstruction of rationality which orthodox economists find useful and capable of articulation within a mathematical framework, which they exploit in a variety of novel ways. In addition there is, within a Quinean context, always more than one way of explicating common-sense terms like rationality.

In this connection an example may be offered. William James, one of the father's of American pragmatism, referred to decisions which were 'momentous, lived and forced'. Take a high-technology firm working at the frontiers of nanotechnology. To date the firm has poured hundreds of millions of euros into its R&D. Over the last two years it has narrowed down its major research programme to two different techniques, let us say lithography using X-rays and lithography using electron beams. Now one of these lines has to be closed down. However, the scientists do not know which technique is likely to be optimal and argue that in eighteen months or so they would be in a much better position to evaluate the relative merits of the alternatives. The firm, under pressure of rival competition, cannot afford to wait. Its decision is 'momentous, lived and forced'. Moreover, the R&D is so novel, past experience is no guide. In Keynesian terms the decision is beyond the parameters of risk; it is in the realm of the uncertain. Is the company irrational in making its decision? Hardly, but it will get little help from the orthodox theory of rationality as encapsulated in Popper's rationality principle. And within a Quinean framework the privileging of rationality is, as we have argued, neither justified nor viable.

A Wittgensteinian challenge to the rationality principle

Popper's defence of the rationality principle is also challenged by a later Wittgensteinian approach. In our view, Popper's defence of the rationality principle belongs to a tradition extending at least from the writings of John Stuart Mill. In particular, this Millieau tradition claims that some rationality principles are so basic as to be beyond dispute. This is reflected in Robbins' discussion of how the 'propositions of economic theory, like all scientific theory, are obviously deductions from a series of postulates', and that the 'chief of these postulates are all assumptions involving in some way simple and indisputable facts of experience relating to the way in which the scarcity of goods is the subject-matter of our science actually shows itself in the world of reality' (Robbins 1932: 78). Hence, the main postulate of the theory of value for Robbins is the fact that individuals can arrange their preferences, while that of the theory of production is that there is more than one factor of production. Likewise, the main postulates of the theory of dynamics is that we are not certain regarding future scarcities. For Robbins:

> These are not postulates the existence of whose counterpart in reality admits of extensive dispute once their nature is fully realised. We do not need controlled experiments to establish their validity: they are so much the stuff of everyday experience that they have only to be stated to be recognised as obvious.
>
> (Robbins 1932: 79)

Here we can refer to Wittgenstein's later work, *On Certainty* (Wittgenstein 1969), in which he engages G.E. Moore's celebrated defence of common-sense realism on the one hand and the Cartesian sceptic on the other, to buttress Robbins' thesis that orthodox economic principles of rationality are 'so much the stuff of everyday experience that they have only to be stated to be recognised as obvious'. In *On Certainty*, Wittgenstein makes clear that some positions are so basic to our everyday forms of life that there is no viable way in which they could be doubted. As Kenny (1973: 208) points out, according to Wittgenstein, various types of doubt are ruled out: there are some propositions about which we cannot doubt but about which we are not mistaken. The contrast to be drawn is between madness and a mistake: in a mistake there is false judgement, whereas in madness no judgement is exercised. For instance, to doubt that my friend hasn't sawdust in his head would be madness, not a mistake (Wittgenstein 1969: 281). However, for Wittgenstein, 'to say that something cannot be doubted, or cannot be the subject of a mistake, is not the same as to say it can be *known*' (Kenny 1973: 211 italics in original). For Wittgenstein, 'I know that p' makes sense only when, for instance, 'I do not know', or 'I doubt', or 'I will check up that …' and so on make sense. In short, Wittgenstein disagreed with Moore that there are indubitable propositions that are *known*, but he agreed that there are special, empirical-like propositions that are 'solid' or 'stand fast' and cannot be doubted (Wittgenstein 1969: 112, 116, 151). These special basic propositions are not axioms in the sense that axioms are the point of departure in a deductive system. Neither do they provide grounds for our language-games. Rather, they are integral to our actions and 'it is our acting which lies at the bottom of the language-game' (Wittgenstein 1969: 204).

Robbins' defence of the core of rationality could be reconstructed along these Wittgensteinian lines. Thus, neoclassical principles of rationality, although technically not known, cannot be doubted. They are basic. They 'stand fast' for us in that they are rooted in our social actions, which in turn constitute our forms of life. Robbins' own turn of phrase is opposite: 'they are so much the stuff of everyday experience that they have only to be stated to be recognised' (Robbins 1932: 79). In other words, some subset of the rationality principles of orthodox microeconomics forms the basis of human action in the economic world and therefore it is either unreasonable or impossible to doubt these principles. They constitute an immutable core of rational actions in economics. In the context of a changeable external economic reality, rational actions must be governed by some set of basic principles. The philosophy of the later Wittgenstein could then be argued to provide a defence of a changeable external economic environment at a macro-level, but when applied at the micro-level it buttresses the immutability of the core of orthodox or neoclassical rationality.

Despite the initial plausibility of this application of Wittgenstein's on what is basic to the rationality principles of orthodox economics, we argue that, on a more careful analysis, it is not justifiable. In the *Philosophical Investigations*, Wittgenstein warns us that a main cause of philosophical disease is a one-sided diet of examples. He also warns us not to think that there must be some common core; rather we should look at the broadest range of relevant examples available and see whether there is something common or not. When, for example, we look at the well-ordering axioms of orthodox rationality theory, which assumes that each agent has a complete and transitive preference ordering of all possible choices, we see that it holds only for simple problems of decision-making. According to Savage, 'the behaviour of people is *often* at variance with the theory. The departure is sometimes flagrant' (Savage 1954: 20 our italics). However, if behaviour is often at variance with orthodox theory, then of course the theory cannot be basic in the Wittgensteinian sense of basic. As we have already seen, Wittgenstein gives priority to forms of life. In looking at forms of life, Wittgenstein was looking for what is basic to human actions in these contexts. Savage's point is precisely that the standard axioms of choice are not basic in this sense: they are not the 'the stuff of everyday experience'.

More generally, the philosophy of the later Wittgenstein is utterly incompatible with the orthodox economics picture of rationality. This incompatibility hinges on a web of presuppositions underlying the neoclassical theory. We focus on three of these presuppositions, namely the neoclassical assumptions of a universal core of rationality, methodological individualism which includes introspection, and optimisation or more generally algorithmic calculation.

Let us consider, first, the assumption that there must be a universal, generative core to economic rationality. This assumption is buttressed by the reductionist demand for the basic building blocks of economic rationality. Just as there are basic generative axioms in Euclidean geometry, there must be basic axioms to economic rationality. The later Wittgenstein's anti-essentialism undermines this reductionist picture. Just as the reduction of pure mathematics to logic fails to capture the richness and creativity of mathematics, the axiomatic reduction of economic rationality to the core neoclassical axioms fails to capture the complexity and innovative character of rationality. The prescriptive core of neoclassical rationality becomes obsolete. In place of this reductionist core, a Wittgensteinian will put the emphasis on, first, the heterogeneity of forms of life and the complex differences in rationality in these contexts and, second, on the search for family resemblances between these, rather than an essentialist core. Thus a Wittgensteinian will emphasise the necessity for observational field studies of rationality. In these studies, in place of prescriptively engaging in an obsessive drive for a single or unified abstract theory of rationality, economists will look for family resemblances between various classes of economic decision-making in various economic domains, whether it be consumption, saving, investment, production or trade. Subsequently, they will identify families of parameters governing rational decision-making in different economic sectors and investigate the complex ways in which these interact, evolve or change. The orthodox prescriptive core is replaced by the observational studies of economic decision-making in its rich, socially divergent contexts.

We turn second to methodological individualism and its psychological privileging of introspection. A specific kind of methodological individualism informs neoclassical economics; each individual is postulated to have a private mind to which each has privileged access through introspection. Thus, as Hausman points out, the core principles of rationality are privileged by introspection (Hausman 1992b: 14). Moreover, each rational agent is postulated as an independent atomistic individual against the background of the natural world. Thus the social world is a constructed derivative, with social contract theories from Hobbes to Rawls coming to mind. Language is also accidental, serving the primary purpose of expressing our independently existing thoughts and passions, which are private mental events. The later Wittgenstein devoted considerable time and effort to this nineteenth-century picture of ourselves. In this later Wittgensteinian approach, dynamic public languages inextricably woven into public actions constitute the human world. The focus is on public forms of life. The individual, in this framework, is not conceptualised against the backdrop of the physical universe, rather it is the social forms of life which provide the backdrop against which the individual is viewed. In addition, and contrary to the nineteenth-century picture, rationality is not essentially private. It resides in our public, dynamic and changing language-games.

This Wittgensteinian approach has major ramifications for the study of rationality in economics. First, introspection, with its privileged access to the fixed internal principles of the mind, is redundant. Introspection, as noted above, is closely associated with nineteenth-century and earlier philosophies of the mind that postulate introspection as an infallible means of privileged access by each individual to the inner private contents of one's mind, to which no other person has access. A Wittgensteinian emphasis on public language-games that are social, combined with the Wittgensteinian thesis of the impossibility of a private language, renders these introspective philosophies obsolete. Introspection is a philosophical fiction and therefore cannot privilege any principles of rationality. Introspection, which acted as an infallible guarantor of neoclassical rationality, is a myth. This, in turn, liberates economics from the inhibiting influence of its prescriptivism in the domain of rationality.

Second, it liberates economics from the constraints of methodological individualism. The different variants of methodological individualism are philosophically centred on the individualistic turns taken by both classical rationalism and empiricism. However, twentieth-century philosophy of language accomplished nothing short of a paradigm shift. This paradigm shift is clearly reflected in the philosophy of the later Wittgenstein. The shift is from the individual to the social and from private, inaccessible, individual minds to public language-games or forms of life. These public forms of life are rooted in a social, non-reductionist ontology. In this Wittgensteinian perspective there is no philosophical or methodological anxiety about the status of a Keynesian macro-level of analysis. However, the neoclassical reductionist mentality, which requires the subordination of the macro- to the micro-level, where individualistic parameters reign supreme, is deemed to be both unnecessary and misguided. Third, any economic theory of rationality will have to integrate social learning into its core. The challenge is to look and observe how people learn to be rational and then to construct insightful models of this activity. The picture of an atomistic individual against the backdrop of nature is fruitless here. In contrast, the Wittgensteinian framework opens up a rich variety of approaches ranging from detailed socio-historical analysis to computer simulation studies and complexity theory, with the appropriate emphasis on local, regional and transnational factors. In short, the reductionist programme, whereby all economic rationality is reduced to the neoclassical core is abandoned, thereby opening the door to a rich and variegated range of conceptual and analytical possibilities.

Finally, we turn to Wittgenstein's efforts to undermine the implicit assumption that rational decision-making is basically a matter of calculation, an assumption that is central to the orthodox programme of rationality. In this programme, a rational economic agent is a maximiser, a self-interested calculator. A later Wittgensteinian approach rejects this assumption. A number of considerations derived from Wittgenstein can be invoked to show that rationality and calculation are quite distinct. There is, first, the fact that in his philosophy of mathematics, Wittgenstein rejects all foundational programmes that attempt to reduce mathematical calculation to logic. Mathematical calculation is to be seen in the context of pre-existing human language-games or forms of life and not as the product of a non-contextualised Platonic world of pure reason. The notion of pure reason is for the later Wittgenstein nothing but a mythical creation of a misguided philosophy. Mathematical calculation for Wittgenstein presupposes human language-games. Consequently, rationality is not reducible to calculation.

Then there is the emphasis which the later Wittgenstein puts on learning. In particular, the process of how we learn to calculate in mathematics presupposes a vast social network of human interactions that precede this learning. Moreover, this network has rationality already deeply embedded in it. We need to examine critically therefore how we learn to be rational. In this Wittgensteinian context, learning rationality in very different contexts along with its dynamic path dependency are crucial to an understanding of rationality. These considerations are, however, missing from the reductionist neoclassical programme. Again, for Wittgensteinians, rational decision-making is undetermined by algorithms or calculi. For instance, when there is a conflict in logic or mathematics, we can frequently resolve the conflict by showing an error in the calculation or the application of the algorithm. However, when there is a conflict about a qualitative issue, we do not bring the conflict to an end in the same manner. This latter type of conflict is not the outcome of miscalculation. In any event the procedures for dealing with miscalculations are irrelevant when it comes to talking someone out of an irrational decision. For instance the efforts by which an economist attempts to persuade a politician from making politically opportunistic decisions which violate principles of rational policy-making will be very different from those used to explain a miscalculation in solving a differential equation. Finally, it is irrational to judge when one is not competent to do so, but again this is not analogous to a miscalculation in differential geometry. For these and other considerations, a Wittgensteinian drawing from his later work, will reject the neoclassical reductionist programme. As Putnam succinctly stated it, ‘this conception of rationality is deeply embedded in a scientism inherited from the nineteenth-century which attempts to erode the issue of giving a sane and human description of the scope of reason’ (Putnam 1981: 126). How, then, are we to model rationality in economics? A Wittgensteinian framework will not prohibit the creative modelling of rationality, whether through mathematics or otherwise. It will however caution that in constructing mathematical models of rationality, economists must be alert to the limited nature of these models. This is particularly the case if this modelling is underlain by a reductionist programme as reflected in the orthodox economic theorising of rationality. At its most fundamental, the Wittgensteinian approach calls seriously into question a unified body of economic doctrine in this domain, and makes a cogent case for the necessity of a more pluralistic approach to economic theorising as is now discernible in the field of economic methodology (Salanti and Screpanti 1997).

Conclusion

Popperian scholars have been actively engaged for some considerable period in attempting to clarify Popper’s contribution to the methodology of the social sciences. This involves two separate, but related, tasks. One is to reconcile the rationality principle as formulated in Popper’s strong version of the zero-principle with the principle of adequacy of action or his weak version of the zero-principle as contained in his situational analysis framework. The second task is concerned with reconciling his rationality principle and situational analysis with his more general philosophy of science, in particular his doctrine of falsifiability and other aspects of his general philosophy. In both cases Popper has bequeathed methodologists of the social sciences with a number of considerable and challenging tasks. The fact that Popper has not provided a very satisfactory theory of rationality as the behavioural basis of economics is hardly surprising. He appealed after all to the orthodox economic theory of rational action complete with its limited, restrictive and underlying reductionist perspective. His rationality principle, as defined in his earlier or strong version of the zero-principle certainly provides a benchmark which acts as a powerful regulative methodological principle, but is substantively vacuous or even empirically false. His shift to a principle of adequacy of action, which underlies his situational analysis is ambiguous as between a subjective or objective reading of the aims and information of the agent interacting with their environment which constitute the core of the situational analysis.

The appeal for Popper of the most advanced social science, i.e. economics, must arguably be rationalised by reference to other considerations. It provided him with an individualist basis of approach, while appearing to provide a distance from the psychologism to which he was vehemently opposed. This was of very considerable importance to Popper as we demonstrated earlier in this chapter. His indebtedness to Austrian economics, particularly under the influence of Hayek, provided him with the conceptual framework which facilitated his assault on historicism. The intellectual origins of this development go back to the *Methodenstreit*, and the methodological disputes between the German Historical School and the Austrian School, the latter under the leadership of Carl Menger. Popper, in the context of his own time, following his break from socialism, and even briefly communism, was motivated by his own emerging political agenda of opposition to authoritarianism and totalitarianism in the form of communism and fascism. He was able to draw on this larger and earlier intellectual debate between the two competing methodologies of the social sciences that preoccupied central European economists over an extended period. In this context Popper was a good Austrian.

However, in developing his own distinctive methodological framework for the social sciences, Popper has not provided us with a very satisfactory theory of rationality as a behavioural basis for economics. He was not, apart from a small number of exceptions, prepared to seriously engage the work of leading contemporary philosophers. This is surprising and intriguing, particularly in the second or later period of his interest in the methodology of the social sciences, i.e. in the 1960s. If he had engaged with the implications of Quine and Wittgenstein's work for the theory of rationality, we have argued in this chapter that Popper's position would have been seriously challenged. Presumably this would not have presented him with a major problem, since engagement with problems and problem solving was at the core of his own philosophy. In the event we will never know his responses to these challenges, but the reconfiguration of rationality theory in the light of these considerations, in addition to reconciling the internal issues of Popper's own contribution remain major tasks for the social sciences.

Notes

1 Souter's contribution should be seen in the context of the debate that was occurring in the 1930s largely as a result of the publication of Lionel Robbins' seminal essay of 1932 (Robbins 1932). Talcott Parsons reviewed the work of both Robbins and Souter in Parsons (1934). Parsons warned that 'economic imperialism … results not only in enriching these neighbouring 'countries', which of course it does, but [also] in putting some of them into a strait jacket of 'economic' categories which is ill-suited to their own conditions' (Parsons 1934: 512).

2 On the ambiguities and weaknesses of rational choice theory see Sen (1977, 1985, 1987, 1997, 2002), Sugden (1991), Arrow *et al.* (1996), Walsh (1996), Laville (2000), Lindenberg (2001), Viskovatoff (2001).

3 See the Symposium on 'Rationality and Methodology' in the special issue of *The Journal of Economic Methodology*, Vol. 4, Number 1, June 1997. It contains papers by Anand and Runde (1997), Binmore (1997), Mariotti (1997), Colman (1997), Russell (1997), Lawson (1997).

4 The paper that Popper is referring to is Hayek's 'Economics and Knowledge', published in *Economica*, Vol. 4, February 1937, pp. 33–54, which was reprinted in Hayek's *Individualism and Economic Order* (Chicago, IL: University of Chicago Press, 1948).

5 It is not clear when Popper presented this paper at Hayek's seminar, but presumably it was later in 1936. In any event its publication was delayed by the fact that he sent it to *Mind*, but it was rejected. It was eventually published in three parts in *Economica*,Vol. XI, no. 42 and no. 43, 1944 and Vol. XII, no. 46, 1945 respectively.

6 Popper's hostility to the fundamental thesis of historicism goes back to the winter of 1919–20, but the main outline of his anti-historicist position was not completed until 1935 (Popper 1957: iv). See Notturno (1999) for an interesting episode in Popper's career immediately after the First World War which influenced his political disposition.

7 Interestingly at this juncture, Popper refers to the use of the 'null hypothesis' as used in a paper by J. Marschak on 'Money Illusion and Demand Analysis', published in *The Review of Economic Statistics*, Vol. 25, No. 1, February 1943, which he compares as sharing a similarity with what Hayek, following Menger, called the 'compositive' method.

8 See Popper (1957), particularly Section 32, pp. 152–9.

9 For an account of how *The Open Society* grew out of *The Poverty of Historicism* see Popper (2002: 130), Simkin (1993).

10 For an interesting assessment of this work after half a century, see Jarvie and Pralong (1999).

11 A footnote in the text refers to the use of the word [objective], where the impression is given that [objective] was inserted in the English edition. The footnote refers the reader to later work, more specifically to Popper's paper 'On the Theory of the Objective Mind', which we refer to later in the chapter.

12 It has been noted that this was the last occasion on which he refers to methodological individualism (Hedstrom *et al.* 1998: 348). See also Agassi (1960).

13 This is an intriguing concept which was not developed by Popper. See Agassi (1975) and Jarvie (1972).

14 The full text of this lecture was not published until 1994 (Popper 1994). The text published in 1994 differs in a number of minor points, deemed to be of little interest, from the text of the lecture delivered at Harvard on 26 February 1963 (Hedstrom *et*

al 1998: 361 fn. 10). The 1994 published version also contains two new sections, which were added in 1963 and 1964 respectively. An extract from the 1963 lecture was published in French under the title 'La Rationalité et le statut du principe de rationalité in *Les Fondements Philosophiques des Systèmes Économiques: Textes de Jacques Rueff et Essais redigés en son Honneur*, ed. E.M. Claasen (Paris: Payot, 1967), pp. 142–50. This book was a *Festschrift* for the celebrated French economist, Professor Jacques Rueff. This extract was translated into English and published in *A Pocket Popper*, ed. D. Millar (Fontana Paperbacks, 1983), pp. 357–65 under the title 'The Rationality Principle'.

15 Uncharacteristic of Popper, who could hardly be accused of being unduly burdened by excess modesty, he immediately continues after this statement: 'You will understand my fear that you may, as economists, find my views trivial – if not altogether out of date' (Popper 1994: 154). By all accounts Popper's self-deprecating tactic was prescient, to the extent that 'Popper's speech did not make too much of an impression on the Harvard community is clear from the fact that Abram Bergson, when we interviewed him did not recall that Popper had ever been at Harvard (interview with Bergson on 6 August 1997)' (Hedstrom *et al.* 1998: 362 fn. 10). It should be noted that it was Bergon who had invited Popper to Harvard and was then in charge of organising the political economy lectures, under whose rubric Popper's lecture was delivered.

16 One strongly suspects that a large part of his Harvard audience of economists were deeply imbued with the values of instrumentalism, given the influence of Milton Friedman's paper 'The methodology of positive economics', which had been published ten years earlier (Friedman 1953).

17 Popper illustrates his thinking by way of an example, which stands arguably as one of the most lucid examples in the philosophy of the social sciences, with the help of a pedestrian whom Popper confers with the endearing name of Richard (Popper 1994: 166–8).

18 This is section 12 of Popper (1994), pp. 177–8.

19 The rationality principle and situational analysis has generated an extensive literature. For the more recent important contributions see *Papers from the Vienna Workshop on Popper's Situational Analysis and the Social Sciences*, Part I in *Philosophy of the Social Sciences*, Vol. 28, Number 3, September 1998, while Part II of the Workshop Papers are contained in *Philosophy of the Social Sciences*, Vol. 28, Number 4, December 1998, under the guest editors Egon Matzner and I.C. Jarvie. These excellent collections of papers contain many of the most important references to earlier work on the rationality principle and situational analysis from philosophers, economic methodologists, sociologists and other social scientists. Since the publication of these papers in 1998, see Hacohen (2000), Oakley (2002).

20 This lecture was originally delivered in German in an abbreviated version, and was published in the same year, 1968 in *Akten des XIV International Kongresses fur Philosophie*, Vol. 1, University of Vienna, Verlag-Herder, Vienna, pp. 25–53. This is now published as Chapter 4, 'On the Theory of the Objective Mind', in Popper (1972), pp. 153–90. This chapter includes additional material, originally published in German in 1970 in *Schweizer Monatshefte*, Vol. 50, No. 3, pp. 207–15.

21 For an overview on the debates on methodological individualism, see Udehn (2001).

22 These issues are discussed in P.F. O'Gorman's chapter in this volume.

23 This was based on the distinction between 'laws of coexistence' (corresponding to statics) and 'laws of succession' (corresponding to dynamics) which was central to Comte and J.S. Mill's work on historical change and development.

24 See Koertge (1974, 1975, 1979).

25 Wade Hands has produced the most comprehensive, philosophically nuanced and methodologically informed survey of the field of economic methodology available to date, in addition to his cogent arguments for a 'new economic methodology'.

26 See Hahn (1996) which addresses Hausman's position, and Kuenne (1974, 1986, 1998) for a more general statement of the restrictiveness of current orthodox theoretical frameworks.

References

Agassi, J. (1960) 'Methodological individualism', *British Journal of Sociology*, 11: 244–70.

—— (1975) 'Institutional individualism', *British Journal of Sociology*, 26: 144–55.

Anand, P. and Runde, J. (1997) 'Introduction', *Journal of Economic Methodology*, 4: 1–23.

Arrow, K.J., Perlman, E. and Schmidt, C. (eds) (1996) *The Rational Foundations of Economic Behaviour*, London: Macmillan.

Becker, G. (1957) *The Economics of Discrimination*, Chicago, IL: University of Chicago Press.

Binmore, K. (1997) 'Rationality and backward induction', *Journal of Economic Methodology*, 4: 23–41.

Boland, L. (1981) 'On the futility of criticising the neoclassical maximisation hypothesis', *American Economic Review*, 71: 1031–6.

Colman, A. (1997) 'Salience and focusing in pure coordination games', *Journal of Economic Methodology*, 4: 61–81.

Conrad, A. and Meyer, J.R. (1958) 'The economics of slavery in the antebellum South', *Journal of Political Economy*, 66: 95–130.

Cross, R. (1982) 'The Duhem-Quine thesis, Lakatos and the appraisal of theories of macroeconomics', *Economic Journal*, 92: 320–40.

Downs, A. (1957) *An Economic Theory of Democracy*, New York: Harper and Row.

Foley, D.K. (1998) 'Introduction', in P.S. Albin (ed.) *Barriers and Bounds to Rationality*, Princeton, NJ: Princeton University Press.

Frege, G. (1968) *The Foundations of Arithmetic*, trans. J.L. Austin, Oxford: Blackwell.

Friedman, M. (1953) 'The methodology of positive economics', in M. Friedman *Essays in Positive Economics*, Chicago, IL: University of Chicago Press.

Friedman, J. (ed.) (1996) *The Rational Choice Controversy: Economic Models of Politics Reconsidered*, New Haven, CT: Yale University Press.

Green, D.P. and Shapiro, I. (1994) *Pathologies of Rational Choice Theory: A Critique of Applications in Political Science*, New Haven, CT: Yale University Press.

Hacohen, M.H. (2000) *Karl Popper – The Formative Years 1902–1945*, Cambridge: Cambridge University Press.

Hahn, F.H. (1996) 'Rerum cognoscere census', *Economics and Philosophy*, 12: 183–95.

Hands, D.W. (2002) *Reflection Without Rules: Economic Methodology and Contemporary Science Theory*, Cambridge: Cambridge University Press.

Harsanyi, J.C. (1977) *Rational Behaviour and Bargaining Equilibrium in Games and Social Situations*, Cambridge: Cambridge University Press.

Hausman, D.M. (1992a) *The Inexact and Separate Science of Economics*, Cambridge: Cambridge University Press.

—— (1992b) *Essays on Philosophy and Economic Methodology*, Cambridge: Cambridge University Press.

—— (1998) 'Problems with realism in economics', *Economics and Philosophy*, 14: 185–213.

Hechter, M. and Kanazawa, S. (1997) 'Sociological rational choice theory', *Annual Review of Sociology*, 23: 191–214.

Hedstrom, P., Swedberg, R. and Udehn, L. (1998) 'Popper's situational analysis and contemporary sociology', *Philosophy of the Social Sciences*, 28: 339–64.

Heijdra, B.J. and Lowenberg, A.D. (1986) 'Duhem-Quine, Lakatos and research programmes in economics', *The Journal of Interdisciplinary Economics*, 1: 175–87.

Hesse, M. (1970) 'Quine and a new empiricism', in G.N.A. Vesey (ed.) *Royal Institute of Philosophy Lectures 3: Knowledge and Necessity*, London: Macmillan.

Hogarth, R. and Reder, M. (eds) (1986) *Rational Choice: The Contrast between Economics and Psychology*, Chicago, IL: University of Chicago Press.

Jarvie, I.C. (1972) *Concepts and Society*, London: Routledge and Kegan Paul.

Jarvie, I. and Pralong, S. (1999) *Popper's Open Society after Fifty Years: The Continuing Relevance of Karl Popper*, London: Routledge.

Kenny, A. (1973) *Wittgenstein*, Middlesex: Penguin.

Keuth, H. (2005) *The Philosophy of Karl Popper*, Cambridge: Cambridge University Press.

Koertge, N. (1974) 'On Popper's philosophy of social sciences', in K.F. Schaffner and R.S. Cohen (eds) *Boston Studies in the Philosophy of Science*, Vol. 20, Dordrecht: Reidel.

—— (1975) 'Popper's metaphysical research program for the human sciences', *Inquiry*, 18: 437–62.

—— (1979) 'The methodological status of Popper's rationality principle', *Theory and Decision*, 10: 83–95.

Kuenne, R.E. (1974) 'Towards an operational general equilibrium theory with oligopoly: some experimental results and conjectures', *Kyklos*, 27: 792–820.

—— (1986) *Rivalrous Consonance: A Theory of General Oligopolistic Equilibrium*, Amsterdam: North Holland.

—— (1998) *Price and Non-Price Rivalry in Oligopoly*, London: Macmillan.

Lakatos, I. (1970) 'Falsification and the methodology of scientific research programmes', in I. Lakatos and A. Musgrave (eds) *Criticism and the Growth of Knowledge*, Cambridge: Cambridge University Press.

Laville, F. (2000) 'Should we abandon optimisation theory? the need for bounded rationality', *Journal of Economic Methodology*, 7: 395–426.

Lawson, T. (1997) 'Situated rationality', *Journal of Economic Methodology*, 4: 101–25.

Lindenberg, S. (2001) 'Social rationality versus rational egoism', in J. Turner (ed.) *Handbook of Sociological Theory*, New York: Kluwer Academic Publishers/Plenum.

Mariotti, M. (1997) 'Decisions in games: why there should be a special exemption from Bayesian Rationality', *Journal of Economic Methodology*, 4: 43–60.

Notturno, M.A. (1999) '*The Open Society and Its Enemies*: authority, community and bureaucracy', in I. Jarvie and S. Pralong (eds) *Popper's Open Society after Fifty Years*, London: Routledge.

Oakley, A. (2002) 'Popper's ontology of situated human action', *Philosophy of the Social Sciences*, 32: 455–86.

Parsons, T. (1934) 'Some reflections on "the human nature and significance of economics"', *Quarterly Journal of Economics*, 48: 511–45.

Popper, K.R. (1957) *The Poverty of Historicism*, London: Routledge and Kegan Paul.

—— (1963) *Conjectures and Refutations: The Growth of Scientific Knowledge*, London: Routledge and Kegan Paul.

—— (1972) *Objective Knowledge: An Evolutionary Approach*, Oxford: Clarendon Press.

—— (1976) 'The logic of the social sciences', in T.N. Adorno (ed.) *The Positivist Dispute in German Sociology*, London: Heinemann.
—— (1994) *The Myth of the Framework: In Defence of Science and Rationality*, ed. M.A. Motturno, London: Routledge.
____ (2002) *Unended Quest: An Intellectual Autobiography*, London: Routledge.
Putnam, H. (1981) *Reason, Truth and History*, Cambridge: Cambridge University Press.
Quine, W.V.O. (1953) *From a Logical Point of View*, New York: Harper and Row.
—— (1960) *Word and Object*, Cambridge, MA: MIT Press.
Robbins, L. (1932) *An Essay on the Nature and Significance of Economic Science*, London: Macmillan and Co.
Russell, T. (1997) 'The rationality hypothesis in economics: from Wall Street to Main Street', *Journal of Economic Methodology*, 4: 83:100.
Salanti, A. and Screpanti, E. (eds) (1997) *Pluralism in Economics: New Perspectives in History and Methodology*, Cheltenham: Edward Elgar.
Savage, L. (1954) *The Foundations of Statistics*, New York: Wiley.
Sawyer, K.R., Beed, C. and Sankey, H. (1997) 'Underdetermination in economics: the Duhem-Quine thesis', *Economics and Philosophy*, 13: 1–23.
Sen, A.K. (1977) 'Rational fools: a critique of the behavioural foundations of economic theory', *Philosophy and Public Affairs*, 6: 317–44.
—— (1985) 'Rationality and uncertainty', *Theory and Decision*, 18: 109–27.
—— (1987) *On Ethics and Economics*, Oxford: Blackwell.
—— (1997) 'Individual preference as the basis of social choice', in K.J. Arrow, A.K. Sen and K. Suzumura (eds) *Social Choice Re-examined*, Vol. 1, New York: St Martin's Press.
—— (2002) *Rationality and Freedom*, Cambridge, MA: Belknap Press.
Simkin, C. (1993) *Popper's Views on Natural and Social Science*, Leiden: E.J. Brill.
Souter, R.W. (1933) *Prolegomena to Relativity Economics: An Elementary Study in the Mechanics and Organics of an Expanding Economic Universe*, New York: Columbia University Press.
Sugden, R. (1991) 'Rational choice: a survey of contributions from economics and philosophy', *The Economic Journal*, 101: 751–85.
Udehn, L. (2001) *Methodological Individualism*, London: Routledge.
Vanberg, V.J. (2004) 'The rationality postulate in economics: its ambiguity, its deficiency and its evolutionary alternative', *Journal of Economic Methodology*, 11: 1–29.
Viskovatoff, A. (2001) 'Rationality as optimal choice versus rationality as valid inference', *Journal of Economic Methodology*, 8: 313–37.
Walsh, V. (1996) *Rationality, Allocation and Reproduction*, Oxford: Clarendon Press.
Wittgenstein, L. (1969) *On Certainty*, Oxford: Blackwell.

4 Popper and social explanation

Tony Lawson

Introduction

I want to consider the nature of one possible answer to an important question. For those of us engaged in social explanatory endeavour it may even be the most important research question we face. Certainly this appears to be the case from the perspective of the project to which I, and numerous others, have been contributing in recent years.[1] As formulated, though, it is a question that Popper seems never quite to have addressed despite his interest in social explanation. However, the nature of the particular answer to it on which I shall focus is, I think, very Popperian indeed, both because it is in the broad spirit of Popper's writings and also because Popper provides many, though not quite all, of its central ingredients.

A minor, or supplementary, question I wish to address is whether the current orientation to social explanation in modern economics warrants the label Popperian. Just as Popper often mentioned how his contribution to social explanation drew on economics, the few practising economists who give a nod to the philosophy of social science tend to describe themselves, and/or view modern mainstream economics, as being within the Popperian tradition. In concluding this chapter I briefly examine the appropriateness of this association.[2]

The question

So what, first of all, is the primary question to be addressed here, the one that I take to be so important? It is the following. *How can social explanatory work proceed in an open system context that lacks the possibility of experimental intervention?* Let me briefly explain my terms and indicate why I believe the question to be such an important one. Actually, I shall suggest that although Popper does not pose the question precisely as stated it may have been high on his agenda during the last years of his life. For it practically jumps out of his very last contributions. Certainly I think it to be a question the pursuit of which the later Popper would endorse. Eventually, I will, as I say, propose a somewhat 'Popperian' answer to it.

Ontology

The first point to make is that the question just noted arises as a result of ontological investigation. That is, it arises through a study of the nature of social reality, or social being. A concern with ontology is very much the emphasis of the realist project with which I have been involved for many years now, one often systematised as *critical realism*.[3] For it is a fundamental tenet of this project that the nature of the material we study bears significantly on how we can study it. All methods presuppose an implicit ontology. That is, all methods are appropriate for some conditions but not others. And all materials are such that they can be usefully investigated by some methods but not others. As Karl Marx once observed, 'in the analysis of economic forms neither microscopes nor chemical reagents are of assistance' (*Capital* Vol. I: 90). But the point is a general one.[4] The particular nature of the material of any sphere of reality makes a difference to how, if at all, we can come to know it.

Now I take the social realm to be that domain of phenomena whose existence depends at least in part on us, which, I take it, includes but I suspect is not exhausted by Popper's World 3.[5] And according to the conception I defend (Lawson 1997a, 2003), social reality is found to be in a fundamental sense *open*, which is why, of course, my question above is formulated in such terms. To understand what I mean by open let me first define a closed system. The latter is one in which regularities of the form, whenever event (or state of affairs) x then event (or state of affairs) y (or stochastic near equivalents) occur. Closures are conditions in which correlations hold, in which we find sufficiently strict (deterministic or probabilistic) patterns at the level of *actual* phenomena such as events and states of affairs. The thesis that reality consists only of closures, that all outcomes can, in effect, be accounted for using techniques of correlation analysis, can be referred to as *regularity determinism*.[6] And all forms of explanation which rest on the necessity of positing such closures, typically in conjunction with the stipulating of initial conditions, can be referred to as *deductivist*. Clearly, on this conception deductivism covers most examples of modern micro, macro and econometrics. All are forms of deductivist (closed-systems) modelling.

By interpreting a system as open I mean any that is not closed in the sense described. In an open system, not all events are predictable. It is a system where a knowledge of past events does not of necessity allow any inference as to future events that must come about. And by interpreting the social realm as fundamentally open I mean also to suggest that it is hardly amenable to local closure whether experimentally determined or spontaneous.

However, it is a further feature of the conception I defend that social reality is found to be not only open in the manner described but also *structured*. That is, it comprises not only *actualities* such as actual events and states of affairs, some of which we may directly experience, but also deeper structures, powers, mechanisms, and tendencies, etc., which produce, facilitate or otherwise condition these actualities. Tendencies here are a bit like forces. The category expresses the ways things act irrespective of the *actual* outcome. Gravitational tendencies draw autumn leaves to the ground (or leaves and the ground to each other) even *as* counteracting forces of the wind or aerodynamic tendencies help send them flying over roof tops and chimneys. So actual events are the result of numerous causal forces or tendencies. That, in part, is why the present and future are open. For the context always affects the outcome and the future context is everywhere not yet determined.

This assessment that reality is so structured, i.e. that it is, in the manner described, irreducible to the actual course of events, immediately guides us in the direction of causal explanatory research or *causal explanation*. For whether or not given phenomena are correlated with others at any one level of social reality, they can be *explained* in terms of meaning shown to have been produced or facilitated by their underlying causal structures and conditions. So the ontological conception I defend directs us towards considering how, in economics, we might conduct causal explanatory projects.

Even an analysis of the well-controlled experiment leads us to this conclusion. I say 'even' just because the controlled laboratory situation is the one to which empiricists and others often point when arguing to the contrary that the identification of event regularities is essential to science. For event regularities are regularly associated with experimental work even if they are rare beyond the experimental confines. However, this acknowledged restriction of event regularities to controlled experimental conditions warrants explanation. So too does the further observation that experimental findings are often successfully observed outside of experimental conditions where event regularities are rarely to be found.

The explanation is just that the experimental situation is a humanly engineered contrivance in which single sets of causal mechanisms of interest are insulated from countervailing factors. Any even regularity produced corresponds to the empirical identification of the mechanism; it correlates the triggering event with the mechanism's undisturbed effects. The point here is that even the controlled experiment is not concerned with any event regularity produced *per se*, but with what it serves to identify: an isolated underlying causal mechanism. And of course we can make sense of the successful application of experimental results in non-experimental conditions where event regularities do not occur just by recognising that these results relate to the workings of the mechanism and not the regularity through which it is experimentally revealed. I return to these considerations in due course. For the time being it is sufficient that we recognise that even the experimental situation, when adequately reflected upon, is found to support the idea that science is ultimately concerned with causal explanation.

Now I believe the conception of social reality I have set out, though not identical, is very much in line with that developed by Popper, at least towards the end of his life. I refer in particular, although not only, to the two lectures contained in his *A World of Propensities*, published in 1990, just four years before his death. Before considering this later work, however, I must acknowledge that, prior to it, Popper's emphasis very much reveals *not* a presumption that reality, and in particular social reality, is open, but rather an acceptance that it is reasonably closed, that event regularities do exist. It is Popper's earlier position I want to examine first.

Popper and closed systems

My assessment, as I say, is that early on Popper mostly regards reality as more or less everywhere closed, or at least closable. Thus in the 1940s Popper talks of:

> a really fundamental similarity between the natural and the social sciences. I have in mind the existence of sociological laws or hypotheses which are analogous to the laws or hypotheses of the natural sciences. Since the existence of such sociological laws or hypotheses ... has often been doubted, I will give a number of examples: 'You cannot introduce tariffs and at the same time reduce the cost of living.' – 'You cannot, in an industrial society, organise consumers' pressure groups as effectively as you can certain producers' pressure groups.' – 'You cannot have a centrally planned society with a price system that fulfils the main function of competitive prices.' – 'You cannot have full employment without inflation.'
>
> (Popper 1944: 307)

Despite the impression given that these examples took some effort by Popper in constructing, it is easy enough to suggest counterexamples to all of them: tariffs can be introduced as a country joins a trading block which gives massively expanded markets facilitating scale economies and, perhaps simultaneously, even bringing subsidies from centralised resources; advances in communications technology, including those yet to happen facilitate all sorts of previously unimagined possibilities including many for (i) organising groups of every kind as well as (ii) other forms of planning; and currently in Cambridge UK, according to some accounts and depending on our categories, price inflation, excluding housing, and zero unemployment effectively coexist. The point, though, is that Popper clearly posited closures in his earlier years and seemed almost to imply he regarded them a common place.

It is relevant, too, that closures appear to be a presupposition of his (later) method of *situational analysis* which Popper devised specifically for the social realm. It was Popper's view in setting out this approach that those sciences which study social phenomena cannot explain or predict 'singular events', only kinds or types of event. The point then, according to Popper, is to construct models of typical situations to see, in effect, the general manner in which social events could have occurred.

Popper's idea of a model is clear when he considers examples for the natural realm, and specifically lunar eclipses. He talks of making perspective drawings, or using a lamp for the sun, a wooden earth, and so forth. He is really looking to understand a *type* of mechanism. Even the initial conditions involved are described only as *typical* initial conditions (Popper 1967: 358). To see how the earth and moon move in reality, however, we further need to 'animate' the model. Here Newton's laws of motion are called upon. But basically, the model is explanatory of *how* phenomena can come about.

The trick for the social realm, Popper believes, is to construct models of typical social *situations*:

> The fundamental problem of both the historical and the social sciences is to explain and understand events in terms of human actions and social situations. The key term here is 'social situation'.
>
> The description of a concrete historical *social situation* is what corresponds in the social sciences to a statement of *initial conditions* in the natural sciences. And the '*models*' of the theoretical social sciences are essentially descriptions or reconstructions of typical situations.
>
> (Popper 1994: 166 italics in original)

Popper is here setting out the conditions for his method of *situational analysis*. Models constructed according to it are animated by the *rationality principle*, by the assumption that people always act in a manner appropriate to their situations:

> As for the social sciences … we can construct our models by means of *situational analysis*, which provides us with models (rough and ready ones to be sure) of typical social situations. And my thesis is that only in this way can we explain and understand what happens in society: social events.
>
> Now if situational analysis presents us with the model, the question arises: what corresponds here to Newton's universal laws of motion which, as we have said, 'animate' the model of the solar system? In other words, how is the model of a social system 'animated'?
>
> … it is the central point of situational analysis that we need, in order to animate it, no more than the assumption that the various persons or agents involved act *adequately, or appropriately*; that is to say in accordance with the situation. Here we must remember, of course, that the situation, as I use the term, already contains all the relevant aims and all the available relevant knowledge, especially that of possible means for realising these aims.
>
> Thus there is only one animating law involved – the principle of acting appropriately to the situation …
>
> (Popper 1967: 358–9 italics in original)

These models assume, in effect, closed systems, rendering the explanatory schema as a whole a form of deductivism (Caldwell 1991; Runde 1996; Koertge 1975, 1979), one systematised by Spiro Latsis as *situational determinism* (Latsis 1976).

An example of a supposed social event regularity Popper explicitly acknowledges at this stage is 'the theory of profit maximisation, [whereby] the businessman maximises his (monetary) profits by a policy of marginal cost pricing' (Popper 1994: 182). But basically, in situational analysis, the situation of the agent is assumed to be of a sort that there is but one 'adequate or appropriate' course of action, and the agent is assumed to take it. In essence the model, including (or along with) the 'rationality principle', provides the closures or (set of) event regularity(ies), whilst a description of a given situation constitutes the initial conditions (always required in deductivist explanation). Putting the two aspects together, predictions are deduced regarding individual behaviour. In this way the models are tested. Popper acknowledges that the process may not always be clear-cut. But the method allows deductive testing after a fashion:

> Tests of a model, it has to be admitted, are not easily obtainable and are not usually very clear-cut. But this difficulty arises even in the natural sciences. It is connected, of course, with the fact that models are always and necessarily somewhat rough and schematic over-simplifications. Their roughness entails a relatively low degree of testability. For it will be difficult to decide whether a discrepancy is due to the unavoidable roughness, or to a mistake in the model. Nevertheless we can sometimes decide by testing, which of two competing models is the better.
>
> (Popper 1994: 170)

If Popper thought in 1967 and earlier that deductivist testing of this sort was less than clear-cut his ontological assessments of later life most likely, and certainly should have, led him to be more cautious still, to the point, I think, of abandoning this approach more or less entirely. Let me now turn to his later writings and in particular his *A World of Propensities* (1990).

Propensities and open systems

Popper's central category here, as the title of his book leads us to expect, is *propensity*. The category was not entirely new to him at this point in time of course. For in 1956 Popper had published his 'propensity theory of probability'.[7] But in 1990, on recalling this earlier work, Popper writes:

> This theory has further grown so that it was only in the last year that I realised its cosmological significance. I mean that we live in a *world of propensities*, and that this fact makes our world both more interesting and more homely than the world as seen by earlier states of the sciences.
>
> (Popper 1990: 9)

Popper explains:

> Propensities, it is assumed, are not mere possibilities but are physical realities. They are as real as forces, or fields of forces. And vice versa: forces are propensities. They are propensities for setting bodies in motion. Forces are propensities to accelerate, and the fields of forces are propensities distributed over some region of space and perhaps changing continuously over this region (like distance from some given origin). Fields of forces are fields of propensities. They are real they exist.
>
> (Popper 1990: 13)

There is scope for some confusion here. Unlike the categories of my own project, Popper's propensities are aspects not of structures or objects but of situations. They are 'objective probabilities'. Where a cause acts in isolation to produce its direct effect we have the propensity 1. Where countervailing forces act in competition with some other causes Popper seems to suggest that the propensity of its typical effect being actualised is less than 1:

> The propensity 1 is the special case of a classical force in action: a cause when it produces an effect. If a propensity is less than 1, then this can be envisaged as the existence of competing forces pulling in various opposed directions but not yet producing or controlling a real process. And whenever the possibilities are discrete rather than continuous, these forces pull towards distinct possibilities, where no compromise may exist. And zero propensities are, simply, no propensities at all, just as the number zero means 'no number'.
>
> (Popper 1990: 12)

I am not entirely convinced by Popper's emphasis on, or use of the category, propensities here. But the important point is that in developing his account Popper reveals an attachment to a conception of reality inclusive of forces and countervailing forces, including those that shift. The result is a perspective in which reality is viewed as open, where the thesis I have stylised *regularity determinism* is rejected as false:[8]

> Now, in our changing real world, the situation and, with it, the possibilities, and thus the propensities, change all the time … Our very understanding of the world changes the conditions of the changing world … All this amounts to the fact that *determinism is simply mistaken*: all its traditional arguments have withered away and indeterminism and free will have become part of the physical and biological science.
>
> (Popper 1990: 17 italics in original)

A few lines after providing examples of features of reality that fit with his theory, Popper adds:

> In all these cases the propensity theory of probability allows us to work with an *objective* theory of probability. Quite apart from the fact that we do not *know* the future, the future is *objectively not fixed*. The future is *open: objectively open*. Only the past is fixed; it has been actualised and so it is gone. The present can be described as the continuing process of the actualisation of propensities; or, more metaphorically, of the freezing or the crystallization of propensities. While the propensities actualize or *realize* themselves, they are continuing processes … Propensities, like Newtonian attractive forces, are invisible and, like them, they can act: they are actual, they are real.
>
> (Popper 1990: 18 italics in original)

Or as Popper writes in the *Introduction* to his collection of essays systematised as *The Myth of the Framework*:[9] 'The future is open. It is not predetermined and thus cannot be predicted – except by accident. The possibilities that lie in the future are infinite' (Popper 1994: xiii).

The question that clearly arises is how in such a world we do explanatory work. Popper does not get around to considering this. When, in his *A World of Propensities*, he does turn to questions of method he focuses only on theoretical physics. Here he basically notes that in some cases laboratory experimentation is possible. These are situations he associates with 'natural laws of a deterministic character' (Popper 1999: 22) and in others it is not. Only in the case of planetary movements do spontaneous closures or naturally occurring laboratory-like situations occur:

> Only the system of our planets is so well isolated from all the extraneous mechanical interference that it is a unique, natural laboratory experiment. Here, only the *internal* disturbances interfere with the precision of Kepler's laws … In most laboratory experiments we have to exclude many disturbing extraneous influences such as change of temperature or the normal moisture of air. Or we may have to create an artificial environment of extreme temperatures – say, near to absolute zero …
>
> But what does all this show us. It shows us that in the non-laboratory world, with the exception of our planetary system, no strictly deterministic laws can be found. Admittedly, in certain cases such as the planetary movements, we can interpret events as due to the vectorial sum of forces that our theories have isolated. But in an actual event such as, say, the fall of an apple from a tree, this is not the case. Real apples are emphatically not Newtonian apples. They fall usually when the wind blows. And the whole process is initiated by a biochemical process that weakens the stem so the often repeated movement due to the wind, together with the Newtonian weight of the apple, lead to a snap of the stem – a process we can analyse but cannot calculate in detail.
>
> (Popper 1990: 24)

Actually, it is possible to *explain* why experimental work is mostly impracticable in the social realm, although Popper does not go so far as doing so. I mentioned earlier that Popper's (implicit) social ontology and that which I defend are rather similar in viewing reality as open and structured. The conception I argue for elsewhere does, however, go somewhat further than that of Popper in portraying social reality as also highly *internally related*, and intrinsically *processual*, amongst other things. By internally related I mean that aspects of reality are what they are and can do what they do in virtue of the relations in which they stand to others. Students and teachers (or the positions in which they stand) are internally related to each other, as are (the positions of) employers and employees, landlords and tenants, and so on. The result is a holistic conception that cannot easily be carved up into isolatable atomistic bits. By saying social reality is intrinsically processual I mean that its very nature is that of process. It does not first exist and then experience change; change is intrinsic to its mode of being. Think of language. We do not create it, for it precedes us. But nor is it fixed and determining of what we say. Rather it both conditions our speech acts and also is reproduced or transformed through them. Being continually reproduced or transformed is essential to its mode of being. But on reflection we can see this is true of all aspects of social structure.

So we are left wondering how explanatory endeavour might proceed in a social realm which, *prima facie* at least, is not at all similar to the planetary system, and wherein controlled experimentation seems hardly feasible. Given the fundamental openness of the social system and the recognition that the method of situational logic or situational analysis requires local closures, it is difficult to discern how we can proceed.

We arrive once more, then, at the conclusion noted earlier, that the nature of society is such as to be not amenable to study through either controlled experimentation or Popper's situational analysis. Popper, I think, had reached a point where he would have accepted this. If not then, as I say, the comments he made, supplemented by the ontological conception sketched above and defended elsewhere, suggests he should have accepted this. One way or another, in any case, we arrive at the question posed at the outset, and singled out as rather important. How might social explanatory work proceed in an open system context that lacks the possibility of experimental intervention?

Critical rationalism

One answer to this question, I now want to suggest, rests heavily on adopting an orientation similar to Popper's *critical rationalism*. The latter is the name given to Popper's long-standing stipulation that a critical orientation is essential to science, an orientation that requires the scientist to seek for errors and to learn from them. This, of course, is where Popper and critical realism come together most easily. It is not for nothing that both projects identify themselves explicitly with the term *critical*.

Now the critical perspective of which I talk is not at all a recent one for Popper. Although earlier he mostly emphasised versions of it appropriate to closed systems, namely falsificationism and later situational analysis, and although these are the only versions most economists at best have tended to notice (Boland 1997), his critical rationalism has been present throughout. For example, in 1944 we find Popper arguing as follows:

> According to this piecemeal view, there is no clearly marked division between the pre-scientific and the scientific experimental approaches, even though the more conscious application of scientific, that is to say, of critical methods, is of great importance. Both approaches may be described, fundamentally as utilizing the method of trial and error. We try; that is, we do not merely register an observation, but make active attempts to solve some more or less practical and definite problems. And we make progress if, and only if, we

> are prepared to *learn from our mistakes*: to recognise our errors and to utilise them critically instead of persevering in them dogmatically. Though this analysis may sound trivial, it describes, I believe, the method of all empirical sciences. This method assumes a more and more scientific character the more freely and consciously we are prepared to risk a trial, and the more critically we watch for the mistakes we always make. And this formula covers not only the method of experiment, but also the relationship between theory and experiment. All theories are trials; they are tentative hypotheses, tried out to see whether they work; and all experimental corroboration is simply the result of tests undertaken in a critical spirit, in an attempt to find where our theories err.
>
> (Popper 1944: 314–15)

Clearly at the relatively high level of abstraction these comments are pitched the basic position argued for applies as much to explanatory work in the social realm as any other. Indeed Popper continues:

> For the piecemeal technologist or engineer these views mean that, if he wishes to introduce scientific methods into the study of society and into politics, what is needed is the adoption of a critical attitude, and a realisation that not only trial but also error are necessary. And he must learn not only to expect mistakes but consciously to search for them. We all have an unscientific weakness for being always in the right, and this weakness seems to be particularly common among professional and amateur politicians. But the only way to apply something like scientific method in politics is to proceed on the assumption that there can be no political move which has no drawbacks, no undesirable consequences. To look out for these mistakes, to find them, to bring them into the open, to analyse them, to learn from them, this is what a scientific politician as well as a political scientist must do. Scientific method in politics means that the great art of convincing ourselves that we have not made any mistakes, of ignoring them, of hiding them, and of blaming others for them, is replaced by the greater art of accepting the responsibility for them, of trying to learn from them, and of applying this knowledge so that we may avoid them in the future.
>
> (Popper 1994: 315)

So Popper was always in favour of analyses being subjected to criticism and learning from error. Still, it can be argued, this is hardly enough. Though attractive, it can be said that Popper's attention to criticism and learning from error provide little content about how to proceed. Certainly this appears to be the consensus of those few economists who have even noticed his critical rationalist stance (Caldwell 1991: 26–7). As Wade Hands observes:

> The real problem for critical rationalism is not that one can say very much against it, but rather that one cannot say very much with it. Critical rationalism

> is a view which seems palatable by virtue of its blandness, the epistemological analog of the ethical mandate to 'live the good life'.
>
> (Hands 1992: 37)

Certainly if we accept the ontological conception systematised as critical realism, Popper's stipulations appear to be of very little help indeed. For when faced with a social reality as complex as described how can we even begin to undertake explanatory endeavour? How specifically might criticism and error play a role? In a closed systems context Popper was able to be more explicit or definite. Perhaps too much so. Certainly his stipulations on falsificationism and situational analysis are read this way by some. But how do we begin even to proceed with explanatory endeavour in the social realm as understood here? What kind of trials and errors can we make? Certainly, if we are talking about aspects of dynamic or evolving totalities we are not in a position to experiment in the sense of manipulating aspects of our objects. So how can we expect to make explanatory progress at all?

Clarifying the question

I believe we can make explanatory progress, but that in order to do so we first need to be slightly more precise in formulating the nature of our problem. The earlier discussion of the situation of controlled experimentation can help us here. I have identified the task before us as one of causal explanation. Specifically, it is to determine how we might uncover aspects of the social structures, mechanisms and conditions responsible for social phenomena in which we are interested. Now reflection on the earlier analysis of the controlled experimental situation reveals that there are three interlinked aspects or parts to the problem that arise here, three relative disadvantages facing non-experimental research. For experimentally based causal explanatory endeavour can be usefully viewed under the aspects of (i) identifying an event regularity; (ii) forming causal hypotheses that can account for the regularity; and (iii) discriminating between competing hypotheses consistent with the regularity. It is in relation to these three activities that the problem of social or, more generally, non-experimentally aided explanation can be viewed.

To elaborate, there is first of all the difficulty of determining how an explanatory project is to be initiated if, or where, event regularities of the sort engineered in controlled experimental conditions are not in evidence. How do we know where to start?

Second, if somehow it proves possible to initiate an explanatory project in a meaningful fashion, there arises the question of how to direct any causal explanatory research. It is easy to demonstrate that experimentally produced event regularities correspond to situations where a single (set of) intrinsically stable mechanism(s) is effectively insulated from countervailing mechanisms. Causal hypotheses are, in this very particular case, directed at the underlying mechanism experimentally insulated. In an open system such as human society, the relative paucity of regularities of the causal sequence sort reflects the fact that events or outcomes are mostly each determined by a multiplicity of causes, with the possibility that at least some of the latter will be highly transient as well as unstable. From the perspective of this understanding, a *prima facie* problem of causal research in the social realm, is with determining how it is possible to pick out one particular cause from the conceivably very many acting on any phenomenon in which we might be interested.

Third, to the extent that an understanding of a single (set of) causal mechanism(s) can be pursued at all, there arises the likely task of discriminating between competing accounts of it, where such arise. In the experimental laboratory background factors can be varied in a controlled and systematic manner. What options are available in the non-experimental situation? Clearly because we are concerned with causal explanation rather than with correlation analysis *per se*, the criterion for selecting amongst any competing hypotheses will not be predictive accuracy but explanatory power. We can accept the hypothesis which makes sense of the widest range of phenomena within its scope. But in the absence of event regularities, what sort of empirical phenomena might we now expect to call upon in assessing the relative explanatory power of competing hypotheses where held?

It is this three-part problem of the openness of knowing how even to *start* the explanatory process in the absence of event regularities of the sort produced in controlled experiments, of determining how to *direct* causal reasoning, and of being able to *select* amongst such competing alternative hypotheses as may be formulated that remains to be addressed, and on which I propose to focus in much of the remainder of this chapter. First, I outline one possible solution to the noted three part problem as developed in critical realism. I then turn to indicate why I take this answer to be rather Popperian.

A sketch of an answer

So where might we start in providing an answer to the multi-faceted problem identified? The answer I have focused upon elsewhere can be referred to as *contrast explanation*. According to it, the trick is to seek to explain why two outcomes were not the same as each other when we had good reason to expect that they would be. Put differently it is to ask in respect of one of the outcomes *not* 'why did *x* occur?', but 'why did *x* happen rather than *y*?', where *y* occurred elsewhere in circumstances regarded as similar. The starting point of the exercise, indeed, is a surprise that two outcomes are not the same, or that one is 'x rather than y'. The object then is to explain the difference.

Two conditions are clearly required for such an explanatory approach. The first is just that over some region that I refer to as the *contrast space*, we had good reason to expect outcomes of a certain kind to have a similar causal history and so to be much the same. In other words, the first condition is an informed, if often tacitly held or implicit, judgement about conditions operating over some particular region, which may stretch over geographical space, time, cultures and so forth, where the range of the contrast space will be larger or smaller depending on context. All that is required of any judgement is that it be suitably informed. It is not necessary that the judgement be wholly correct. A correct judgement is specifically a condition of learning by way of identifying a new mechanism coming into play. This scenario, though, is but a special case of contrast explanation. The second condition is merely that *a posteriori* we are surprised, concerned, or otherwise interested to find that things do not turn out as expected.

I shall indicate below that such conditions are found to hold quite widely. First let me address the prior question as to how, where the noted conditions hold, such a contrastive approach to explanation might be expected to help. Consider again our three part problem of explanation, turning first to the puzzle of how we might even initiate a causal explanatory project.

Initiating the explanatory process and interest relativity

An entry point can be occasioned by feelings of surprise, doubt, concern or interest, that accompany some contrastive observations. Where we possess knowledge of sorts, and form expectations, we can be surprised by what occurs. Here, then, we have an obvious basis for initiating an analysis. Surprising contrasts serve to draw attention to the possibility that, and to indicate a 'location' where, a hitherto unknown or unidentified causal factor is, or may well be, in play. In an open and highly internally-related system this is rather important. Without such surprising or otherwise *interesting* contrastive observations it is difficult to imagine how investigatory research can proceed in any meaningful or systematic fashion at all.

The notion of *interest* here denotes a relative assessment of course. Further it tends to presuppose a prior (equally relative) assessment of a scenario as *uninteresting*. For a contrast tends to be interesting precisely in situations where its absence would have been regarded as somewhat uninteresting in the sense of expected or taken for granted.[10] Many taken-for-granted things are going on all the time. We often only notice that they have been when something different occurs.

Prior to the 1980s, the sight of cows standing and walking around the field was mostly not of great interest to someone living in the British countryside. Indeed it was an unexceptional common place. It is because of this, however, that the later observation of many cows appearing to lose the ability to stand and walk, with the onset of 'mad cow disease' was interpreted as 'interesting' to the point of disturbing.

As I walk down the street in which I live, people walk past, and birds fly in the air. I usually take it all for granted. But I would be quite interested if a passing fellow human being suddenly propelled herself or himself into the stratosphere, and even if certain birds of a particularly nervous disposition stayed on the ground and chose to pass me by.

So, when certain phenomena are described as uninteresting this must often be recognised as an achieved view, a relative and knowledgeable perspective marking a site where potentially very interesting things may yet arise. The interesting is a realisation of that potential.

In sum, if it is usually a mistake to take anything completely, or even largely, for granted, we can now see that it is often just because we do so that contrast explanation can go to work. Contrasts tend to be considered interesting precisely because, and where, their prior absence was, at that time, regarded as uninteresting in the sense of 'taken for the ordinary'. So the first component of the three-part problem of openness is met in contrast explanation. The fundamental feature is the element of *surprise*, *doubt*, or, more generally, *interest* in 'surprising contrasts', a feature presupposing a concerned and knowledgeable orientation. It is the human interest that gets the explanatory project going.

Directing the explanatory process

The second problem, the issue of directionality, is resolved as much by the *contrastive* side of interesting or surprising contrastive observations as by the interest or surprise. For just as an event regularity produced in the experimental laboratory *prima facie* marks the site of a single (set of) causal mechanism(s) in play, so a surprising contrast *prima facie* directs us to a single (set of) causal mechanism (s). It directs us to the mechanism(s) explaining the *discrepancy* between outcomes, or between outcomes and expectations, that accounts for the contrast 'x rather than y'.

Consider, once more, the situation of cows and the case of 'mad cow disease'. Consider first someone concerned with explaining any and all aspects of a cow's state or behaviour. Conceivably, any aspect of the cow, its mouth, teeth, legs, tail, parents, all factors that entered into the evolution of cows, and ultimately many factors going back to any big bang, have had a causal impact and so are explanatory of some aspects of the behaviour or general state of cows. Explaining the behaviour or state of cows, in truth, is not a meaningful proposition.

However, consider the situation of someone familiar with cows, who is surprised and concerned to discover that, say, in local herds (this, and perhaps all previous herds, is the contrast space) some, but only some, are showing symptoms of the disease. By attempting to explain *not* the state of cows *per se*, but the observed contrast, i.e. why these cows are ill and those are not, factors which are common to all cows can be standardised for, or factored out, allowing the possibility of identifying the specific or most direct cause of the (symptoms of the) disease.[11]

Discriminating between causal hypotheses

Finally there is the question of how the third component of the earlier noted three-part problem of openness is (or might be) met. This is the problem of determining, in the absence of event regularities of the sort produced in experimental laboratories, a type of evidence that might usefully be brought to bear in selecting amongst any competing hypotheses. This problem arises most clearly in a situation where we believe a hitherto unaccounted for causal mechanism is responsible for some surprising contrast. And one sort of evidence we might meaningfully seek is precisely sets of contrasts on which our competing hypotheses bear.

Consider the farmer who expected crop yields to be roughly uniform throughout the field but discovers that they are significantly higher at one end. If a river passing by is hypothesised to be the cause, then it may be sensible to check whether, in other fields through which the river passes, crop yields are higher in regions closest to it. If the hypothesis entertained is that shade from trees causes the higher yields it may be possible to examine other fields to assess whether yields are higher where there is shade. And so on. In the case of each hypothesis in contention, inferences are drawn concerning contrasts that we might expect to find. In each case it is inferred that if the hypothesis is correct, yields will mostly be higher in the region of the contrast space closest to the hypothesised mechanism in question. The hypothesis that performs best in terms of accounting for the widest range of relevant contrastive observations can, with reason, be accepted as the better grounded.[12]

Facilitating explanatory research in the social domain

Now the central thesis I want to defend is that the conditions for contrast explanation hold for the social realm in particular. Fundamental here is the general point that a condition for contrast explanation is a *rational judgement* that the contrast space is sufficiently homogeneous. or, more precisely, that events throughout it share a similar causal history. For it is only on the basis of an informed judgement about the nature of a contrast space that a contrast can be recognised or interpreted as significant.

Contrast spaces are underpinned by expectations of continuity in social life, by expectations that causal processes are such that regularities, strict or particular, of the form 'what happens here happens there' are justified. In fact such regularities abound in social life. They underpin all observations of continuity: that prices of stamps, television licences, etc., are in general everywhere the same in the UK; that the school curriculum is identical throughout schools in England; that goods everywhere are bought and sold; and so forth. There are definite bounds to all such regularities of continuity, and all are partial. But their nature is often of a sort that an expectation of continuity is knowledgeably formed, that a contrast space is rationally delineated.

The explanatory process gets underway, however, when an expectation of some sort turns out to have been in error. When this happens we can learn in two ways at least. It may be that a new causal mechanism is operating over only part of the contrast space. Or it may turn out that we were wrong from the outset in formulating a contrast space in a particular way. That is, it may often turn out that a surprising a posteriori contrast is the result not of a change in circumstances, say the emergence of a new causal factor, but of an error in our previous understanding of the nature of the contrast space. But if so, on examining the cause of the contrast we may well learn that, and how, our original judgement was wrong.[13]

How specifically might this discussion bear on practices of social-explanatory research? Very often, in our day-to-day encounters, observed discrepancies between our best judgements and what happens gives rise to a sense of *surprise* (or even shock) as I have noted. This will be the case, for example, when an acquaintance breaks accepted conventions of polite behaviour, or the UK high street shop does not open on Monday morning as usual, etc. And it will be the case, too, when people travel further afield. For example, a first trip by a British person to Naples brings the 'surprise' that almost no one stops at most red traffic lights.

However, for the social researcher alive to the conditions of contrast explanation, the relevant orientation may well be an informed *curiosity* more often than *a posteriori* surprise or shock. In particular, through recognising both (i) that actual or expected event regularities (of whatever degree of strictness) can, and eventually regularly do, break down, yet nevertheless (ii) that existing (fallible) knowledge of certain specific or local conditions (contrast spaces) often suggests uniformity (similarity of causal histories) as our most grounded assessment, the social researcher may search out such scientifically significant contrast spaces just to see if noteworthy contrasts after all occur. In a sense, the social researcher will often be knowledgeably seeking out situations in which either they are surprised, or he or she knows it would have been reasonable (given existing knowledge claims) to have been, and that others probably will be surprised at the sorts of observations recorded.

For example, by exploring whether changes in given structures, e.g. the introduction of minimum wage legislation, or the legalisation of Sunday trading, impact in a uniform way throughout a given region such as the UK, it may be possible, where discontinuities or differences are observed, to uncover previously insufficiently understood differences in specific social mechanisms, e.g. the employment process, reflecting, in particular, the nature of their internal relationality to local context, and so obtain a less partial account than hitherto of the mechanisms at work.

In other words, in such situations it is not that a researcher necessarily expects the legislation to impact in the same way in all areas, merely that her or his prior knowledge is such as to have no specific reason to expect of any two sub-regions that the impact will be greater in one than in the other. If after the event a significant difference is observed it is likely that something of note can be determined by pursuing the explanation. Similarly, by focusing on movements in specific phenomena, say house prices or productivity growth rates, or whatever, it may be found that there are marked differences in outcomes over two (or more) regions, where current understanding would have led the researcher to expect greater homogeneity.

On occasion such a development may lead to the uncovering of a previously unrecognised causal factor. For example, recent increases in house prices in Cambridge (UK) appear to have been significantly higher in the south of the city. The implicit contrast involved here seems to have been caused by the phenomenon of an increase in the number of house buyers wanting to live in Cambridge, but work in, and so commute to, London. This is an option recently made feasible by the speeding up of the rail link between the two cities, with the railway station situated in the south of Cambridge.

On other occasions, the knowledge acquired may be of factors already recognised but insufficiently understood. For example, differences in productivity growth rates may reflect the fact not of a new causal factor coming into play, such as a faster railway system, but of new developments in technology being assimilated differently according to the different existing systems of industrial relations, or local levels of technical knowledge, or forms of support industries, throughout the regions of the contrast space.

A further possible basis for contrast explanation arises where a researcher's understanding of the conditions of recent developments, say trend growth rates or whatever, lead her or him to the view that identified trends are likely to continue unabated, or from other information could with reason be expected to continue. A marked downturn, or upturn, would then constitute a contrast with extrapolated outcomes, suggesting a *prima facie* case of a new and identifiable causal factor having come into play. In short, it is through recognising that generalisations about concrete social circumstances and processes will usually have limits, and through exploring how specific generalisations break down in areas where our current understanding suggests they could nevertheless have held, that we can learn, by way of contrast explanation, of hitherto unknown or insufficiently understood factors that make the difference.

In a world that is open and complex, unforeseen developments are always occurring. But by starting from a position where specific changes or developments are not foreseen, those changes that do occur provide points from which it seems feasible to initiate an explanatory investigation, and concerning which, explanatory successes seem likely.[14]

In truth, indeed, we are confronted with noteworthy contrasts of this nature almost everywhere. Is it not significant, for example, that in the modern day UK girls perform significantly better in single sex schools than in mixed ones; that in all schools, girls are beginning to outperform boys academically, when until very recently boys performed significantly better than girls; that teenage pregnancy rates at the start of the twenty-first century are reported to be significantly higher than elsewhere in Europe; that men usually get paid more than women for identical work; and so on. In all such cases, the prior expectation need not have been that conditions are everywhere exactly the same, merely rather more similar throughout the relevant contrast space than is found to be the case. All that is required for the explanatory process to be initiated is that the contrasts observed are striking enough to suggest that something systematic is going on, given the contrast spaces involved, and that the causes of the contrasts are identifiable. I conclude from all this that contrast explanation holds out the promise for an adequate causalist approach to social science even accepting the social ontology I defend, including an absence of conditions to facilitate experimental enquiry.

The essence of the method set out is clearly that we learn by getting things knowledgably wrong. Thus, I am here rejecting positivistic or, more generally, monistic accounts of knowledge, i.e. accounts wherein knowledge is the accumulation of incorrigible facts. And I am reaffirming the familiar realist insight that knowledge, although concerned with an at least partly independent reality or intransitive 'objects', is a two way process. Through confronting 'objects' of study we learn not only about them but simultaneously about ourselves, including, in particular, the errors of our current thinking, as well, no doubt, something of our social-cultural situations, values, and so forth. Knowledge is intrinsically a transformational process. And it is a process of transformation in which the continuous absenting of errors of various sorts is fundamental. Although the analytical moment, the elaboration and utilisation of surface patterns, has a role, explanatory research does not reduce to it. Rather the knowledge process is fundamentally dialectical.

Back to Popper's critical rationalism

So what does any of this have to do with Popper's *critical rationalism*? The answer is quite a lot. Indeed, not only is contrast explanation consistent with Popper's emphasis on (self) criticism and learning from errors, I think Popper provides many of the components of the approach I have defended. The major insight that is missing from Popper is an explicit orientation to contrast explanation and its central categories. But otherwise all the components are provided. To demonstrate this let me concentrate once more on Popper's 1990 book, albeit this time on the second of the two essays entitled *Towards an Evolutionary Theory of Knowledge*.

First recall the two essential preconditions of any contrastive explanatory exercise. The first is a knowledgeable stance regarding the likely causal uniformity over some contrast space. The second is a set of outcomes within this contrast space which surprises or interests us. So does Popper emphasise the idea of a contrast region? Not exactly. But his starting point is a knowledgeable orientation, and more specifically a recognition that *existing knowledge is a prerequisite for further knowledge*, i.e. for *learning*. Indeed, I do not know of any philosopher who emphasises this point more strongly. Moreover in his evolutionary theory of knowledge he generalises this assessment to all other life forms as well. Perhaps the more contentious aspect in Popper's position is the proportion of our knowledge we do not learn or acquire at all but is *a priori* or, as Popper interprets the latter term 'inborn'. Popper writes:

> Most knowledge of detail, of the momentary state of our surroundings, is *a posteriori* … But such a posteriori knowledge is impossible without *a priori* knowledge that we somehow must possess before we can acquire observational or a posteriori knowledge: without it, *what our senses tell us can make no sense*. We must establish an overall frame of reference, or else there will be no context available to make sense of our sensations.
>
> (Popper 1990: 46 italics in original)

This is clearly a Kantian position, although Popper claims to go far further than Kant in supposing that 99 per cent of all knowledge is inborn.[15] The point here, though, is that Popper explicitly stresses the role of knowledge as a condition of further knowledge. Although Popper emphasises that a condition of possibility of *a posteriori* knowledge is *a priori* knowledge, he would not rule out, although he does not always emphasise, the role of already acquired *a posteriori* knowledge in facilitating additional such knowledge. I guess I would stress this feature more than Popper does.[16]

How, in Popper's scheme of things, does existing knowledge make advances in learning possible? According to my own account, systematised above as contrast explanation, existing knowledge, beliefs and expectations make surprises or interesting observations possible. Current understanding leads us to have expectations of certain sorts, specifically that outcomes in a contrast space stand in a particular relation to one another. The basis for learning arises when these expectations turn out to be in error. As I have suggested we may not even be conscious of our knowledge and expectations; until things surprise us by being contrary to an expectation sub-consciously held, we may have regarded things in a very taken for granted way. But it is the disappointment of expectations that moves us to explanatory work all the same. Popper takes a similar view:

> Our own unconscious knowledge has often the character of unconscious *expectations*, and sometimes we may become conscious of having had an expectation of this kind when it turns out to be mistaken.
>
> (Popper 1990: 31 italics in original)

What accounts for the mistake or the sense of surprise? According to Popper: 'when we are surprised by some happening, the surprise is usually due to an unconscious *expectation* that something else would happen' (Popper 1990: 32). This of course is close to a formulation of contrast explanation, it is based on an implicit questioning of 'why this happening rather than that'. And Popper well recognises the role of disappointed expectations in science:

> But in all sciences, the experts are sometimes mistaken. Whenever there is a breakthrough, a really important new discovery, this means that the experts have been proved wrong, and that the facts, the objective facts, were different from what the experts expected them to be.
>
> (Popper 1990: 34)

So has Popper had the basis of an answer to the question formulated at the outset all along? The answer I think is both yes and no. Yes at least in that some of the various components, a knowledgeable orientation, disappointed expectations, are in Popper; although not the notion of a contrasts pace, of a region rationally assessed to be covered by a similar causal history. But without a question being appropriately formulated there is nothing very clear to answer. Whatever else critical realism adds to Popper's contributions on these matters it provides a framework that allows us to determine the important question, to provide an appropriate formulation of it, thereby in turn allowing a suitable combination of the existing components into an answer.

Of course even this latter sort of reasoning is somewhat Popperian. For, as Popper himself stresses, a major part of the science process lies in detecting or formulating the problem to be answered or resolved:

> a new theory is only rarely thought up by more than a few people, even when there are many who agree on the refutation of the old theory. The few are those who *see the new problem*. Seeing a new problem may well be the most difficult step in creating a new theory.
>
> (Popper 1990: 49 italics in original)

And this brings me to a further point of interest. If we agree with Popper that seeing a problem is crucially important, and if a condition of seeing a problem, of getting the explanatory enterprise going, is the experience of disappointed expectations, this argues for a more inclusive academy than we currently find, especially within economics. For the things that surprise us, or rather the expectations which we hold that can be disappointed, necessarily vary very much with our situations. Only those who do *not* expect, or do not accept as 'normal' that; all the best jobs to go to men, most of the wealth of the world to accrue in the hands of the few, peace will regularly be sacrificed in the interests of one group gaining the resources of another, economists will regularly forsake the real world in the interests of appearing to be skilled in mathematics, will be concerned by, and prepared to question, the situations we find around us. So for wide-ranging explanatory work we need to bring all points of view into the academy. For, as I say, what it is that strikes us as surprising, depends very much on our situated practices and prejudices and so immediate values. It seems that Popper would agree with this too:

> All organisms are problem finders and problem solvers. And all problem solving involves evaluations and, with it, values. Only with life do problems and values enter the world. And I do not believe that computers will ever invent important new problems, or new values.
>
> (Popper 1990: 50)

Final comments

Let me, in conclusion, address the remaining question raised at the outset, for it allows me to sum up my assessment of Popper's basic orientation as it bears on social explanation. The second question posed was whether the current orientation to social explanation in modern economics warrants the label Popperian. Now modern economics is a subject which is not in a healthy state. Its methods, mainly those of mathematical formalism, are not very successful. But its results, though questionable, are rarely challenged. Economists choose mostly to live with the situation, rather than to seek to transform it. The few who attempt to do anything different, and specifically to learn from error, are largely ignored. Consider the recent observations of Richard Lipsey, a mainstream, not a heterodox, economist:

> … anomalies, particularly those that cut across the sub-disciplines and that can be studied with various technical levels of sophistication, are tolerated on a scale that would be impossible in most natural sciences – and would be regarded as a scandal if they were.
>
> (Lipsey 2001: 173)

Or consider Leamer's (1978) observations regarding the widespread discrepancy between the theory and practice of econometrics:

> The opinion that econometric theory is largely irrelevant is held by an embarrassingly large share of the economics profession. The wide gap between econometric theory and econometric practice might be expected to cause professional tension. In fact, a calm equilibrium permeates our journals and our meetings. We comfortably divide ourselves into a celibate priesthood of statistical theorists, on the one hand, and a legion of inveterate sinner-data analysts, on the other. The priests are empowered to draw up lists of sins and are revered for the special talents they display. Sinners are not expected to avoid sins; they need only confess their errors openly.
>
> (Leamer 1978: vi)

The truth, then, is that Popper the critical rationalist is hardly understood by economists at all. Rather than pursue existing methods in the name of Popper, it is time, I believe, for a more critical orientation to be taken. Specifically, something more is required than the tired insistence that given methods are fine, or that errors can be lived with. And to the point, a more genuinely Popperian response is needed. Or at least a response is required that fits with Popper's critical rationalism. The aspect of modern economics that warrants criticism is not the making of errors but the widespread reluctance to learn from them, including the pretence that they do not matter. Errors provide a scientific opportunity. This anyway is a position described and defended here and elsewhere (Lawson 2003). And I think it entails replacing the Popperianism of modern mainstream economists with the quite different Popperianism of Karl Popper.

Notes

1 See especially the contributions in Fleetwood (1999).
2 What I cannot do is explore the details of the many ways in which Popper has influenced methodological discussion in economics. But for a sample of the literature the reader might consult Blaug (1980, 1985, 1990); Boland (1982); Caldwell (1984); Hands (1985, 1991, 1992); Hausman (1985, 1988); Hutchison (1956); Latsis (1972, 1976, 1983); de Marchi (1988a, 1998b).
3 I am not the first economist to be comparing critical realism and Popper: see Runde (1996).

4 From this perspective social scientists cannot just take natural scientific methods and apply them to the social realm. The usefulness of borrowing from the natural sciences depends on the nature of the methods and the subject material to be investigated. Popper also seems to accept this latter orientation to ontology, at least here and there. Although in modern economics Popper is mostly interpreted as being concerned with methods by which theories are to be rationally appraised, he occasionally explicitly acknowledges that how we can proceed depends on what we are dealing with. Thus for example he writes as early as 1936 that:

> Whether a [social-scientific] student of method upholds anti-naturalistic or pro-naturalistic doctrines, or whether he adopts a theory combining both types of doctrine, will largely depend on his views about the character of the science under consideration, and about the character of its subject matter.
>
> (Popper 1936: 290)

5 Popper writes:

> By 'World 3' I mean the world of the products of the human mind. Although I include works of art in World 3 and also ethical values and social institutions (and thus, one might say, societies), I shall confine myself largely to the world of scientific libraries, to books, to scientific problems, and to theories, including mistaken theories.
>
> (Popper 1982: 114)

He continues two pages further on:

> The proposition the truth of which I wish to defend and which seems to me to go a little beyond common sense is that not only are the physical World 1 and the psychological World 2 real but so also is the abstract World 3; real in exactly that sense in which the physical World 1 of rocks and trees is real: the objects of World 2 and of World 3 can kick each other, as well as the physical objects of World 1; and they can also be kicked back.
>
> (Popper 1982: 116)

6 Or, as Popper preferred to call it, *scientific determinism*:

> '[S]cientific' determinism, that is to say, the doctrine that the structure of the world is such than any event can be rationally predicted, with any desired degree of precision, if we are given a sufficiently precise description of past events, together with all the laws of nature.
>
> (Popper 1982: 1–2)

7 For a good discussion see Runde (1996).

8 Popper, I think, always did reject determinism. But in the earlier period he seemed optimistic that rough and ready forms of deductivist explanation would be adequate.

9 Or as he writes elsewhere:

> This is of fundamental importance; for it shows that nature, or the universe to which we belong, and which contains as parts the Worlds 1, 2, and 3, is itself open; it contains World 3, and World 3 can be shown to be intrinsically open.
>
> (Popper 1982: 129)

10 And if there is a sense in which the uninteresting is a condition for the interesting, it is equally the case that the unsurprising can be a condition of the surprising, the expected a condition of the unexpected, the ordinary, a condition of the extra-ordinary, and so on.

11 Now is this enough for our needs? It certainly helps us get at a causal mechanism. But what if we want to learn more about the event that emerges? More specifically, if contrast explanation is directed by an interesting contrast to a specific mechanism

which, along with others, co-produces a phenomenon, is there any way of identifying other causal conditions of the phenomenon in question?

If we do indeed want to further our understanding of an open-system (multiply determined) event, i.e. to identify several of the causes bearing on it, one possible strategy is to seek out different interesting contrasts or 'foils' involving it.

Consider an example I explore in depth in Lawson (1997a). The primary outcome (or the 'fact' or actuality of interest) upon which I chose to focus is the UK's productivity record in the early post World War II period. The point is that various aspects of this phenomenon can be determined by setting it against a variety of contrasts or foils, and seeking then to explain the contrast.

If the selected foil is the UK's productivity record before the war, the more recent productivity performance (our primary concern) is found to be superior. Thus we can ask why the recent record is *superior* to, rather than the same as, that before the war. And the likely answer to this contrastive question is the postwar expansion of world demand in the period of reconstruction.

However, if the selected foil or contrast is instead the early postwar productivity record of certain countries of the continent of Europe, say of the old West Germany, the postwar UK productivity performance, our topic of interest, is found to be mostly inferior. In this example, our contrastive phenomenon turns on the discrepancy in cross-country performances. We are concerned to determine why the UK fared so much *worse* than counties like West Germany (rather than as well). The likely answer to this contrastive question is the UK's relatively unique stream of localised (as opposed to centralised) collective bargaining, with its in-built slow responsiveness to change (see Lawson, 1997a: Chapter 18).

It is not necessary, here, that the reader accepts the explanations offered of the noted contrastive questions. It is enough that the example demonstrates that where different foils are involved, where different contrastive observations are used to initiate explanatory research, different causal mechanisms bearing on the object of our focus (here UK postwar measured productivity performance) are likely to be uncovered. The more contrastive questions we can pose which involve a given phenomenon x, the more, potentially, we learn about its different causes. The feasible result is a range of causal knowledge that might eventually be synthesised to give a more rounded and deeper understanding of the concrete phenomenon of our investigations.

Of course, none of this throws any general insight on the process of retroductive inference, whereby we might move from (an account of) a given phenomenon to a (hypothesis about) an underlying cause. The problem of deciding how to make this move remains a matter of context. But there is no difficulty that arises with retroduction in the context of contrast explanation that does not arise in all other situations as well. The move from phenomenon to cause rests on a logic of analogy and metaphor, luck and ingenuity, here as everywhere else. Any problems of retroductive inference are not specific to non-experimental situations.

12 Of course, because the world is open, things will rarely, if ever, be clear cut. Even where a river usually brings positive benefits there may be countervailing factors (such as floods or up-stream spillage of industrial pollution). The rational course of action is to persevere with the hypothesis that has the greater explanatory power, that accommodates the widest range of evidence, and to see if its explanatory failures, where they exist, can be accounted for by countervailing factors, and so on. If they cannot be, the response which is most appropriate will depend on the context. Science everywhere is a messy business. But there is no difficulty here that is insuperable in principle.

13 Of course, in the special case where the contrast space stretches from the current point in time into the future, and it is expected that things will continue much as they are, the *a posteriori* outcome of getting the contrast space wrong, and that of an unforseen causal mechanism coming into play may amount to the same thing.

14 This, of course, is more or less the opposite emphasis to that of mainstream modellers who attempt to assume away or gloss over discrepancies as 'noise'.

15 Popper acknowledges his agreement with Kant on the existence of *a priori* knowledge and adds:

> But I am going much further than Kant. I think that, say, 99 per cent of the knowledge of all organisms is inborn and incorporated in our biological constitution. And I think that 99 per cent of the knowledge taken by Kant to be a posteriori and to be 'dated' that are "given" to us through our senses is, in fact, not a posteriori, but *a priori*.
>
> (Popper 1990: 46)

16 Treating features of other life forms as homologous to those of humans, Popper talks of all life forms as possessing *a priori* or inborn knowledge:

> Philosophers and even scientists often assume that all our knowledge stems from our senses, the 'sense data' which our senses deliver to us. They believe (as did, for example, the famous theorist of knowledge, Rudolf Carnap) that the question 'How do you know?' is in every case equivalent to the question 'What are the observations that entitle you to your assertion?' But seen from a biological point of view, this kind of approach is a colossal mistake. For our senses to tell us anything, we must have prior knowledge. In order to be able to see a thing, we must know what 'things' are: that they can be located within some space; that some of them can move while others cannot; that some of them are of immediate importance to us, and therefore are noticeable and will be noticed, while others, less important, will never penetrate into our consciousness: they may not even be unconsciously noticed, but they may simply leave no trace whatever upon our biological importance. But in order to do so, it must be able to use adaptation, expectation: prior knowledge of the situation must be available, including its possibly significant elements. This prior knowledge cannot, in turn, be the result of observation; it must, rather, be the result of an evolution by trial and error. Thus the eye itself is not the result of observation, but the result of evolution by trial and error, of adaptation, of non-observational long-term knowledge. And it is the result of such knowledge, derived not from short-term observation, but from adaptation to the environment and to such situations as constitute the problems to be solved in the task of living; situations that make our organs, among them our sense organs, significant instruments in the moment-by-moment task of living.
>
> (Popper 1990: 37 italics in original)

References

Blaug, M. (1980) *The Methodology of Economics: or How Economists Explain*, Cambridge: Cambridge University Press.

Blaug, M. (1985) 'Comment on D. Wade Hands' "Karl Popper and economic methodology: a new look"', *Economic Philosophy*, 1: 286–8.

Blaug, M. (1990) 'Reply to Hands', *Review of Political Economy*, 2: 102–4.

Boland, L.A. (1982) *The Foundations of Economic Method*, London: Allen and Unwin.

—— (1997) *Critical Economic Methodology: A Personal Odyssey*, London and New York: Routledge.

Caldwell, B.J. (1984) 'Some problems with falsification in economics', *Philosophy of the Social Sciences*, 14: 489–95.

—— (1991) 'Clarifying Popper', *Journal of Economic Literature*, 29: 1–33.

Fleetwood, S. (ed.) (1999) *Critical Realism: Development and Debate*, London: Routledge.

Hands, D. Wade (1985) 'Karl Popper and economic methodology: a new look', *Economic Philosophy*, 1: 83–99.

—— (1991) 'Popper, the rationality principle and economic explanation', in G.K. Shaw (ed.) *Economics, Culture and Education: Essays in Honor of Mark Blaug*, Cheltenham: Edward Elgar.

—— (1992) 'Falsification, situational analysis and scientific research programs: the Popperian tradition in economic methodology', in N. de Marchi (ed.) *Post-Popperian Methodology of Economics: Recovering Practice*, Boston, MA: Kluwer Academic Publishing.

Hausman, D. (1985) 'Is falsification unpractised or unpractisable?', *Philosophy of the Social Sciences*, 15: 313–19.

—— (1988) 'An appraisal of Popperian economic methodology', in N. De Marchi (ed.) *The Popperian Legacy in Economics*, Cambridge: Cambridge University Press.

Hutchison, T.W. (1956) 'Professor Machlup on verification in economics', *South Economic Journal*, 22: 476–83.

Koertge, N. (1975) 'Popper's metaphysical research programme for the human sciences', *Inquiry*, 18: 437–62.

—— (1979) 'The methodological status of Popper's rationality principle', *Theory and Decision*, 10: 83–95.

Latsis, S. (1972) 'Situational determinism in economics', *British Journal for the Philosophy of Science*, 23: 207–45.

Latsis, S. (ed.) (1976) *Method and Appraisal in Economics*, Cambridge: Cambridge University Press.

Latsis, S. (1983) 'The role and status of the rationality principle in the social sciences', in R. Cohen and M. Wartofsky (eds) *Epistemology, Methodology and the Social Sciences*, Vol. 71, *Boston Studies in the Philosophy of Sciences*, Dordrecht: D. Reidel.

Lawson, T. (1997a) *Economics and Reality*, London: Routledge.

—— (1997b) 'Critical issues in *Economics as Realist Social Theory*', *Ekonomia*, (Special Issue on critical realism), 1: 75–117; reprinted in S. Fleetwood (ed.) (1999) *Critical Realism in Economics: Development and Debate*, London: Routledge.

—— (2003) *Reorienting Economics*, London and New York: Routledge.

Leamer, E.E. (1978) *Specification Searches: Ad hoc Inferences with Non-experimental Data*, New York: John Wiley and Sons.

Lipsey, R.G. (2001) 'Success and failure in the transformation of economics', *Journal of Economic Methodology*, 8: 169–201.

De Marchi, N. (1988a) 'Popper and the LSE Economists'. in Neil De Marchi (ed.) (1988) *The Popperian Legacy in Economics*, Cambridge: Cambridge University Press.

—— (ed.) (1988b) *The Popperian Legacy in Economics*. Cambridge: Cambridge University Press.

Marx, K. (1974) *Capital*, Vol. 1, London: Lawrence and Wishart.

Mill, J.S. (1974) *A System of Logic, Ratiocinative and Inductive: Being a Connected View of the Principles of Evidence and the Methods of Scientific Investigation*, in J.M. Robson (ed.) *Collected Works of John Stuart Mill*, vols. 7 and 8, Toronto and London: University of Toronto Press and Routledge and Kegan Paul.

Popper, K.R. (1936) 'Historicism', in D. Miller (ed.) (1985) *Popper Selections*, Princeton, NJ: Princeton University Press.

—— (1944) 'Piecemeal social engineering', in D. Miller (ed.) (1985) *Popper Selections*, Princeton, NJ: Princeton University Press.
—— (1967) 'The rationality principle', in D. Miller (ed.) (1985) *Popper Selections*, Princeton, NJ: Princeton University Press.
—— (1982) *The Open Universe: An argument for Indeterminism*, in W.W. Bartley, III, (ed.) *Postscript to The Logic of Scientific Discovery*, London: Hutchinson.
—— (1990) *A World of Propensities*, Bristol: Thoemmes.
—— (1994) *The Myth of the Framework*, M.A. Notturno, (ed.) London and New York: Routledge.
Runde, J. (1996), 'On Popper, probabilities and propensities', *Review of Social Economy*, 54: 465–85; reprinted in S. Fleetwood (ed.) (1999) *Critical Realism in Economics: Development and Debate*, London: Routledge.

5 Metaphysics and growth through criticism

Giulio Giorello and Matteo Motterlini

Introduction

The aim of this chapter is to re-appraise and further articulate Popper's views on metaphysics and the growth of knowledge through criticism. A prevailing Popperian view is that, while metaphysics as such does not form a part of science, it is a fruitful external source of scientific ideas. These scientific ideas are used in the construction of a theory which, according to the same prevailing view, is subject to strict falsificationism. We reject this prevailing view, and argue that disagreement and debate concerning the metaphysical core and heuristic power of different research programmes is a prerequisite for scientific progress. Moreover, in place of the rhetoric of strict falsificationism, we maintain that the clash of different research programmes competing for supremacy in the same arena defines the framework for scientific testing. To support this thesis we look at a number of disagreements in the history of science, namely Galileo versus Aristotelians on atomism, heliostaticism versus geostaticism, and general relativity versus non-relativity views of gravitation. This analysis defines a framework as a family of rival research programmes and researchers working within the same framework may differ with respect to the heuristic power of such programmes. Our position is that researchers in this scenario may not only disagree, but do so, we argue, if there is to be a Popperian growth in knowledge through criticism.

In particular we argue that Popper's notion of 'criticisable metaphysics' combined with Whewell's concept of 'metaphysics of a better kind' shall replace Popperian strict falsificationism. Moreover, we maintain that by separating Duhem from Quine and by appealing to Duhem's action of 'bon sense' of the individual scientist, we see how science includes testing. Finally we argue, in light of Duhem's challenge, the Lakatosian distinction between hardcore and heuristic is not as absolute as some Lakatosians believe and that this is not a view for research programmes.

From Popper to Whewell

Popper's refusal to consider metaphysics as meaningless nonsense is what has distinguished his views from those of the members of the *Wiener Kreis* since the very beginning. In 1934 Popper was already aware that the fine line of demarcation should not be traced between meaningless sentences and meaningful sentences, but between empirically *refutable* statements and unfalsifiable ones. Popper's rehabilitation of metaphysics went further in the *Postscript to the Logic of Scientific Discovery*. Here he claimed that metaphysics holds a close relation with the scientific enterprise. From a *historical* point of view, metaphysical theories or, in John Watkin's (1958) words, 'haunted-universe doctrines', have played a creative role within the development of science. From a *heuristic* point of view, metaphysics provides scientists with important regulative ideas. Moreover, in expressing ways of seeing the world, it co-ordinates ways of exploring it. Metaphysical conjectures, therefore, provide programmes for the future development of science in fixing its problems and in suggesting directions to be undertaken in resolving these problems.

The question then arises on how we ought to (rationally) appraise *irrefutable* theories. 'If a metaphysical theory is a more or less isolated assertion, no more than the product of an intuition or an insight flung at us with an implied "take or leave it"', then Popper claims that 'it may well be impossible to discuss it rationally' (Popper 1982: 200). In fact, a metaphysical theory can be criticised by showing its own inconsistency or the inconsistency between some of its consequences and an established scientific result. It is thus possible to demarcate '*within metaphysics*' rationally worthless metaphysical conjectures from metaphysical ideas that deserve to be seriously entertained (Popper 1982: 211).

As an example, let us take the classical doctrine of atomism, a tenacious and fruitful metaphysical research programme. Historically, in order to oppose physical atomism, the Peripatetics put forward the argument about the diagonal and the side of the square being incommensurable (i.e. not measurable as integer multiples of the same unit): if p is the number of atoms of the diagonal and q the number of the atoms of the side of the square, the fraction p/q establishes the ratio of the diagonal with the side. But from Greek geometers we know that if we suppose that the square root of 2 is posed equal to some fraction p/q (where it is always possible to suppose that p and q have no common factor) a contradiction is implied in a few steps (Stillwell 1989: 8–9).

The historian, however, is asked to give an account of the tenacity of atomism despite these and other objections. A 'sophisticated' defensive strategy of atomism is not different from that adopted by Einstein in 1905 in reference to the contrast between electromagnetism and Galilean relativity: namely, to declare 'apparent' this inconsistency and to attempt a conciliation by giving up some other 'set' of our mental constructions. In Einstein's case this implied the abandonment of the ordinary conception of space and time. In Galileo (1638) the defensive strategy consisted in dealing with finite segments, such as the diagonal and the side of the square, as if they were *infinite* aggregates of *indivisible* 'parts'.

In *Il Saggiatore* (1623), on the one hand, Galileo conceived of light as being composed of atoms absolutely indivisible; and, on the other hand, he conceived the standard physical bodies as made of some *minima* ('*minimi quanti*'). In Galileo (1638), however, we witness an important shift in the concept of the atom itself. In order to explain the cohesion of bodies and the transitions of phase changes in physical states, each finite portion of matter is presented as a lattice made by an *infinite* number of atoms spaced out by voids (*vacui*). If a finite portion of matter is composed by an infinite number of atoms and voids, then atoms are not 'minima' anymore, as in Galileo (1632). In fact, they are now dimensionless elements ('*parti non quante*') or infinitely small elements. The same holds for the voids, which are also characterised as infinitely small ('*vacui non quanti*').

Therefore, Galileo (1638) conceived a finite continuum as (i) indefinitely divisible '*in partes semper divisibiles*', but also as (ii) composed an infinite number of indivisible elements. If, in principle, we could really perform the process of division *ad infinitum* we would eventually be left with such indivisible elements or atoms. But, unlike God, we are unable to perform or merely conceive a division like that. In fact, the fine structure of matter is beyond human understanding: infinite aggregates and infinite numbers can only be grasped by the Creator's mind. This is how a number of traditional paradoxes, many of which are listed in Galileo (1638), are left aside by theological considerations, and how Galileo was vindicated in making use of the idea of an infinite number of elements of a continuum to describe matter and motion with the help of geometrical representations and numerical formulas.

Interestingly, Galileo's revised atomism acts like a scientific *manifesto* (Regge 1995), i.e. it suggests the problems which are to be temporarily abandoned and those which could be faced with a reasonable hope of success. It is important to notice that in Galileo's revised theoretical framework, the conception of the continuum works as an explanation of the continuum or, viewed from a different perspective, the Galilean *manifesto* contains an explanation of the successful portion of its rival Aristotelian programme (since the continuum is a standard tenet of the Aristotelian opposition to traditional atomism). To show that atomism is fully compatible with ordinary geometry, Galileo '*shrank*' the idea of a 'part' of a continuum in order to consider the geometrical point as an infinitely small part of it, but he also '*stretched*' the concept of 'number' in order to include among numbers the infinite.

From a strict falsificationist point of view, Galileo's move would have to be appraised negatively as a typical case of an immunising strategy. In retrospect, however, this move certainly worked out fine in putting forward the basis of a new kinematics. More generally, it disclosed the way in which a quantitative theory of physical change can be developed. Moreover, Galileo's theory of indivisibles suggests relevant tools for dealing with mathematical problems as the determinations of areas and volumes (Giusti 1980).

To sum up: the whole atomism was a metaphysical research programme criticised by Aristotelians on the basis of its inconsistency with Euclidean geometry. Galileo modified an important feature of atomism by shifting the concepts of 'atom' and of 'number' to deal with the contradiction. In his opinion geometry applies to physical matter conceived as an atomistic structure. But the old paradoxes of infinity could have been redirected against such a revised form of atomism, if it were not for some sort of 'theological' scepticism which blocked them to permit geometers and scientists to use the theory of indivisibles both in solving classical geometrical problems and in building models of physical processes, thus providing a crucially important contribution to the growth of knowledge.

This reconstruction of a historical case is mainly intended to undermine the emphasis on refutation and to draw attention to the validity of the following insight by William Whewell, an ancestor of Popper's rehabilitation of metaphysics. For Whewell, it is not by avoiding metaphysics that we make science of a better kind; on the contrary, it is the metaphysics of a better kind which makes science better.

> Some writers are accustomed to talk with contempt of all past controversies, and to wonder at the blindness of those who did not first take the view which was established at last. Such persons forget that it was precisely the *controversy*, which established among speculative men that final doctrine which they themselves have quietly forgotten; and because systems and books, and language itself have been accommodated peculiarly to the expression of accepted truth. Again, some persons condemn all that we have here spoken of as the discussion of ideas, terming it *metaphysical*; and this spirit, Comte has spoken of as the 'metaphysical period' of each science, that which precedes the period of 'positive knowledge'. But as we have seen, that process which is termed 'metaphysical' – the analysis of our conceptions and the exposure of their inconsistencies, – accompanied with the study of facts – has always gone on most actively in the most *prosperous* periods of each science. There is, in Galileo, Kepler, and Gassendi, and other fathers of mechanical philosophy, *as much of metaphysics as in their adversaries. The main difference is, that the metaphysics is of a better kind.*
>
> (Whewell 1840: 378 italics in original)

We have just seen precisely the reasons according to which Galileo's metaphysics was better than those of his antagonists. With hindsight we know that these reasons were good ones. But these reasons would not have been good enough for a strict falsificationist scientist at the time of Galileo, who would have judged his theory refuted according to his endorsed epistemological desiderata.

To conclude this section, we are thus suggesting a way to reconcile this historical episode with its epistemological analysis by viewing Galileo's strategy as progressive. This requires leaving aside Popper's strict falsificationist pattern and the idea of criticism as refutation of falsifiable (scientific) theories. However, we are retaining Popper's idea of 'criticisable metaphysics' very much in line with Whewell's insights. We shall now turn to a further criticism of the former and an illustration of the latter by means of another related scientific dispute.

From Popper to Duhem

Compared with the influential claim by Pierre Duhem that 'an experiment in physics can never condemn an isolated hypothesis but the whole theoretical group'

(Duhem 1954: 183), falsification seems *prima facie* to be born *refuted*. Of course, Duhem's argument would not be a problem for Popper's so called *methodological* falsificationism, if we regard such a theoretical group of hypotheses as finite. But, as Duhem argued, this is not often the case in the sciences:

> Experimental contradiction does not have the power to transform a physical hypothesis into an indisputable truth; in order to confer this power on it, it would be necessary to enumerate completely the various hypotheses which may cover a determinate group of phenomena; but the physicist is never sure he has exhausted all the imaginable assumptions.
>
> (Duhem 1906: 109)

Thus falsification cannot just be a matter of routine; it is not a simple combinatorial process. Yet, Popper (1963: 238–9, 243) opposes this to what is usually referred to as, 'Quine's holistic view of empirical testing'. According to this view, our statements about the external world face the tribunal of sense experience not individually but only as a 'corporate body'. Popper's argument is that 'we can be reasonably successful in attributing a refutation to *definite* portions of the theoretical maze', and that this fact 'must remain inexplicable for one who adopts Duhem's and Quine's views on the matter' (Popper 1963: 243).

The first point to notice here is that Popper is not fair to Duhem in this respect. It is indeed the case that, according to Quine, scientists cannot refute definite portions of their theories, but this is not so for Duhem. On the contrary, Duhem (1906) explicitly argued that a good scientist is able to detect the 'error' and to bring the analysis a step further. 'Refutation' is therefore to switch from the theory as a whole to something which is more simple and elegant than the former. However, what we get right, according to Duhem, is only a matter of the wisdom ('*bon sense*') of a singular scientist (Vullemin 1979: 599; Gillies 1993: 141–2; Maiocchi 1990).

Curiously enough, this could also have been Popper's way out of the problem posed by his own methodological approach, were it not for the fact that Popper (1983: section 22) conflated the problem of guessing which premises of the theoretical group are responsible for the falsification with the problem of finding a new theory. As for the latter, we are told in the *Logic of Scientific Discovery* there is no rational solution; 'there is no such thing as a method of having new ideas' (Popper 1959: 32).[1]

Leaving aside the exegetical issue, the essential aspect of the matter is the 'Homerical challenge' that scientists very often must face, that is, 'to sail safely between the Scylla of intellectual prejudice which makes us reject [relevant] evidence not readily integrated without preconceived notions, and the Charybdis of irrelevance' of presumed anomalies (Martin Deutsch, quoted in Galison 1987: 74).

Let us return to Galileo's story. In particular to the impact of his astronomical observations on the scientific community of the time. As is well known, in his *Sidereus Nuncius* (1610) Galileo reported details of the Moon's surface that he interpreted as valleys and mountains. He also reported about the vast expansion of the Universe and about the Milky Way which was found to consist of aggregates of individual stars. He then, most surprisingly, noted that Jupiter had four satellites, and in 1611 (after the publication of *Sidereus Nuncius*) that Venus went through phases, like the Moon. All these phenomena were in favour of the Copernican system only in as much as they provided argument *against* the rival system.

The Moon's topography, for example, clearly raised doubts about the traditional Aristotelian dogma of the distinction between terrestrial and celestial regions, imperfect and corruptible in the former, perfect and immutable in the latter. Another, and more important, visible analogy with the Copernican model was offered by the four satellites of Jupiter. These 'four moons' (or 'pianeti Medicei' as Galileo named them to pay homage to his protector) were found to move roughly in circular orbits around a planet placed at the centre. They therefore offered to plain view a miniature Copernican system with a centre of revolution at Jupiter and not at the Earth. Add to all these the 'fact' that Galileo probably regarded as the most impressive event confirming the correctness of Copernican astronomy, namely the phases of Venus (Drake 1978). But despite the fact that Galileo, contrary to Osiander's instrumentalist interpretation, believed in the essential truth of the Copernican system, he was probably aware that such new data alone could not have decided unambiguously between heliostaticism and geostaticism.

By way of example, let us review the role of the evidence provided by Venus. At the time of the initial diffusion of Copernican ideas, Venus's phases were presented as a case *against* Copernicus. They were indeed implied by the Copernican hypothesis, but not yet observed. In this contest, Galileo's observational discovery of the phases may be interpreted as successfully deviating the arrow of *modus tollens* from the Copernican hypothesis itself to some other auxiliary conditions. In retrospect, it was therefore a good 'decision' of Copernicians not to dismiss their hypothesis, but to tenaciously defend it against the 'sensible evidence'. The observations by telescope of the phases, however, did not turn Copernicus's hypotheses into one 'indisputable truth', contrary to Galileo's claims, since Venus's phases were also consistent with Tycho Brahe's middle ground system and some particular version of Ptolemy's system as well (Ariew 1984).[2] Nevertheless these phases were 'an indication of objective progress' of the Copernican system (Lakatos and Zahar 1976). But again, how are we to interpret this kind of progress?

After all the phases of Venus provided neither a (more or less crucial) confirmation of Copernicus' theory, nor a (more or less crucial) refutation of Ptolemy's. Rather they are a refutation – the *refutation of a refutation* of an important objection to the former (Feyerabend 1975: Chapter 6; Morpurgo-Tagliabue 1980: 170). This gives an indication of progress neither in the sense of an 'inductivist' (or positivistic) methodology, nor in terms of a strict falsificationist methodology; yet it is a mark of 'objective progress' in as much as it contributed to open the way to a fruitful research programme, like the Copernican one, an alternative both to the 'regressive' Aristotelian-Ptolemaic programme and to the compromise system of Brahe.

Furthermore, Galileo's strategy in arguing for heliostaticism by refuting those objections which invalidated Copernicus is even clearer in the light of his chief contribution to the victory of Copernicanism, namely the 'new' science of motion. Once more, Galileo's foundation of the new mechanics does not amount to any 'crucial' or 'direct' confirmation of the Copernican system; rather it defuses an important counterexample to it regarding the motion of the Earth. That is the well-known peripatetic argument according to which the Earth, if moved, must leave every object behind, and that a freely falling body must hit the ground somewhat behind the vertical point. The vindication of the Copernican system precisely entails the necessity of demolishing such arguments and Galileo accomplished this task in terms of what is now known as the principle of the relativity of motion – which, roughly, states that a stone dropped from the top of a moving ship's mast would not be left behind because the stone shares the ship's motion; and by analogy that the stone dropped from a tower shares the Earth's motion. (For a historical reconstruction see Sparzani 2003: 116–59.)

The Copernican system thus required the dissolution of the 'standard' way of thinking, and this requirement generated the 'new science' of motion and, in particular, the principles which seem most remote to the experience of everyday life, namely the principle of inertia and the principle of relativity. From this respect Galileo's *Discourses Concerning the Two New Sciences* is no less Copernican than the *Dialogue Concerning the Two Chief World Systems*.

Moreover, it is worth emphasising that the arguments in support of the new astronomy are not so much a positive demonstration of a theory as a removal of obstacles that prevented its acceptance. But the main difficulty in defending Copernicus's viewpoint was precisely the paradox of those two mechanical consequences which seemed to result from it. Galileo's contribution did not render the Copernican system 'absolutely certain'. Neither did his contribution mark the moment at which it became 'demonstrated' for the first time in history. Rather it offered a consistent ground for new enquiries: the very possibility of further articulating a 'progressive' research programme. Galileo accomplished the task of the scientist (and philosopher) who must overcome common sense and carry the problem into a new research programme where its solution may become possible.

Back to the future: Lakatos and beyond

We have seen that Galileo introduced changes concerning the nature of observation and 'natural' ideas or commonsense about motion, namely in fields apparently far from mathematical astronomy. Superficially this seems a corroboration of Quine's holistic view, i.e. what is actually tested is a great 'corporate body' of knowledge. But we cannot conclude that such a corporate body is the whole of science. In fact, what scientists really want to change is indicated by what they decide to maintain. The change itself is thus dependent on the identification of what Lakatos (1970) has labelled the 'metaphysical core of a *scientific* research programme', which consists of sets of assumptions that researchers committed to the programme protect against negative evidence. Implicit or explicit decisions make these assumptions metaphysical in Popper's sense (Zahar 1989: 21). What has to be done in the face of counter-evidence is provided by the positive heuristics, which 'consists of a partially, articulated set of suggestions or hints on how to change, develop the "refutable variants" of a research programme, how to modify, sophisticate, the "refutable" protective belt' (Lakatos 1970: 50).

In accordance with Duhem's analysis, Lakatos claims that some negative outcomes of tests do not necessarily constitute a refutation, for they can be ascribed to some incorrect auxiliary assumptions. Consequently, crucial experiments, which are important for Popper, play no role in Lakatos's sophisticated falsificationism, i.e. they cannot decide 'instantly' between two competing theories. Indeed, Kuhn's characterisation of 'normal science' has forcefully drawn attention to the fact that theories are retained by the scientific community well after their presumed refutation, often thanks to some influential metaphysics (Kuhn 1963).

However, once the (naïve Popperian) mono-theoretic pattern of the growth of science has been substituted by a pluralistic one, and once the rationale underlined by Duhem's challenge has been taken into full account, it has to be noticed that the distinction between hardcore and heuristics is rarely 'as absolute as Lakatos imagined' (Zahar 1989: 22). Moreover, we argue, that this is not necessarily a vice in Lakatos's methodological stand point.

From the beginning of our case-study (that is from Galileo's *Dialogo*), the relativity principle has seemed both vague and metaphysical, but this apparent vice turned out to be a virtue when Einstein (1905) removed the 'apparent' inconsistency between the relativity principle and the constancy of light velocity, 'sacrificing only' the Galilean rule of adding velocities (and incorporating in the heuristics the requirement that all physical laws are to be Lorentz-covariant).

At the core of Einstein's General Relativity (1916) we still find the relativity principle, i.e. the frames belonging to some class are all physically equivalent; but Einstein (1916) 'extends this principle from the set of inertial frames to that of all possible ... systems' (Zahar 1989: 266). The correspondent prescriptive import amounts to not distinguishing between inertial and non-inertial frames. In positive heuristic terms, this can be regarded as the constraint of general covariance together with a requirement of 'organic unity', roughly speaking, 'all phenomena should be subsumed under one embracing-theory' (Zahar 1989: 24; 265–70; 302–3).

A further look at the structure and dynamics of research programmes will clarify the role played by heuristic considerations. In particular, heuristics allow us to embed some important facts in the deductive structure of the programme in a way similar to that described by Lakatos concerning lemmas or auxiliary principles or subconjectures in mathematics. More particularly, researchers decide that some 'principles' in mathematics or 'laws' in physics ought to function as constraints in building up a series of more sophisticated theories.

Newton's *Principia* (1869, 1713), for example, requires that any theory of gravitation would have to account for Kepler's laws termed as phenomena (see Book III). The extent to which these 'facts' are approximately true in the Newtonian universe is clarified by a relevant part of Newton's heuristics; namely the theory of perturbations. Moreover, in the case of Special Relativity, Einstein's starting point was an analysis of the 'fact', discovered by Faraday, that in electromagnetic induction the observed results depend on the relative velocity of conductor and magnet, not on their absolute motion in the ether. In the case of General Relativity the starting point was the analysis of the 'fact' that all bodies (near the surface of the Earth) fall freely with the same acceleration (Zahar 1989: 270, 303). In this Galileo's famous result is involved: 'a two-fold constancy … the same body has a constant acceleration throughout its time of fall; and all bodies, irrespective of their mass and composition, experience the same acceleration at the same point of their trajectory. The first constancy was rejected by Newton, but the second can be deduced from Newtonian theory', provided that one 'blandly assumes that the gravitational and inertial masses are equal' (Zahar 1989: 270–71). But in Einstein's programme this 'lemma' is something which needs to be vindicated. In 1912 Einstein exposed the problems as follows:

> I started from the most obvious viewpoint, namely that the equivalence between inertial and gravitational masses should be explained in terms of a fundamental identity between these two primitive quantities of matter, viz. energy. From a physical standpoint, the presence of a state gravitational field should be considered as essentially identical with an acceleration of reference frame.
>
> (Einstein 1912: 1063, translated and quoted in Zahar 1989: 273)

To sum up: the 'equivalence principle' entails that, in a gravitational field, all test particles irrespective of their internal structure and composition experience the same acceleration ('universality of free fall') exactly as it happens in the case of the so-called apparent forces. 'Since a trajectory in the presence of apparent forces is but a different description of a straight line, it follows naturally the question whether it is possible to introduce a new concept of 'straight' line able to describe also motion in the presence of gravity' (Bertotti 1989: 65). This was the route that brought Einstein to 'abandon flat space and adopt Riemannian geometry as the basis of a new revolutionary theory of gravitation' (Zahar 1989: 200).

Einstein's programme was not developed in isolation. In the long run Special Relativity 'superseded' its competitors but, as far as General Relativity is concerned, we cannot unambiguously derive the same conclusion. In fact, the classical tests of General Relativity (the excess perihelion shift of Mercury, the deflection of light by a mass and the gravitational redshift) can also be accounted by different relativistic approaches (Will 1986).

Let us recall that in the 1960s the 'supremacy' of Einstein's General Relativity was challenged by researchers moving from an alternative *manifesto*, the so-called Mach's principle, i.e. the conjecture that laws and physical constants determining the behaviour of bodies in a laboratory are not absolute but depend upon the global dynamic of the whole universe, in particular, from matter at great distance (Brans and Dicke 1961). This point of view would also lead to a violation of the principle of equivalence (Dicke 1962). Other alternative theories of gravity were then advanced, mainly characterised by different field equations and different geometries to that of General Relativity, but still satisfying the equivalence principle and explaining the motion by the principle of geodetic (for a survey see Will 1986). Finally, 'a "theory of gravitation theory" was developed ... to study and classify all theories of gravitation in as unbiased a manner as possible. Pioneered by Robert H. Dicke and Kenneth Nordtvedt, Jr, this "theory of theories" could also be put to powerful use analyzing the new high-precision experiments, and suggesting future experiments made possible by further technological advances' (Will 1979: 25).

To conclude: in such a *framework* characterised by a family of alternative theories of gravitation, some 'principles' used in the construction of General Relativity are challenged (e.g. the principle of equivalence). But researchers still seem to agree that a weak version of these is required for each programme involved in the framework, for example that each gravitational theory must embody the universality of free fall (Will 1979: 27). For decades this *framework* has represented the major incentive for the design of tests and the discovery of new facts or of an interpretation of 'old' phenomena in a 'new' light. At last, rather paradoxically, 'this enormous experimental effort has corroborated Einstein's General Relativity, usually accepted for other reasons in former phases of its growth' (Bertotti 1989: 74).

However paradoxical, the story is not without a moral: it is because of the competition of different programmes that scientists do not take for granted the 'classical' tests (e.g. the perihelion of Mercury) of a particular point of view (e.g. General Relativity); but they are forced to devise various experiments and a new arena for the comparison of the rival proposals. Moreover, this is how the *Homerical challenge* can be met: it is a rational attitude to stick to some 'preconceived idea', if, at the same time, one encourages other researchers to work on some objections to them. It is also 'scientifically acceptable' to support some (alleged) anomalies in the light of different explanatory principles in order to develop an alternative view, if, at the same time, one is ready to stimulate the defence of the challenged core. This is of course a plea for a 'competitive tolerance'. In the disposition of Kip Thorne's slogan: Monday, Wednesday, and Friday we believe in General Relativity, while Tuesday, Thursday and Saturday we believe in Brans Dicke theory. Sunday we go to the beach' (Quoted in Will 1986: Chapter 8).

Our analysis therefore suggests that in science different research programmes fighting for supremacy in the same arena define a *framework* for experimental tests. As Poincaré (1902) suggested, science is certainly cumulative at the phenomenological level, but strong differences are produced at the top theoretical explanation. The usual picture, according to which different 'paradigms' consist of completely incomparable worlds (each of them encompass their own 'facts'), misses the point that often programmes start from the same set of 'facts' and 'bifurcate' when they state their metaphysical commitments, in accordance with Whewell's insight referred to earlier.

Moreover, the agreement about some (presumed) facts does not imply total agreement: in accordance with Duhem's analysis, scientists working in the same framework make different choices. Thus, a framework is nothing but a family of rival research programmes, and researchers working in the same framework may disagree about the heuristic power of such programmes. Indeed, not only may they disagree *but* they also must do so: this is the condition for the Popperian *growth through criticism*. Moreover, herein lies our views of Popper's major legacy (deprived of much of its rhetoric on falsificationism): scientists, researchers and philosophers, should be worried when there is little debate, not when the debate is particularly intense. After all, a poet so dear to Popper, such as Novalis, wrote that science as a definite achievement is a myth, exactly 'as the philosophical stone', but good philosophy (and science) is like 'the Copernican system: it takes away fixed points, and transforms everything quietly at rest in something floating'.

Notes

1 See Lakatos's 'Lectures on Scientific Method at the LSE', in Motterlini (1999). Here Lakatos claims that as far as Popper's major contributions to philosophy are concerned, the falsifiability criterion 'is a step back from Duhem', and his solution to the problem of induction 'is a step back from Hume' (p. 89).

2 More into details, the discovery that Venus passed through different phases (like the Moon) would have established the revolution around the Sun not only of this planet but of 'all the planets' ('tutti li pianeti'). However, we have to pay attention here: 'All the planets' could also not include the Earth. Indeed, the very existence and qualitative appearances of the phases of Venus do not constitute a disproof for geostaticism. It is in fact still possible to account for the phases of Venus into a Ptolemaic framework (as Kepler was perfectly aware of). Of course, this requires some modifications in Ptolemaic astronomy, but it is at least debatable whether these modifications are such that they would invalidate all of the Ptolemaic astronomy. Ariew (1987) has shown that the theory of Venus under the Ptolemaic system requires that the line of sight from the earth to the Sun also goes through the centre of the epicycle of Venus. The actual location of the centre of the epicycle of Venus on this line of sight is left open (this is why various Ptolemaics have held differing opinions about whether Venus is above or below the Sun). The correction required by Galileo's observations of Venus would be the fixing of the centre of Venus' epicycle at the Sun. There are no further implications to be derived from this and, certainly, one cannot conclude anything definitive concerning the behaviour of the Earth and the fixed stars. Moreover the correction seems minimal here and it is almost the same as accepting the Tychonic system which, in its turn, was also able to account for the absence of the stellar parallax.

References

Ariew, R. (1984) 'Galileo's lunar observations in the context of medieval lunar theory,' *Studies in History and Philosophy of Science*, 15: 213–26.

—— (1987) 'The phases of Venue before 1610', *Studies in History and Philosophy of Science*, 18: 81–92.

Bertotti, B. (1989) 'La teoria della relatività generale a confronto con l'esperienza', in U. Curi (ed.) *L'opera di Einstein*, Ferrara: Gabriele Corbino & Co.

Brans, C. and Dicke, R.H. (1961) 'Mach's principle and relativistic theory of gravitation', *Physical Review*, 124: 925–35.

Dicke, R.H. (1962) 'Mach's principle and equivalence', in *Proceedings of the International School of Physics*, New York.

Drake, S. (1978) *Galileo at Work: His Scientific Biography*, Chicago, IL: University of Chicago.

Duhem, P. (1906) *La théorie physique: Son objet et sa structure*, trans. P. Wiener (1954) *The Aim and Structure of Physical Theories*, Princeton, NJ: Princeton University Press.

Einstein, A. (1905) 'Zur Elektrodynamik bewegter Körper', *Annalen der Physik*, 17, ser. 4: 891–921.

—— (1916) 'Die Grundlage der allgemeine Relativitätstheorie', *Annalen der Physik*, 49: 769–822.

Feyerabend, P.K. (1975) *Against Method*, London: NLB.

Galileo, Galilei (1638) 'Discorsi e dimostrazioni matematiche intorno a due nuive scienze' in G. Favero (ed.) *Le Opere di Galileo Galilei*, Firenze 1890–1909, Vol. VIII.

—— (1610) *Sidereus Nuncius*, in G. Favero (ed.) *Le Opere di Galileo Galilei*, Firenze 1890–1919, Vol. III.

—— (1623) *Il Saggiatore*, in G. Favero (ed.) *Le Opere di Galileo Galilei*, Firenze 1890–1909, Vol. VI.

—— (1632) 'Dialogo sopra I due massimi sistemi del mondo', in G. Favero (ed.) *Le Opere di Galileo Galilei*, Vol. VII.

Galison, P. (1989) *How Experiments End*, Chicago, il: University of Chicago Press.

Gillies, D. (1993) *Philosophy of Science in the Twentieth Century: Four Central Themes*, Oxford: Blackwell.

Giusti, E. (1980) *Bonaventura Cavalieri and the Theory of Indivisibles*, Rome: Cremonese.

Kuhn, T. (1963) 'The function of dogma in scientific research', in A.C. Crombie (ed.) *Scientific Change*, London: Heinemann.

Lakatos, I. (1970) 'Falsificationism and the methodology of scientific research programmes', in I. Lakatos and A. Musgrave (eds) *Criticism and the Growth of Knowledge*, Cambridge: Cambridge University Press. Reprinted in J. Worrall and G. Currie (eds) (1978) *The Methodology of Scientific Research Programmes*, Vol. I of the *Philosophical Papers of Imre Lakatos*, Cambridge: Cambridge University Press.

—— (1978) *The Methodology of Scientific Research Programmes: Philosophical Papers Vol. I*, J. Worrall and G. Currie (eds) Cambridge: Cambridge University Press.

Lakatos, I. and Musgrave A. (eds) (1970) *Criticism and the Growth of Knowledge*, Cambridge: Cambridge University Press.

Lakatos, I. and Zahar, E. (1975) 'Why did Copernicus's programme supersede Ptolemy's?', in R. Westman (ed.) *The Copernican Revolution*, Berkeley, CA: University of California Press.

Maiocchi, R. (1990) 'Pierre Duhem's *The Aim and Structure of Physical Theory:* A Book against Conventionalism', *Synthese*, 83: 385–400.

Morpurgo-Tagliabue, G. (1981) *I Processi di Galileo e l'Espistemologia*, Rome: A. Armando.

Motterlini, M. (ed.) (1999) *For and against Method: Including Lakatos's Lectures on Method and the Lakatos-Feyerabend Correspondence*, Chicago, IL: University of Chicago Press.

Poincaré, H. (1902) *La Science et l'hypothese*, Paris: Flammerion.

Popper, K.R. (1934, 1959) *Logik der Forschung*, Vienna; translated as *The Logic of Scientific Discovery*, London: Hutchinson.
—— (1963) *Conjectures and Refutations*, London: Routledge and Kegan Paul.
—— (1982) *Quantum Theory and the Schism in Physics*, in W.W. Bartley, III (ed.) *Postscript to the Logic of Scientific Discovery*, London: Hutchinson.
—— (1983) *Realism and the Aim of Science*, in W.W. Bartley, III (ed.) *Postscript to the Logic of Scientific Discovery*, London: Hutchinson.
Quine, W.V.O. (1951) 'Two dogmas of empiricism', *Philosophical Review*, 60: 20–43; reprinted in *From a Logical Point of View* (1961), Cambridge, MA: Harvard University Press.
Regge, T. (1995) *Infinito: Viaggio ai Limiti dill'Universe*, Milan: Mondadori.
Stillwell, J. (1989) *Mathematics and its History*, New York: Springer-Verlag.
Sparzani, A. (2003) *Relativita, Quante Storie: Un Percorso Scientifico e Letterario tra Relativo e Assoluto*, Turin: Boringhieri.
Vuillemin, J. (1979) 'On Duhem's and Quine's Theses', *Grazer Philosophische Studien*, 9: 69–96; reprinted in L.E. Hahn and P.A. Schilpp (eds) (1986) *The Philosophy of W.V. Quine in Library of Living Philosophers*, La Salle, IL: Open Court Publishing.
Watkins, J. (1958) 'Confirmable and influential metaphysics', *Mind*, 67: 344–65.
Whewell, W. (1840) *The Philosophy of the Inductive Sciences*, in G. Buchdahl and L. Laudan (eds) (1967) *The Historical and Philosophical Works of William Whewell*, Vol. VI, London: Cass.
Will, C. (1979) 'The confrontation between gravitation theory and experiment', in S. Hawking and W. Israel (eds) *General Relativity: An Einstein Centenary Survey*, Cambridge: Cambridge Universiy Press.
—— (1986) *Was Einstein Right?*, New York: Basic Books.
Zahar, E. (1989) *Einstein's Revolution: A Study in Heuristic*, La Salle, IL: Open Court Publishing.

6 Conjectures on a constructive approach to induction

John McCall

Introduction

Karl Popper was one of the most influential philosophers of the twentieth century. There are many original and profound ideas that could and indeed should be celebrated. However, there is one idea which preoccupied Popper throughout his illustrious career and yet remained flawed and incomplete. Induction is this wayward notion which we have decided to discuss and hopefully repair.

We begin with a brief statement of Popper's views on induction. As we will see it is the hallmark of his critical rationalism and permeates his massive contribution to scientific methodology. The influence of Popper's induction in statistics is assessed with significance testing the primary example. Its connection with Kuhn's thought has been noted by Kuhn himself and we summarise Kuhn's reactions. After considering some other critiques, we present an alternative view of induction based on the ideas of Ramsey, Polya, Poincaré, Quine, Hofstadter, and, especially, deFinetti and his dynamic inductive creation – exchangeability.

Popper on induction

Popper's views on induction were profound and can be found in most of his major works. His position can be easily summarised. The logical problem of induction is a consequence of three principles: (1) a natural law cannot be proven by observation or experiment. As Born observes 'the statement of law – B depends on A – always transcends experience. Yet this kind of statement is made everywhere and all the time, and sometimes from scanty material' (as quoted in Popper 1963: 54). (2) The second principle is also present in Born's statement and is simply the fact that science uses laws 'everywhere and all the time'. Popper notes that Born resembles Hume on his astonishment that these laws are frequently founded on 'scanty material'. Popper augments Born with (3) the *principle of empiricism*: 'In science only observation and experiment may decide upon the *acceptance or rejection* of scientific statements, including laws and theories' (Popper 1963: 54 italics in original). These three principles appear to be incompatible, but Popper maintains that they 'do not clash'. His key insight is that science never accepts a theory or law once and for all. Instead, laws and theories are always tentatively embraced, that is, all laws and theories are conjectures, or *tentative* hypotheses and new evidence may lead to their rejection. Furthermore, this rejection does not invalidate or exclude the old evidence, which prompted acceptance in the first place. This smacks of Bayes's theorem. The crucial observation of tentative acceptance guarantees that 'the *principle of empiricism* can be fully preserved'. However, '*only the falsity of the theory can be inferred from empirical evidence, and this inference is a purely deductive one*' (Popper 1963: 55 italics in original). In showing that these three principles are compatible, Popper claims that he has solved Hume's problem of induction.

Popper goes on to claim that, with Hume there is no such logical entity as inductive inference. Induction is *invalid* in every sense. On the other hand, he disagrees with Hume's opinion that induction is a fact and is necessary. 'The belief that we use induction is simply a mistake. It is a kind of optical illusion. What we do use is a method of trial and the elimination of error'. This method resembles induction but is totally different. Once again this can be compared with Bayes's theorem. Popper concludes: 'In brief *there is no such thing as induction by repetition*' (Popper 1972: 7 italics in original). Another position which Popper regards as 'thoroughly mistaken' is that '*Our senses are the main if not the only source of our knowledge of the world*'.

Popper decomposed Hume's induction problem into two problems: (1) '*The logical problem. Are we rationally justified in reasoning from repeated instances of which we have had experience to instances of which we have had no experience?*' He claims Hume's answer is no. (2) '*How is it that nevertheless all reasonable people expect and believe that instances of which they have had no experience will conform to those of which they have had experience?*' Hume's brief answer is because of 'custom or habit' (Popper 1972: 4). Popper agrees with Hume on (1) and disagrees with (2). Popper considers two pragmatic problems of induction: '(1) Upon which theory should we rely for practical action, from a rational point of view? (2) Which theory should we prefer for practical action, from a rational point of view?' (Popper 1972: 21). His answer to (1) is that 'from a rational point of view we should not "rely" on any theory, for no theory has been shown to be true, or can be shown to be true'. His answer to (2) is: 'we should prefer the best tested theory as a basis for action' (ibid.: 21–2).

There are several points worth contemplating relative to Popper's view of induction: (1) Induction cannot be separated from probability. Yet in these definitive remarks Popper ignores probability.[1] (2) At several points Popper seems to be using a version of Bayes's theorem. (3) Popper's dismissal of the senses as the source of knowledge is controversial. (4) Popper's views have had an enormous influence on significance tests and confidence intervals in the everyday practice of statistics. (5) Popper's quest for objective, scientific, rational solutions is doomed and caused much mischief.

Critical appraisals of Popper's views on induction

After emphasising that his views on science are 'very nearly identical' to those of Popper, Kuhn (1977) presents several trenchant critiques of Popper's philosophy. He maintains that 'Sir Karl has characterised the entire scientific enterprise in terms that apply only to its occasional revolutionary parts' (ibid.: 6). Furthermore, 'a careful look at the scientific enterprise suggests that it is normal science, in which Sir Karl's sort of testing *does not* occur …' (ibid.: 6). These remarks are not compatible with the remarkable influence of Popper on statistical practice, which in many ways is the most normal of sciences. According to Howson and Urbach (1989), the Popperian ambition is to develop a view of science which is both objective and non-probabilistic and in this context significance testing and estimation, which form the bulk of so-called classical methods of statistical inference, are pre-eminent.

Howson and Urbach believe that this pre-eminence is undeserved. The logical foundation of tests and confidence intervals are missing. This is currently being corrected as more and more statisticians and applied workers in almost all fields are adopting Bayesian methods instead of the flawed 'objective' procedures.

Returning to Kuhn we find the following revelation:

> Again and again [Popper] has rejected the "psychology of knowledge" or the "subjective" and has insisted that his concern was instead with the "objective" or "the logic of knowledge." The title of his most fundamental contribution to our field is *The Logic of Scientific Discovery*, and it is there that he most positively asserts that his concern is with the logical spurs of knowledge rather than the psychological drives of individuals.
>
> (Kuhn 1970: 7)

Kuhn concludes his essay with glimmers of hope that Popper will embrace social-psychological imperatives that he sometimes mentions, but also not fully perceive. This has proven to be a false hope!

Ayer also criticises those who claim that scientists do not employ inductive reasoning. They overlook the fact 'that an enormous amount of inductive reasoning is built into our language' (Ayer 1992: 255). He also notes that any successful method of forming our expectations must be inductive:

> The question at issue is not so much *whether* the future will resemble the past, since if the world is to continue to be describable at all, it must resemble it in some way or other, but *how* it will resemble it. What we want and cannot obtain, except by circular argument, is a justification for our actual interpretation of the past; a justification for adhering to a special corpus of beliefs.
>
> (Ayer 1992: 255 italics in original)

We cannot obtain it according to Hume. Yet Hume *never claimed* that the result is 'that beliefs should be abandoned'.

Quine offers an interesting defence of induction:

> To trust induction as a way of access to the truth of nature … is to suppose, more nearly, that our quality space matches that of the cosmos … [But]

> why does our innate subjective spacing of qualities accord so well with the functionally relevant groupings in nature as to *make our inductions* tend to come out right?
>
> (Quine 1969: 126 italics in original)

Quine turns to Darwin. 'If people's innate spacing of qualities is a gene-linked trait, then the spacing that has been made for the most successful inductions will have tended to predominate through natural selection. Creatures inveterately wrong in their inductions have a pathetic but praiseworthy tendency to die before reproducing their kind'. Similarly, firms who consistently embrace incorrect inductions tend to go bankrupt and entrepreneurs *should have difficulty* reconstituting the firm.

We finally mention some comments by Bird on falsification and induction. Bird observes that according to Popper if a favoured hypothesis is falsified, scientists do not initiate new programs. Instead, they search for new conjectures and try to falsify them. The Popper process of conjecture and refutation resembles Darwinian natural selection. Bird maintains that Popper's unwillingness to use induction poses many problems. Popper tried to show that one theory (while not true) may be closer to the truth than another. But this judgement requires induction. Bird poses the following conundrum:

> A number of philosophers … argued that theory dependence is ubiquitous and Popper agreed. But if we do not know the theories in question to be true, as Popper holds, then he is committed to agreeing that we do not know the truth of any observation claim either. So, if we don't know any observations, we don't know that any hypotheses are falsified. And so Popper is committed to a very radical form of scepticism indeed.
>
> (Bird 2000: 5)

An alternative approach to induction

Classification and the search for similarities via metaphor are primary functions of the mind. The birth and evolution of language, society, and mind hinge on these creative activities. The evolution of language in each human repeats the process by which society first acquired language. Classification and the search for similarities are crucial to learning and indispensable to perception, induction, poetry, and science. We believe with Jesperson:

> Man is a classifying animal: in one sense it may be that the whole process of speaking is nothing but distributing phenomena, of which no two are alike in every respect, into different classes on the strength of perceived similarities and dissimilarities. In the name-giving process we witness the same ineradicable and very useful tendency to see likenesses and to express similarities in the phenomena through similarity in the name.[2]
>
> (Jesperson 1922: 88)

The evolution of mathematics, the language of science, is also founded on classification and similarity search by metaphor. Cassirer (1944) draws a sharp distinction between mathematics and the other languages; the former is objective and free of metaphor, whereas the latter is subjective and contaminated by metaphor. He fails to see the creative power of metaphor and its basic role in the development of mathematics and the sciences. While Cassirer acknowledges that we must repudiate mechanical determinism, he claims: 'the true scientific determination of number is not liable to these objections'. This attitude is, no doubt, the source of the disdain which many philosophers have towards the metaphorical aspects of classification and similarity in the 'non-scientific' realms. These arenas have been infiltrated by uncertainty and metaphor and can never achieve the objective stature of science and mathematics. After Chaitin *et al.*, the grounds for this scientific arrogance have disintegrated. Mathematics is special and indeed divine-like in that it makes what it rearranges and assembles. But its creativity is lodged not in determinism, but in metaphor and chance. No science is more brilliant than evolutionary biology where chance is clearly the source of its creativity. Scrutiny of the more abstract sciences shows not only that they have been pierced by chance, but that it is precisely this penetration which yields their creativity.

Metaphor adopts a new vision of the relations among the entities being studied. Metaphor *searches* for new connections which are more visible from its novel perspective. This search and discovery process is the crux of all metaphors. Through search and discovery, metaphors spin a web of fresh connections among entities that were previously thought to be dissimilar. This web or network was a vital source of communication among our ancestors who first used metaphor. Information flowed through the network as the family adapted to changing circumstances. Families observed their similarities as the metaphoric search process saw other families as extensions of the natural family. This revelation gave rise to another communication network alerting each family to information gathered by other families. It is this exchange of information which is the source of conventions, customs, and other civilising influences. Just as children learn within each familial network, so too do families extract information from the interfamily network that is crucial to its survival and civility. Indeed, these information networks are the *sine qua non* of a viable, civilised society. Language is itself a metaphorical process. Thus the genesis of a communication network occurs as the language which flows through these networks develops in a metaphorical fashion. As the connections among society's members thicken, there is a simultaneous development and strengthening of the brain's neural networks. The key observation (due to Vico) is that language, society, and mind interact with one another fostering the evolution and enrichment of each.

Metaphor releases us from the chains of the literal. The cost of this freedom is that each and every conversation requires induction for comprehension. Metaphor confers richness and riskiness to conversations and writing. Listeners and readers must search for meaning. Thus each conversation or letter entails a creative interpretation. The induction and search affiliated with communication via metaphoric language is the source of this creative interpretation. It is the prelude to meaning. This may seem to reduce communication to a puzzling enterprise entailing onerous problem solving. On the contrary, man is a metaphorical animal and as such thrives on resolving metaphorical missives. Induction may be the 'scandal of philosophy', but it is also the essence of human communication; and just as randomness is essential for evolution, so is risk essential for precise communication.

Language is a combinatoric process. It is also evolutionary. Each metaphor is itself engaged in a birth and death, evolutionary drama. Its birth is marked by a creative addition to language. As the metaphor ages, it loses its vitality and eventually becomes as dull as literal utterances, which signals its approaching death. It should be noted, however, that resurrection is a frequent occurrence among dead metaphors!

Metaphors are frequently used in the formation of scientific theories. The description of these theories is almost always replete with metaphors. Indeed, the creativity of many theories is sparked by this metaphoric invasion. Most of the definitions and portraits of metaphor are modifications or extensions of Aristotle's metaphorical pronouncements in his *Poetics* that the 'greatest thing by far, is to be a master of metaphor. It is the one thing that cannot be learned; and it is also a sign of genius' (para. 22, 1459: 5–8.). Capacity to think metaphorically 'is a sign of genius since a good metaphor implies an intuitive perception of similarity of dissimilars' (ibid.: para. 22, 1459: 5–8), while 'Metaphor consists in giving the thing a name that belongs to something else' (ibid.: para. 20, 1457: 5–8).

In these definitions, and most of those founded on Aristotle, the comparison of a metaphor is a passive process. In fact, metaphor and the perception and memory on which it leans are all active *search processes*. The mind explicitly considers alternative names and chooses the one that makes the best metaphor. Both perception and memory are also active search processes. Perception has a vast array of entities to focus on and choose from. It searches these candidates and chooses the most appropriate for the situation at hand.[3] Memory is also a process of looking for just the right word for matching with a seemingly dissimilar word and thereby creating a metaphor.

The discovery of these new similarities enriches the language and bestows prowess on the model. These discoveries do not appear out of the blue. They must be searched for. This insight suggests that metaphor and model formation be set in a dynamic search setting. The connections discovered by this process form a stochastic web which is a dynamic birth and death process. As new links are generated by the metaphorical process, old links lose their vitality and die. A network vitalised by metaphoric search enhances induction and learning. This dynamic perspective reveals an entirely new set of empirical tests, which were previously unnoticed.

It should also be noted that the essence of learning from experience (Bayes's theorem) is search activity that organises experience into controlled and uncontrolled segments. The uncontrolled applies Bayes's theorem directly; the controlled are organised into dynamic, sequential, search activities. Bayes's theorem is decomposed and joined to the search processes. All are united to produce the information essential for survival. The sequential search paradigm belongs to the economics of information. We agree with Deacon (1977) that the impetus for language was provided by hunting and mating strategies rooted in a basic economic problem – the acquisition of information which served individual self-interest.[4] Thus, the core problems in anthropology, linguistics, and Bayesian statistics are economic.

After Descartes it was a postulate that metaphor and analogy detracted from the certainty and stability of scientific enterprises. Clear and distinct ideas were the only legitimate inhabitants of these discovery processes. Any activity that was uncertain or contingent, like history, poetry, business, and sociology, brazenly used a metaphoric language thereby proclaiming its non-scientific and subjective status. These Cartesian beliefs have been challenged by many since Vico's solitary rebuttal. Nevertheless, Descartes is alive and well in many academic disciplines seeking scientific stature. Yet, as we saw, no human activity can claim to be a discovery process without making constant use of metaphor and analogy. To make use of any human language is to be metaphorical. This is also true of the scientific language: mathematics! Any extended conversation is replete in metaphors which transfer the illumination achieved in one area to another that was previously dark. Induction is the switch which turns on the light as these transfers take place. Mary Hesse (1966) claims that both a theory of metaphor and a theory of induction deal with basically the same subject matter. According to Griswold (1999), Adam Smith regarded 'life in a market society is an ongoing exercise in rhetoric'. Indeed, exchange may be viewed as a debate between buyer and seller with price and quantity the persuasion parameters. The debate continues until either the items of exchange – money and goods – are deemed interchangeable by both parties or an impasse occurs and negotiation stops.

Finally, we must mention Peirce as a precursor to de Finetti. His views on induction fluctuate over his lifetime. But it seems that he would regard his notion of weight of evidence to be a substantial contribution. This idea was rediscovered by Alan Turing and I.J. Good and is, of course, closely tied to de Finetti's notions of learning and induction. Peirce was also the first to attempt to elicit subjective or personal probabilities.[5] Like de Finetti, he thought that urn models revealed the essence of induction. Hacking (1990) observes that for Peirce 'the rationale [for induction] can always be cast into the same logical form as the beanbag'.

In his recent book, Hauser (1996) states that similarity is important for the many disciplines involved in communication. These include: neurobiology, evolutionary biology, cognitive and development psychology, linguistics, and anthropology. Earlier Tversky (1977) maintained that similarity is crucial to theories of knowledge and of behaviour. For instance it is indispensable in each individual's initial classification of objects and in the formation of concepts. It underlies our accounts of stimulus and response generalisation in learning and pattern recognition. Similarity also is of paramount importance in economics. It percolates throughout the theory and empirical study of every economic subdiscipline.

In spite of its importance in the physical, social, and life sciences, similarity has been subject to scathing attacks by philosophers and linguists. One of the most trenchant critiques was by Nelson Goodman (1972) who maintained that 'similarity is invidious, insidious, a pretender, an imposter, and a quack'. This invective was based on his claim that the similarity of A to B is poorly defined in that the *respects* in which A is similar to B are rarely specified and furthermore similarity lacks a frame of reference. In their important article, Medin, *et al.* (1993) rehabilitate similarity with respect to its demolition by Goodman, by showing that respects 'are determined by processes internal to comparisons'. They show that similarity is not an unconditional concept. When similarity is invoked without regard to Goodman's respects, or what might be called *contextual conditions*, then similarity is indeed a 'pretender'. However, when one accounts for these *contextual conditions*, similarity is transformed from an unconditional to a conditional concept and its ubiquity is justified. The imposter has become a legitimate prince.

The problem of conditioning ramifies through the tree of life and is most evident in probability and applied statistics or data analysis. Indeed, Mallows maintains:

> The main challenge of applied statistical work is that of taking proper account of contextual issues. Good techniques are not enough; nor are good computer programs, nor powerful theorems. A major intellectual attraction of the discipline is the subtlety of the interplay between the formed statistical procedures and the imperfectly understood substantive questions. The formulation of clean questions is often an important part of the inquiry.
> (Mallows 1998: 2)

In Draper *et al.* (1995), the concept of similarity is analysed. They use a series of important examples to show the crucial manner in which judgements of similarity are used in data analysis and inferences. Their goal is to formalise how similarity measures should be constructed and utilised. Because of its close resemblance to de Finetti's exchangeability, they call similarity 'descriptive exchangeability'. A judgement of similarity entails four different concepts. For example, suppose we wish to judge whether those who drive cars in Los Angeles are similar to the population of drivers in the USA. Then the four concepts specify:

(1) A description of each set
(2) A measure of the difference (distance) between the two sets
(3) A calliper for appraising the size of the differences
(4) Deciding which comparisons should be made.

What is crucial is that the context is present in all four of these concepts, which together define similarity. Mallows (1998: 5) emphasises that 'the statistician's understanding of the context can and must be used in choosing the set of pairs of subsets to be compared'. Frequently, it is not possible to make these four judgements on actual data. This is the critical point where analogy or metaphor come into play to obtain exchangeability from similarity. Throughout his writings on induction and exchangeability, de Finetti highlighted the role of analogy:

> If analogy leads to a certain symmetry in our opinion, which we call 'exchangeability,' then we are, in consequence, willing to be influenced more and more by the observed frequency as the size of the experience increases. Here ... homogeneity is in a sense a favourable circumstance. In order to obtain a satisfactory evaluation of the probability of a future ... event on the basis of an observed frequency, the situation is better if the experience is larger and if the events observed are more homogenous with the one we are interested in.
>
> (de Finetti 1972: 180)

According to de Finetti, the dominant theme in this discussion of homogeneity (similarity) and indeed the kingpin of his entire philosophy[6] is: 'The necessity of taking into account all that is known, regardless of what method or source produced it'.

In Draper *et al.* (1995), the authors considered judgements of similarity between available data and data which was unavailable. Mallows notes: 'We saw no way to avoid a leap of faith, which necessarily will not be supported directly by data, whenever such a judgement is made. We believe that all extrapolation from known to unknown involves such a leap' (Mallows 1998: 5). An important and prescient article by Smith (1984) anticipates the developments in Draper *et al.* and also predicts the spectacular applications of Markov Chain Monte Carlo methods in providing an approximate solution to the problem of estimating prior distributions. Smith's major points include: (a) a concise capitulation of de Finetti's philosophy: 'To be sure, the object of the scientists' attention may well be assumed external, objective reality: but the actuality of the scientific process consists in the evolution of scientists' *beliefs* about that reality'. A lengthy and compelling defence of this view can be found in de Finetti's majestic *magnus opus* (de Finetti 1974–5); (b) The ambiguous statements of everyday language are replaced by precise definitions in such a way that close contact to 'the touchstone of actual personal experience' is retained. The goal is to acquire unambiguous statements which are sensible. To accomplish (a) and (b), Bayesian thinking about the foundations of statistics has been strongly influenced by Peirce's pragmatism[7] and operationalism.[8] Peirce's pragmatism admonishes the decision-maker to focus attention on all conceivable practical outcomes in order to obtain 'clear thinking'. According to Bridgman (1936), the practical conveys concrete meaning when physical or mental concepts are defined such that the nexus with both physical and mental operations is preserved.

The operational meaning of 'degree of belief' flows directly from Ramsey's prescription that the measure of belief be inextricably tied to action. Smith emphasises that whether one is engaged in inference or decision-making one must choose among competing alternatives. In designing the axioms of choice, coherence of actions must be reflected in consistency of the axioms. Coherence is simply the requirement that the axioms never be inconsistent in that they lead to inevitable losses regardless of the action chosen.

There are many sets of consistent axioms. They are equivalent in their implications which include: the degree of beliefs associated with events should combine according to the laws of probability; Bayes's theorem is applied to convert old beliefs into new beliefs in the light of new information; and preferences among alternatives behave as if each alternative was assigned a numerical utility and then ordered according to expected utility.

In his comments on similarity, Smith, in keeping with Goodman's objections notes that there are problems in defining similarity without becoming enmeshed in a web of circularity. The subjectivist avoids these entanglements by recognising that any claim of 'similarity' among different events is a 'personal judgement, requiring … an operational definition of what is meant by "similar"'. He goes on to claim that this requirement of an operational definition 'finds natural expression in the concept of exchangeability'. In this way, he anticipates the articles by Draper *et al.* (1995) and Mallows (1998).

Exchangeability

De Finetti discovered exchangeability in 1931. His famous representation theorem shows how Bayesian subjective statistics can be joined to classical statistics. As we will see, exchangeability is closely related to the similarity which is the defining characteristic of metaphor and analogy. The vitality of the Bayesian approach flows from exchangeability. The essence of the Bayesian approach is to extract as much pertinent information as is possible from a particular sample. This entails conditioning the information with respect to the context that obtains. This is precisely what exchangeability accomplishes. Practical economists may find that either the informational framework of exchangeability is helpful in thinking about concrete problems, or that approximations to exchangeability are useful in that most particular art: data analysis.

It must be observed that de Finetti (1974–5) distinguishes sharply between the *Bayesian standpoint* and *Bayesian techniques*. The former occurs in everyday life as well as in statistics and decision-making. Many applications from a Bayesian standpoint entail little formal mathematics. A qualitative revision of beliefs as new information unfolds is all that is required. *Bayesian techniques* on the other hand sometimes grow into 'imposing mathematical machinery', are applied in the standard Bayesian manner, and frequently lost sight of the 'specific features of each particular case and the true opinion of the person concerned'. De Finetti observes that the two approaches are closely related in that the former is the logical framework and the latter the mathematical tool in 'the theory concerning the way in which our opinions (or beliefs) must be modified (according to Bayes's theorem) when new information is attained. Nevertheless, in practice, the overlap of the fields of the published applications inspired by the Bayesian standpoint and of those making use of Bayesian techniques seems rather narrow'. De Finetti regards the *Bayesian standpoint* as 'an almost self-evident truth'. On the other hand, *Bayesian techniques*, while they do produce admissible decision rules, the validity of each is with respect to 'a particular initial opinion … Any conclusion is arbitrary if the choice responds to arbitrary formal criteria … rather than to personal advice'.

The subjective and objective approaches to probability differ in several important ways. The most important distinction is that the subjectivist considers probability as a relation between a statement and a body of accumulated evidence. The numerical value assigned to probability is called a *degree of belief*. The *degree of belief* may differ among individuals even when they possess the same body of evidence. These differences reflect the uniqueness of individuals in their evaluation of uncertain situations. In contrast, the empirical frequency view of probability maintains that there is the long-run relative frequency attached to an event. A more sophisticated version of the empirical objective approach considers probability as a theoretical construct, where its meaning is derived from the rules used in its application. Kyburg and Smokler (1964) cite Braithwaite (1953) as exemplifying this approach. Briathwaite presents a theoretical model in which the probability of an event is a parameter. The empirical content is determined by a 'rule of rejection'. If the samples drawn reveal a particular structure, the theoretical model concerning the event is accepted. The key to these objective approaches is their insistence that the probability of a particular event is similar to a statement about lengths and weights. It is this vision which endows statistics and probability theory with scientific stature.

The subjective approach to probability allows any degree of belief in a particular statement, but restricts the distribution of degrees of belief. Four concepts are crucial to the subjective approach: 'degrees of belief', coherence, Bayes's theorem, and exchangeable events. *Degrees of belief* consists of a propensity to make particular choices in objectively defined choice situations.[9] Coherence is related to *degrees of belief*. Bayes's theorem was published posthumously in 1764. According to Stigler (1982, 1986) Bayes's essay is one of the more difficult works to read in the history of statistics. As a consequence, his assumption that an unknown probability is distributed uniformly *a priori* has been misread by many illustrious statisticians including: Karl Pearson, R.A. Fisher, Harold Jeffreys, and Ian Hacking.

Bayes's problem was to find: $P(a < \theta < b \mid X = p)$, where X is a binomially distributed random variable and there are n independent trials. The probability of success on a single trial is θ. In his solution he uses a billiard table analogy: a ball W is rolled across a unit square table and its stopping point is uniformly distributed over the table. The x coordinate of the stopping point is called θ, which is uniformly distributed over (0, 1). A second ball is rolled in like fashion n times. If its stopping point is to the left of W, it is a success. Hence, the total number of successes X is binomially distributed. Bayes's answer to this problem is:

$$P(a<\theta<b \mid X=p)=\int_a^b \binom{n}{p} \theta^p (1-\theta)^n - p d\theta \,/ \int_p^n \binom{n}{p} \theta P (1-\theta)^n \, p d\theta$$

Stigler believes:

> that Bayes wished to argue that his 'billiard' table is an apt analogy to other applications where θ is unknown ... The key question is, how does he describe such cases in order that the analogy be judged appropriate? The answer [and this is crucial to the entire Bayesian enterprise] is that it is not through the distribution of θ that we shall judge whether we 'absolutely knew nothing' but through the marginal distribution of *X*.

The distribution of *X* is given by:

$$P(X = p) = \int_0^1 \binom{n}{p} \theta P (1-\theta)^{n-p} \, d\theta = \frac{1}{n+1}, \quad p = 0, 1, \ldots n$$

Stigler concludes: Bayes would emphasise the specification of subjective probabilities, to be sure, but only *probabilities of observables*, such as *X*, rather than *unobservables*, such as θ. *This places Bayes in the de Finetti camp!*

Kyburg and Smokler (1964) maintain that the subjective theory was 'a philosophical curiosity' until de Finetti discovered exchangeability.[10] With its introduction, subjective probability could be linked to classical statistical inference. For example, de Finetti showed that the classical limit theorems remain true when independent sequences are replaced by exchangeable sequences. Regardless of the prior opinion, the revised probability in the light of accumulating experiences converges to the observed relative frequency.

Sequences of identical repetitions are called exchangeable in that your belief or judgement of them is invariant under permutations. From this definition de Finetti proved his famous representation theorem: exchangeable sequences of events are mixtures of Bernoulli sequences. If θ is the parameter of the Bernoulli sequences, θ is uncertain and has a probability distribution which mixes the Bernoulli sequences for different values of θ. The parameter θ is a propensity, an objective property of the sequence; it is not a probability for you, but is a frequency limit. (If θ were known, it would be the probability for any event in the sequence.) Lindley (1978) stresses that, while there is a close connection between frequency views and Bayesian (personalistic) probability, because we usually are studying exchangeable sequences, there is always a personalistic ingredient in the Bayesian view. 'It is you who judges the sequence to be exchangeable'. Then, it follows that 'the frequency limit exists for you'. Notice that independence is a strong assumption. You claim by independence that no information of one event can influence 'Your uncertainty about another. This is assuredly not true for a Bernoulli sequence with unknown chance, for we would all agree that knowledge of the results of some of the events would typically affect our opinion about other events'.

As a simple example, suppose a decision-maker flips a coin 5,000 times and that the proportion of the heads in those 5,000 trials is p'. The individual is asked to guess the probability of a head on the five-thousandth and first trial. Suppose the decision-maker agrees with two statements:

(1) In the next 1,000 trials, the decision-maker is told the total number of heads and tails, but not the specific sequence. If he concludes, that among the possible sequences of heads and tails giving rise to this number of heads and tails, are equally likely, then he agrees with the *exchangeability principle*.

(2) The decision-maker would be surprised if the proportion of heads in the 1,000 trials p_1 was not approximately equal to p'.

If the decision-maker believes these two statements, he should be willing to assign a probability to the event (a head on the next coin toss), i.e. $P(H$ on trial $1{,}001) = p'$.

Pratt *et al.* (1995) give the following justification for statements (1) and (2): If the decision-maker can detect no pattern in the sequence of 5,000 trials and believes that the future will be like the past, then a future sequence of coin tosses will also contain no detectable patterns. Pratt *et al.* point out that exchangeability has produced a dramatic change in the usefulness of the subjective approach. Exchangeability provides a nexus between subjective probability and statistical inference of objective (classical) probability. More than this, de Finetti showed that the subjective theory augmented by exchangeability comprised the foundation for most of the statistical inferences of classical probability. Bayesian statistical procedures, (augmented by exchangeability), are reducible to classical inference. The decisive difference is that the Bayes inference begins with a prior probability distribution and revises it according to Bayes's theorem as new information accumulates. De Finetti demonstrated that a sequence of exchangeable events which 'learns from experience' converges so that the probability assigned to it is the same as the event relative frequency.

A great epistemological achievement by de Finetti was his use of the representation theorem for exchangeability to resolve Hume's induction problem. Everyone practises induction. It is therefore important to have a theorem showing the legitimacy of induction. Exchangeability justifies induction. When de Finetti developed exchangeability, he realised he was solving Hume's problem. He also converted subjective probability from a clever, but seemingly useless, epistemology into a vital, creative programme, whose full effects have not yet been appreciated, especially in economics. After probability, exchangeability is the most important concept linked with chance. Alfred North Whitehead observed in 1924: 'The theory of induction is the despair of philosophy – and yet all our activities are based on it'. Its ubiquity extends to the behaviour of all living things. As Penrose (1994) noted, even the amoebae, which have no neurons, learn from experience and practise induction. *All creative activity is founded on induction*. In perceiving similarity among objects which at first sight seem diverse, exchangeability bears an intimate connection with the metaphorical and analogical.

There is an inextricable nexus joining search and exchangeability (induction). Induction is performed by the five senses in conjunction with the perceptive activity of the brain. The world confronts the mind with an enormous array of signals, most of which are useless.

Ramsey observes: 'We can regard perception, memory, and induction as the three fundamental ways of acquiring knowledge; deduction on the other hand is merely a method of rearranging our knowledge and eliminating inconsistencies or contradictions' (Ramsey 1990: 86). Sixty-one years later, Young states:

> Two things are missing from most lay and philosophical treatments of life and mind. First, they do not show appreciation of the intense and complex continuous internal activity that directs organisms to *search* for means of survival. This incessant pursuit of aims is the essence of the maintenance of life ... Secondly, this continuity of life is made possible only by calling from moment to moment the stored information derived from past history.
>
> (Young 1987: 17 italics in original)

Confining attention to the economic environment decreases the number of signals, but they remain a vibrating hurly-burly. To distil pertinent information from these signals one must search in order to discover informative signals. Without this discrimination, the mind would be overwhelmed by chaotic signals and would doubtless lapse into a deadly passivity. *Search is the essence of induction (exchangeability)*. All the senses search for welfare-enhancing information. Thus, search bestows vitality on the adaptive organisms. It is well known that the optimal policy for sequential search is characterised by a critical threshold ς such that search terminates if and only if the current observation exceeds ς. The calculation of ς employs a martingale argument.

We conclude with a simple proof of de Finetti's representation theorem by Diaconis (1985):

Let P be an exchangeability probability on coin tossing space. There is a unique probability distribution μ on [0,1] such that

$$P(X_1, \ldots, X_n) = \int p^k (1-p)^{n-k} \, d\mu(p)$$

When k successes in the first n trials are observed, the mixing measure for future predictions is proportional to

$$P^k (1-p)^{n-k} \, d\mu(p)$$

As n increases, this measure becomes peaked at the frequency k/n. Hence, predictions about the future are approximately consistent with the distributed trials with parameter k/n. We believe the future will be like the past, i.e. the future is exchangeable with the past. In short de Finetti's representation theorem offers us a pragmatic justification for induction, based on the notion of exchangeability. It legitimates our intuitive expectation that a frequency observed in the future will be close to the frequency observed in the past. In the words of Zabell:

> De Finetti's analysis ... represents a watershed in the probabilistic analysis of induction. It abolishes all reference to the infinite, all reference to the principle

> of indifference, all reference to probabilities of probabilities, all reference to causation … In order to attack it, one must attack the formidable edifice of probability itself. Modern philosophy continues to ignore it at its own peril.
> (Zabell 1989: 305)

Notes

1 Popper has developed a propensity interpretation of probability. For a summary and critique see Howson and Urbach (1989).
2 Jesperson (1922).
3 Hofstadter (1995) correctly insists that perception is accompanied by metaphor.
4 It is enlightening to compare Deacon's vision with Vico's, which is nicely described by Danesi (1993).
5 It is also true that Peirce provided the basic underpinnings of confidence intervals and hypothesis testing. See Hacking (1990) for an excellent portrait of Peirce.
6 George Polya also sees analogy as the key to induction. Like de Finetti, Polya considers induction as learning from experience. He also regards inductive reasoning as 'a particular case of plausible reasoning'. Thus he joins de Finetti's view of induction with Aristotle's definition of metaphor. It is interesting to note that the meaning of the Greek word for metaphor is exchange. Metaphor encompasses any substitution of one synonymous (interchangeable) term for another. The form of metaphor appropriate for prose is analogy.

   Aristotle sought to grasp the very roots of persuasion itself, which required him to ponder the nature of character and emotion and also the method of demonstration in the absence of deductive certainty. Thus persuasiveness becomes for the first time a fully systematic and even scientific exercise; … the study of rhetoric instead of being a philosophical outcast, transcends its humble and practical origins to become an important component in the general study of man.
7 The direct influence of William James on the Italian pragmatists and their profound effect on de Finetti should also be noted.
8 The role of operationalism is nicely described in Lad (1996).
9 See Kyburg and Smokler (1964) for thorough discussions.
10 In his splendid treatise, von Plato (1994) strongly supports this position.

   In sum, those who developed mathematical probability in the 1920s had found no place of note for subjective probability. Physical thought has rendered it almost obsolete it seemed … The scientifically oriented logical empiricists were looking for hard facts rather than individual perceptions of the likelihood of events. Subjective probability was barely alive around 1930.

   One reason for the low status of subjective probability was centred on the paradoxes flowing from LaPlace's Rule of Succession. Keynes adopted a similar rule, the Principle of Indifference and depicted several of its paradoxes. According to Keynes (1921) The Principle of Indifference asserts that if there is no *known* reason for predicating of our subject one rather than another of several alternatives, then relatively to such knowledge the assertions of each of these alternative have an equal probability.

   On the other hand, LaPlace argued that if p is the unknown probability of success in a single trial and if one value of p is no more probable than another, then the Rule of Succession represents the ignorance of p by a uniform distribution.

   De Finetti rejected not only LaPlace's Rule of Succession, but also his entire deterministic edifice. He replaced them with his exchangeable structure, where each individual has his own subjective probability.

References

Ayer, A.J. (1992) 'Hume', in K. Thomas (ed.) *The British Empiricists*, Oxford: Oxford University Press.

Bird, A. (2000) *Thomas Kuhn*, Chesham: Acumen Publishing.

Braithwaite, R.B. (1953) *Scientific Explanation*, Cambridge: Cambridge University Press.

Bridgman, P. (1936) *The Nature of Physical Theory*, Princeton, NJ: Princeton University Press.

Cassirer, E. (1944) *An Essay on Man*, New Haven, CT: Yale University Press.

Danesi, M. (1993) *Vico, Metaphor and the Origin of Language*, Bloomington, IN: Indiana University Press.

Deacon, T.W. (1977) *The Symbolic Species*, New York: Norton.

de Finetti, B. (1972) *Probability, Induction and Statistics: The Art of Guessing*, New York: Wiley.

—— (1974–5) *Theory of Probability: A Critical Introductory Treatment*, 2 vols, New York: Wiley.

Diaconis, P. (1985) 'Bayesian statistics as honest work', in L.M. LeCam and R.G. Olshen (eds) *Proceedings of Berkeley Conference in Honour of Jerzy Neyman and Jack Kiefer*, Vol. 1, Belmont, CA: Thomson Wardswork Press.

Draper, D., Hodges, J.S., Mallows, C.L. and Pregibon, D. (1995) 'Exchangeability and data analysis', *Journal of the Royal Statistical Society*, Series A, 156: 9–37.

Goodman, N. (1972) *Problems and Projects*, Indianopolis, IN: Bobbs-Merrill.

Griswold, C.L. Jr (1999) *Adam Smith and the Virtues of the Enlightenment*, Cambridge: Cambridge University Press.

Hacking, I. (1990) *The Taming of Chance*, Cambridge: Cambridge University Press.

Hauser, M.D. (1996) *The Evolution of Communication*, Cambridge, MA: MIT Press.

Hesse, M. (1966) *Models and Analogies in Science*, Notre Dame, IN: University of Notre Dame Press.

Hofstadter, D. (1995) *Fluid Concepts and Creative Analogies*, New York: Basic Books.

Howson, C. and Urbach, P. (1989) *Scientific Reasoning: The Bayesian Approach*, La Salle, IL: Open Court.

Jesperson, O. (1922) *Language: Its Nature, Development and Origin*, New York: Holt.

Keynes, J.M. (1921) *A Treatise on Probability*, London: Macmillan.

Kuhn, T.S. (1970) 'Logic of discovery or psychology of research?', in I.M. Lakatos and A. Musgrave (eds) *Criticism and the Growth of Knowledge*, Cambridge: Cambridge University Press.

—— (1977) *The Essential Tension*, Chicago, IL: University of Chicago Press.

Kyburg, H.E. and Smokler, H.E. (eds) (1984) *Studies in Subjective Probabilities*, Malabor, FL: Kreiger Publishing.

Lad, F. (1966) *Operational Subjective Statistical Methods*, New York: Wiley.

Lindley, D.V. (1978) 'The Bayesian approach', *Scandinavian Journal of Statistics*, 5: 1–26.

Mallows, C. (1998) 'The zeroth problem', *The American Statistician*, 52: 1–9.

Medin, D.L., Goldstone, R.L. and Gentrer, D. (1993) 'Respect for similarity', *Psychological Review*, 100: 254–78.

Penrose, R. (1994) Shadows *of the Mind: A Search for the Missing Science of Consciousness*, Oxford: Oxford University Press.

Popper, K.R. (1963) Conjectures *and Refutations*, New York: Basic Books.

—— (1972) Objective *Knowledge*, Oxford: Oxford University Press.

Pratt, J.W., Raiffa, H. and Schlaifer, R. (1995) *Introduction to Statistical Decision Theory*, Cambridge, MA: MIT Press.

Quine, W.V.O. (1969) Ontological *Relativity and Other Essays*, New York: Columbia University Press.

Ramsey, F.P. (1990) 'Truth and probability', in D.H. Mellor (ed.) *Ramsey, F.P., Philosophical Papers*, Cambridge: Cambridge University Press.

Smith, A.F.M. (1984) 'Bayesian statistics: present position and potential developments: some personal views', *Journal of the Royal Statistical Society*, Series A, 147: 245–59.

Stigler, S.M. (1982) 'Thomas Bayes's Bayesian inference', *Journal of the Royal Statistical Society*, Series A, 145: 250–8.

—— (1986) The *History of Statistics*, Cambridge, MA: Belknap Press.

Tversky, A. (1977) 'Features of similarity', *Psychological Review*, 84: 327–52.

von Plato, J. (1994) *Creating Modern Probability*, Cambridge: Cambridge University Press.

Young, J.Z. (1987) *Philosophy and the Brain*, Oxford: Oxford University Press.

Zabell, S.L. (1989) 'The rule of succession', *Erkenntnis*, 31: 283–311.

7 Demystifying induction and falsification

Trans-Popperian suggestions

K. Vela Velupillai

Preamble

> By these results [i.e. Hume's answers to what Popper called Hume's 'logical' and 'psychological' problems] Hume himself – one of the most rational minds ever – was turned into a sceptic and, at the same time, into a believer: a believer in an irrationalist epistemology.
>
> (Popper 1972b: 4)

However, we persist in continuing to read this *believer in an irrationalist epistemology*, puzzle over his paradoxical thoughts, ruminate over their unfathomable implications and debate, almost endlessly, about *induction as Hume's Problem*, over two centuries after that great man's speculative thoughts were penned.[1] Should we be doing this, particularly mulling over *Hume's Problem*, almost three quarters of a century after one of the great philosophers of the twentieth-century claimed he had *solved* it? The opening lines of *Objective Knowledge*, assert, with characteristic boldness and without any sense of what may be suspected as false modesty:

> I think I have solved a major philosophical problem: the problem of induction. (I must have reached the solution in 1927 or thereabouts.)
>
> (Popper 1972b: 1)

Almost half a century after he claimed to have 'solved' the problem of induction there was, in the opening pages of the above book, a rueful reflection of the seeming failure of this 'solution' to have penetrated the philosophical discourse of the times:

> However, few philosophers would support the theses that I have solved the problem of induction. Few philosophers have taken the trouble to study – or even criticize – my views on this problem, or have taken notice of the fact that I have done some work on it.
>
> (Popper 1972b: 1)

It would seem possible that 'few philosophers would support the thesis that [Popper had] solved the problem of induction' because they did not think he had solved it. After all some philosophers who did not agree that he had solved the problem of induction were not lesser giants of twentieth-century philosophy, particularly of the philosophy of science – Carnap, Quine, Putnam, Harré and, of course, Kuhn, Feyerabend, Laudan and a legion of other giants of equal stature.

In my admittedly erratic reading of Popper's massive and impressive writings I have never managed to unearth any admission that some, at least, of the many distinguished philosophers who did not agree that he had 'solved' the problem of induction may have been right. Formulating a famous problem, naming it famously and offering a supposedly famous solution to it are all, by any conceivable standard, arduous endeavours. Popper's irritation that the philosophers of his time did not pay attention to his solution or, worse, did not agree that he had solved it, is understandable – if he was an ordinary mortal. He, however, is supposed to be one of the giants of twentieth-century western philosophy who, again famously,[2] propagated the *credo* '*that we can learn from our mistakes*' (Popper 1963: vii),[3] and argued passionately for *open societies* (Popper 1945).

I must admit that I detect something more than an irritation – indeed, an *intolerance* with his contemporaries, particularly of course with Carnap,[4] that his formulation and solution of the problem of induction was not recognised universally and unconditionally. This is brought out most vividly in Quine's majestic description of Popper's contrived 'clash of titans' to bury Carnap's alternative vision of the problem of induction and its solution:

> Popper was counting on a confrontation of Titans. Carnap's latest work was his ponderous one on induction. The first volume had appeared and the second was in progress. Popper decried induction, and he meant to settle the matter. I sensed that he was deploying his henchman, Imre Lakatos and John Watkins, with military precision as the three of them undertook preliminary skirmishes. But the last scheduled session drew to an end without the anticipated culmination. Popper accordingly declared an additional session, next morning, for all who could see their way to staying. It was strictly Popper vs. Carnap, with an audience of twenty-odd in a seminar room. I was carried back to Carnap's confrontation of Lovejoy in Baltimore thirty years before. Again he met vehemence with the mild but ready answer, the same old cool, unruffled reason. It is my splendid last memory of Carnap.
>
> (Quine 1985: 373)[5]

A similar story of almost passionate intolerance of disagreements with his visions, views and theories can be told for those other great concepts with which we even, indeed especially, as *economists*, associate Popper's name, the Popperian credo and a Popperian philosophy: *falsifiability*, the rational underpinnings of *the growth of scientific knowledge*, the impossibility of discovering a *method* (an *algorithm*) for the *logic of scientific discovery*, just to name a few.

An example of this intolerance towards the possibility of falsifying his narrow and logic-based theory and thesis on falsifiability, which I believe illustrates his inability to apply his own precepts consistently, viewed by him to be a cardinal sin, is the way he warned readers not to accept a particular challenge posed by Alan Turing:[6]

> Turing [1950] said something like this: specify the way in which you believe that a man is superior to a computer and I shall build a computer which refutes your belief. Turing's challenge should not be taken up; for any sufficiently precise specification could be used in principle to programme a computer.
>
> (Popper and Eccles 1983: 208)

Why should we not take up 'Turing's challenge'? Should we be afraid that the challenge might 'refute our beliefs'? Surely, the *raison d'être'* of a falsifiable *credo*, buttressed by a philosophy wedded to an untrammelled[7] 'openness', is to be challenged[8] and dethroned. Is this an intolerance or, perhaps, a subjective attachment to personal theories compounded by a fear of some sort? After all, Carnap was 'attacked' almost personally, as if his particular view of inductive probability could not be separated from Carnap's personality.

Above all, however, where I, coming from a Buddhist culture, a Hindu home and a Western education, buttressed also by an undergraduate training in Japan, find a narrowness of vision and a lack of a generosity of spirit, is the lack of attention given to alternative *epistemologies*, even if not *philosophies*.[9] In Buddhist epistemology, for example, there are clear precepts for inductive inference that eschew any reliance on an underlying probabilistic framework. Moreover, as McGinn (2002) has recently pointed out, in an extremely interesting essay, there is the necessity, in any Popperian falsification exercise, to rely on an inductive inference:

> But there is a worse problem for Popper's philosophy: he is committed to inductive verification himself … Consider, too, that falsifying experiments have to be repeatable so that other researches can duplicate the alleged finding. We have to be able to *infer* that if a *falsifying* result has been found in a given experiment it will be found in future experiments … [So] *falsification needs to be inductively justified* if it is to serve as a means of testing theories.
>
> It is generally so justified, of course, but this is not something that Popper can consistently incorporate into his conception of science.
>
> (McGinn 2002: 48 our italics)

In Buddhist epistemology, however, the coupling of any falsification exercise with inductive inference, is tackled in an extremely enlightened manner – enlightened in the sense of trying to inculcate a sense of humility for the human condition in the face of nature's possible intransigence, although there is not that sharp dichotomy between the human being and nature. Popper's seemingly encyclopaedic knowledge exhibits no awareness of alternative epistemologies. His underpinnings are best described in Toulmin's brilliant characterisation.

> All the way across the field, from logic and mathematics to the human sciences and the fine arts, the essential tasks of intellectual and artistic activity were redefined in static, structural, a-historical, non-representational, and wherever possible *mathematical* terms.
>
> Nowhere were the effects of this reformulation more far-reaching than in the philosophy of science… . By the early 1920s it was an unquestioned presupposition for philosophers of science that the *intellectual content* of any truly scientific theory formed a timeless "propositional system," like that of which Russell and Whitehead had given a prototype in *Principia Mathematica*.
>
> (Toulmin 1971: 56 first set of italics added)

In this chapter I try to tackle and suggest some trans-Popperian solutions and approaches to the vexed problems of induction, inductive inference and falsifiability. The points of view I take is that it is this predominance of redefining all human activity in 'mathematical terms' and forming a 'timeless propositional system' that has bedevilled Popperian epistemology. However, it is not that I disagree with this double-reliance; but it is that there are many ways of relying on 'mathematical terms' and even more ways of underpinning scientific theories on 'propositional terms' that are neither 'a-historical' nor 'timeless'.

Finally, to go back to my initial observation about Hume and our centuries old obsession with his writings, the point I wish to make is the following: would we, at the end of this century, still value the writings of Popper as those of one of the giants of twentieth-century philosophy and epistemology, or would he have been buried with other transient giants, who dominated transitorily? Would his status become that of a Herbert Spencer, a Larmarck, even a Lysenko or a Cyril Burt or would it be in that pantheon of the other two great contemporary Austrians with whom he shared the century and some of its fame:[10] Wittgenstein and Freud? Naturally, I do not know and I am not sure I want to know, for if he is fated to share the company and fate of the former, I may not have the courage to read his provocative and inspiring writings.

But, contrary to the other participants at this centennial to honour the great man, I come not to praise him. I am aware, of course, that Popper, had he been alive, would have counter-punched with the ferocity that we have come to associate with him.

Introduction

> [T]the method of falsification presupposes no inductive inference, but only the tautological transformation of deductive logic *whose validity is not in dispute*.
>
> (Popper 1972a: 42 italics added)

Paradoxically, neither of these assertions are, of course, considered true, as the twenty-first century dawns – although the cognoscenti were aware of their dubious validity long before even the twilight of the previous century set in.

Economic methodology, explicitly and implicitly, has been deeply influenced by three of Popper's seminal ideas: falsifiability, the logic of scientific discovery and the twin issues of induction and inductive inference.[11] Of course, all three of the seminal ideas are interlinked and the unified recursion theoretic approach I am able to use, to tackle them analytically, substantiates that particular point. Underpinning them, in almost all their ramifications, is the ubiquitous spectre of *rationality* and *its* concomitants: rational behaviour, the rational scientist, the rational scientific enterprise and the rationality of the autonomous processes of nature. All these seem to have fallen on receptive ears, at various levels and practice, in the economic community.

Paradoxically, however, these three seminal Popperian conceptual contributions, indeed pioneering research programmes, come in the form of negative precepts. Foremost of these negative precepts is, of course, that there is *no* such thing as a *logic* of scientific discovery; that theories can only be refuted and held, at most, provisionally, waiting for them to be refuted; and, then, there was that insistence about the impossibility of inductive probability.

Behind these vehement negative precepts there was, implicitly, the insistence that the epistemologist was confronted by an environment that was lawful, about which theories could be conjectured, albeit provisionally. As pointed out by Harré in his surprisingly pungent 'Obituary' of Popper:

> ... Popper's methodology of conjecture and refutation, based upon the idea of the rationality of rejecting hypotheses which have been shown at a particular time and place to be false, also depends upon an assumption of a form of the uniformity of nature. In his case, it is the negative assumption that the universe will not change in such a way as to make what was disconfirmed today true tomorrow. Popper's methodology of conjecture and refutation makes no headway in the testing of that proposition. His claim to have solved the problem of induction must now be rejected.
>
> (Harré 1994: 32)

It was also the point made by Glymour (1996) in a more specific sense: that Popper had agreed with Plato that knowledge requires a kind of inalterability, but unlike Plato he did not think that the process of science obtains knowledge. I shall not address specific issues of economic methodology from any particular Popperian point of view in this chapter. Instead, I aim, hopefully, to provide less negative visions of two of these great Popperian themes and help disseminate a more positive attitude towards the rich possibilities of pursuing an inductive methodology in the search for laws of scientific discovery, buttressed by a dynamic, algorithmic, reinterpretation of the meaning of falsifiability. Classical recursion theory and applied recursion theory, in the form of algorithmic complexity theory, will be my conceptual and methodological tools in this adventure. Hence, I shall consider the message in this chapter fully within the programme of research I initiated, about twenty years ago, and coined the phrase 'computable economics' to describe it. If, therefore, there is any constructive contribution emanating from it, it will be towards the methodology of that research programme. In that specific sense, then, it is squarely within the scope and title of this volume.

In his 1972 *Addendum* to the 1972 edition of *The Logic of Scientific Discovery,* Popper was quite explicit about the *logical* basis of falsifiability:[12]

> … [T]he content or the testability (or the simplicity …) of a theory may have *degrees*, which may thus be said to relativize the idea of falsifiability (whose logical basis remains the *modus tollens*).
>
> (Popper 1972a: 135 italics in original)

Let me refresh possible rusty memories of unlikely readers about *Modus (Tollendo) Tollens*:

In *Modus (Tollendo) Tollens*, by denying – i.e. *tollendo* – the consequent of an implication we deny – i.e. *tollens* – the antecedent. More formally:

$$\sim Q \,\&\, (P \Rightarrow Q) \Rightarrow \sim P$$

It is immediate that two dubious mathematical logical principles are implicitly invoked in any falsifiability exercise based on *Modus (Tollendo) Tollens: principium tertium non datur* or the *law of the excluded middle* and *proof of contradiction*. This means an adherence to non-constructive methods in all cases involving infinite alternatives. How experiments can be arranged and methods devised to test for falsifiability, even abstracting away from inductive inferential problems, in a non-constructive environment, escapes me. Indeed, how any method to test for falsifiability can be anything other than constructive, *in some sense*, is beyond my understanding.

It is this kind of reliance on traditional logic and a limited knowledge of the vast developments in mathematical logic in the twentieth-century that I find mysterious in a philosopher who seemed to be encyclopaedic in his awareness of so much else. I find no evidence, in my perusal and attempted reading of as much as possible of Popper's voluminous writings, of any awareness, either, of the fact that mathematical logic had itself branched off, in the twentieth-century, into four or five sub-disciplines and, in any case, into: set theory, proof theory, recursion theory and model theory. This is the kind of reason why Glymour, for example, was scathing in his criticism of a class of philosophers in general, but of Popper, in particular:

> With only a little logical knowledge, philosophers in this period understood the verifiable and the refutable to have special logical forms, namely as existential and universal sentences respectively. There was, implicitly a positivist hierarchy … Positivists such as Schlick confined science to and meaning to singular data and verifiable sentences; 'anti-positivists', notably

> Popper, confined science to the singular data and falsifiable sentences. In both cases, what could be known or discovered consisted of the singular data and verifiable sentences, although there is a hint of something else in Popper's view.
>
> (Glymour 1996: 268)

On the other hand, if one feels it is necessary to retain fidelity to Popper's reliance on *Modus (Tollendo) Tollens* as an underpinning for falsifiability exercises,[13] then it seems to me that the best way to do so would be via formalisations using recursion theory. Classical logical principles retain their validity but methods are given algorithmic content which makes them implementable devices in experimental design. This is, therefore, the mathematical framework I shall invoke in this chapter, in spite of the fact that I believe that a thorough constructive approach is epistemologically superior for numerical reasons.

The rest of the chapter is structured as follows. In the next section I try to extract recursion theoretic precepts from Popper's own writings for their eventual formalisations. I try to exploit the subtle differences between recursive and recursively enumerable sets to give a broader, more dynamic, definition of falsifiability exercises. Had space permitted, I would have expanded this subtle distinction to include recursive separability, but that will have to be attempted in a different exercise.

I will try to suggest that what I have, in other contexts and writings called the 'modern theory of induction' is a perfectly adequate framework to justify and solve *Hume's problem*. This framework is based on (classical) recursion theory and, hence, is an appropriate mathematical structure to encapsulate, formally, the heuristic discussions in this chapter. Solving the induction problem recursion theoretically also, almost as a by-product, solves the problems that have bedevilled Popper's formalisation of falsifiability. But only a sketch is given, although there is enough for any serious reader to complete the mathematical arguments.

In the concluding section, I speculate, on the basis of the results and discussions in the chapter, of alternative visions and vistas and on trying to retain a sense of the humble and the steadfast, in the wake of increasing specialisations, intolerances and dogmas in all fields of human endeavour.

Preparing the backdrop for trans-Popperian suggestions

> Popper's mistake here is no small isolated failing. What Popper consistently fails to see if the *practice is primary*: ideas are not just an end in themselves (although they are *partly* an end in themselves), nor is the selection of ideas to 'criticize' just an end in itself …
>
> The method of testing ideas in practice and relying on the ones that prove successful (*for that is what 'induction' is*) is not unjustified. That is an *empirical* statement. The method does not have a 'justification' – if by a justification is meant a proof from eternal and formal principles that justifies

> reliance on the method. But then nothing does – not even, in my opinion, pure mathematics and formal logic.
>
> (Putnam 1974: 268–9 italics in original)

Popper does not seem to have paid much attention to the great achievements in recursion theory, proof theory or model theory to substantiate his case for empirical methodology or for falsification. As to why he did not seek recourse to recursion theory, in the case of inductive inference or the logic of scientific discovery, could it, perhaps, be because such a framework may have cast doubts on his negative critique against these thorny concepts? One can only speculate and I do speculate simply because these three branches of modern mathematical logic provide literally the proverbial 'tailor-made' formalisms for empirically implementable mathematical structures for falsifiability, the logic of scientific discovery and for induction in all its manifestations. I shall discuss recursion theoretic formalisms for falsifiability and the logic of scientific discovery in this section.

There are two characteristically prescient Popperian observations very early on in *Ldf*:

> [I] am going to propose … that the *empirical method* shall be characterized as a method that excludes precisely those ways of evading falsification which … are logically possible. According to my proposal, what characterizes the empirical method is its manner of exposing to falsification, in every conceivable way, the system to be tested. Its aim is not to save the lives of untenable systems but, on the contrary, to select the one which is by comparison the fittest, by exposing them all to the fiercest struggle for survival.
>
> … The root of [the problem of the validity of natural laws] is the apparent contradiction between what may be called 'the fundamental thesis of empiricism' – the thesis that experience alone can decide upon the truth or falsity of scientific statements – and Hume's realization of the inadmissibility of inductive arguments. This contradiction arises only if it is assumed that all empirical scientific statements must be '*conclusively decidable*', i.e. that verification and their falsification must both in principle be possible. If we renounce this requirement and admit as empirical also statements which are *decidable in one sense only* – unilaterally decidable and, more especially, falsifiable – and which may be tested by systematic attempts to falsify them, the contradiction disappears: the method of falsification presupposes no inductive inference, but only the tautological transformations of deductive logic whose validity is not in dispute.[14]
>
> (Popper 1972a: 42)

First, in what other way, if not by means of an *algorithm*, can we understand the processes implied by implementing an *empirical method?*[15]

Second, Popper endeavours to drive a wedge between verifiability and falsifiability in terms of decidability – but, we know, based on *Modus (Tollendo) Tollens*. There is, however, a much simpler way to drive this wedge *and* preserve the algorithmic character of implementable *empirical methods*. Moreover, it will not be necessary to make the incorrect claim that 'the method of falsification presupposes no inductive inference'.[16]

Third, there is the need to be precise about what is meant by a *natural law* and a *scientific statement*, before even discussing the meaning of their *truth* or *falsity*.

I shall take it that Popper means by a *natural law* something as paradigmatic as, for example, *Newton's Laws of Motion* or, at a slightly more sophisticated level, say, the *General Theory of Relativity*. As an economist I have never felt that we have the equivalent of a *natural law*, in the above senses, in economic theory. Perhaps, at a much lower level of sophistication, we may, as economists, invoke one of the popular theories of growth, say the *Solow Growth Model*.

Such *natural laws*, for example Newton's Laws of Motion or at a much more down-to earth level, Solow's Growth Model, are framed, when mathematised, as formal *dynamical systems*. Of such systems we ask, or test, whether, when they are appropriately initialised, they enter the definable *basin of attraction* of, say, a limit point, a limit cycle, a strange attractor or, perhaps, get trapped in the boundaries that separate a limit cycle and a strange attractor. In the case of the Solow Growth Model, theory predicts that the dynamical system, for all economically meaningful initial conditions enters the basin of attraction of a limit point. The theory and its law can, in principle be 'verified'.

However, it is for very few dynamical systems that we can answer the above type of question unambiguously, i.e. 'verifiably'. This is the key point made by Popper in his almost lifelong quest for a kind of scepticism about theories and the natural laws inherent in them. It is just that such a scepticism comes naturally to those accustomed to formalising in terms of proof theory, model theory and recursion theory – i.e. for those working in the domain of the constructive, non-standard or computable numbers.

Moreover, a *natural law* in any of the above senses is, at least from Popper's point of view, which I think is the commonsense vision, is a *scientific statement*, as indeed referred to as such by Popper in the above characterisation. What, next, does it mean to formalise the notion of a *scientific statement?* Clearly, in the form of something like a *well formed formula* in some formal, mathematical, logic. Obviously, what is, then, meant by 'deciding upon the truth or falsity of scientific statement', must also be a commonsense interpretation; i.e. the 'truth' or 'falsity' of the implications of the scientific statement which encapsulates the natural law. I shall assume, therefore, that the set of meaningful scientific statements form an enumerable infinity.

Fourth, Popper claims that the distinction between verifiability and falsifiability depends on allowing for a certain kind of one-way decidability. More precisely, verifiability is characterised by a 'strong' sense of decidability and falsifiability by a somewhat 'weaker' concept of decidability. In Popper's case, of course, the underpinning to formalise the distinction between a 'strong' and a 'weak' sense is *Modus (Tollendo) Tollens*. I seek a more dynamic version of the possibility of such a distinction, simply because many, if not most, meaningful *natural laws* are framed dynamically or as dynamical systems. By 'dynamically', I mean, the implication of the theory, when formulated as a *natural law*, and subject to experimental procedures, generates a sequence of outcomes, usually numerical,[17] which has to be sequentially monitored and tested.

Fifth, there is a need to be absolutely precise about what Popper means, formally, by 'exposing to falsification, *in every conceivable way*, the system to be tested'. How many conceivable ways would there be, given an 'experimental method', to 'expose to falsification the system to be tested'? Suppose, as in conventional economic theory, the domain of definitions is the real number system. Then, in principle, an uncountable infinity of 'conceivable ways' would have to be devised for 'the system to be tested'. This is meaningless in any empirical system.

The best that can be attempted, in principle, is to enumerate a countable infinity of *empirical methods* and for the case, for example, of *natural laws* formalised as dynamical systems, to quantify the notion of *every conceivable way* by varying the initial conditions in a precisely formalised countably infinite, enumerable, mode – i.e. *algorithmically* – but not necessarily subject to the *Church-Turing Thesis*. In other words, *algorithmically* could also be encapsulated within the broader canvas of *constructive mathematics* (or also more narrowly than even recursion theory).[18]

Finally, there is the need to be precise (and sensible) about what Popper could have meant by 'select the one which is by comparison the fittest, by exposing them all to the fiercest struggle for survival'. It is here, contrary to enlightened Popperian critics, that I find that *inductive inference* enters the Popperian world with almost a vengeance. How does one formalise the selection criterion that is suggested by Popper? What could be meant by 'fittest'? Surely not some facile neo-Darwinian formalism via, say, genetic algorithms in the conventional sense.

This is where Glymour and Harré, for example, presumably locate Popper's adherence to the Platonic assumption of the 'inalterability of nature'. For, if not, we cannot, of course, 'expose them *all*' to any kind of test, let alone the more specific test of 'the fiercest struggle for survival'. By the time we come, say, to *scientific statement*, say, #10948732765923, and the *natural law* implied by it, and say *empirical method* #371952867 for testing it, there is no guarantee that our theoretical world picture would not have changed – from the Ptolemic world vision to the Copernican vision. This would mean some of the *scientific statements* had become meaningless and others, not in the original enumerated list, become feasible candidates for testing.

I shall circumvent these issues by suggesting that we interpret Popper's criterion of the 'fittest' by the analogous criterion, in some precise sense formalisable notion, of 'most likely' or 'most plausible' by invoking yet another historical nemesis of Popper: *Ockham*.

In concluding this section, it may be useful to record, at least for the sake of completion, one of Popper's later, more formal, and rather harshly critical statements on *The Impossibility of Inductive Probability*. His joint paper with Miller, begins and ends in almost apocalyptic tones:

> Proofs of the impossibility of induction have been falling 'deadborn from the Press' ever since the first of them (in David Hume's *Treatise of Human Nature* appeared in 1739. One of us (K.P.) has been producing them for more than 50 years.
>
> ... This result is completely devastating to the inductive interpretation of the calculus of probability. All probabilistic support is purely deductive: that part of a hypothesis that is not deductively entailed by the evidence is always strongly countersupported by the evidence – the more strongly the more the evidence asserts. This is completely general; it holds for every hypothesis *h;* and it holds for every evidence *e*, whether it supports *h*, is independent of *h*, or countersupports *h*.
>
> There is such a thing as probabilistic support; there might even be such a thing as inductive support (though we hardly think so). But the calculus of probability reveals that probabilistic support cannot be inductive support.
>
> (Popper and Miller 1984: 687–8)

Mercifully for Popperian theories of falsifiability (and for theories of the growth of scientific discovery), this particular 'chronicle of a death foretold' (*pace* Gabriel García Márquez) is as chimerical as many before it.[19] The recurring puzzle is the following: why was it that Popper seemed to have been unaware of developments in applied recursion theory – i.e. algorithmic complexity theory – that gave a new lease of life to induction and inductive inference by returning to one of Popper's earliest preoccupations: that with the attempts he made to formalise the Richard von Mises' notion of the *kollektiv*, the *frequency theory of probability* and a formalisation of the notion of *randomness* without basing it on probability.

Perhaps his *psychological* commitment to an anti-inductivist stance overcame his scientific predispositions? Even the Gods are fallible, at least in the Hindu mythologies in which I was brought up in!

Recursion theoretic formalisations of trans-Popperian suggestions

> Popper and the positivists agreed that there could not, in any case, be an *algorithm* for carrying out scientific inquiry. Why not? ... For Popper – who quite confused a psychological question with a mathematical issue – it sufficed to quote Einstein to disprove the possibility of a discovery algorithm; for Carnap it sufficed to quote Popper quoting Einstein.
>
> (Glymour 1996: 268–9)

I shall begin this section with a formal proposition which provides the starting point for *selecting*, for any eventual falsifiability exercise, of a *natural law* which may emerge from some *scientific statement*:

Proposition 1 *An event with the highest probability of occurring is also that which has the simplest description.*
The kind of analysis that leads to a formal demonstration of this proposition is as follows. Consider a standard version of the Bayes rule subject to a denumerable infinity of hypotheses, H_i, about the occurrences of events, E, with Probability, P:

$$P(H_i|E) = P(EH_i)P(H_i)/\Sigma_i P(E|H_i)P(H_i) \tag{1}$$

In the above relation, apart from absolutely standard, textbook interpretations of all the variables and notations, the only explicit novelty is the assumption of a denumerable infinity of hypotheses. Thus, in a standard inverse probability or Bayesian exercise, E, the class of 'observed' events and $P(H_i)$ are given. What I would call the standard *induction problem* is to find the 'most probable' hypotheses, H_i, that would 'most probably' lead to the observed event of relevance. There is no way Popper, if he is to formulate his falsifiability exercise, along the lines he suggested in *Ldf*, can avoid at least this aspect of the *induction problem*.

To get the Popperian perspective I need, let me first translate (1) into an equivalent 'optimisation' problem (Popper's 'fittest'!) by simply rewriting it as:

$$-\log P[P(H_i)E] = -\log P(E|H_i) - \log P(H_i) + \log P(E \tag{2}$$

In (2), the last term on the r.h.s. is a short-hand expression for the denominator in (1) which, in turn, is the normalising factor in any Bayesian exercise. Now, finding the 'most probable hypothesis' becomes equivalent to determining that H_i with respect to (w.r.t) which (2) is *minimised*. But, in (2), *log P(E)* is invariant w.r.t. H_i and, hence the problem is to minimise (w.r.t H_i):

$$-\log P(E|H_i) - \log P(H_i) \tag{3}$$

However, it is clear that a problem of indeterminacy or circularity would remain in any such formalisation so long as we do not have a principle of the basis of which P – the so-called *prior* – cannot be assigned *universally*; i.e. independent of any problem cast in the inverse probability mode.

Now let me backtrack and view the problem from a point of view that would lead to the recasting of the induction problem as one in which *Ockham's Razor* becomes a kind of 'dual' to the Bayes rule. The 'inductive enterprise', even in any relevant Popperian sense, is supposed to interpret a class of observations, events, data, etc., in terms of a denumerable infinity of hypotheses in such a way that a general *scientific statement* is formalised as a *natural law* from which, by *deductive* processes, the outcomes with which one began are generated. This is why it is insufficient, inadequate and even disingenuous for Popper to claim that 'the method of falsification presupposes no inductive inference'.

As far as the requirements of the logic of the inductive method is concerned, I shall assume that we need only formalise, at most, a denumerable infinity of outcomes in an observation space. This particular assumption may well be the only one that goes against a Popperian vision of the empirical world.[20] As for the number of hypotheses, there is no incongruence with Popper's visions and assumptions in assuming a denumerable infinity as their upper limit (as argued for in the previous section).

Thus the space of computable numbers is sufficient for this formalisation exercise. Suppose, now, that every element in the outcome space and every potential hypothesis – both being denumerably infinite – is associated with a positive integer, perhaps ordered lexicographically. More precisely and technically speaking, every outcome and hypothesis is, normally, framed as a logical proposition (the former especially when formalised for falsifiability purposes), particularly by Popper with his absolute and almost fanatical faith in classical logic.

Every such proposition can be assigned one of the computable numbers – those that form the domain of recursion theory. Such numbers can be processed by an 'ideal computer', the *Turing Machine*. The 'ideal computer', however, accepts input in 'machine language', i.e. in binary code. Construct, therefore, the list of binary codes for the denumerable elements of the elements of the outcome space and the hypotheses. In other words, every hypothesis (i.e. *scientific statement* – which, in principle, underlies a potential general law that is the aim of an eventual falsification exercise – has a computable number associated with it and the number is represented in *bits*. It has, therefore, an unambiguous *quantitative measure* associated with it. A similar association can be constructed for the elements of the outcome space. Then, the basic result in what I have in other contexts called the *modern theory of induction* is derived by operating the following rule.

Rule of induction

The 'best theory' is that which *minimises* the sum of:

1. the length, in *bits*, of the number theoretic representation of the denumerable infinity of hypotheses;
2. the length, in *bits* of the elements of the space of outcomes, which are also, by assumption, denumerably infinite.[21]

The conceptual justification for this prescription is something like the following. If the elements of the observation space (E in Bayes's rule) have any *patterns* or *regularities*, then they can be encapsulated as *scientific statements* implying *natural laws*, on the basis of some *hypothesis*. The *best law* – i.e. Popper's 'fittest system' – is that which can extract and summarise the *maximum* amount of regularities or patterns in E and represent them *most concisely*. The idea of the *'maximum amount of regularities'* and their representation *'most concisely* captures the workings of *Ockham's Razor* in any inductive exercise. If two hypotheses can encapsulate the patterns or regularities in the data equally well, in some sense, then the above prescription is 'choose the more concise one'.

The final link in this inductive saga is a formula for the *universal prior* in Bayes's rule in terms of recursion theoretic 'regularities':

Proposition 2 *There exists a probability measure m(.) that is universal in the sense of being invariant except for an inessential additive constant such that:*

$$\log_2 m(.) \approx K(.) \ldots (4-A) \tag{4-A}$$

In (4–*A*), *K*(.) is the *Kolmogorov–Chaitin algorithmic complexity* of the *best theory* – once again, Popper's *fittest system* – generated in the operation of the 'rule of induction'. All of the operations and formalisms that generate *K*(.) are known; i.e. there are no probabilistic elements in any step that leads to a value for *K*(.). The measure *m*(.) can be substituted for the *P*(.) in Bayes's rule, for any inverse probability problem.[22]

The above is a trans-Popperian suggestion on how not to avoid the inductive needs of a falsification exercise. What of the falsification exercise itself? The trans-Popperian suggestion for this formalism proceeds as follows. First, three definitions.

Definition 2 *Recursive set*

$S \subseteq N$ *is* recursive iff $\exists$ *a Turing Machine for* deciding *whether any given member of N belongs to S.*

Definition 3 *Decidable set*

A set S is decidable *if, for any given property P(s),* $\forall s \in S$, $\exists$ *a Turing machine such that it halts iff P(s) is valid.*

Definition 4 *Recursively enumerable sets*

$S \subseteq N$ *is* recursively enumerable (*R.E*) iff *it is either empty or the range of a Turing Machine (i.e. the range of a partial recursive function).*

Thus, for any decidable set, we know there will be *effective* experimental methods – i.e. algorithms – to characterise any member of the set. It is clear from the above definitions that a *recursive set is decidable*. This is the universe of the verifiable.

Falsifiability and verifiability are methods, i.e. procedures to decide the truth value of propositions. Popper claims, in view of his allegiance to classical logic and *Modus (Tollendo) Tollens*, that the only viable procedure in a scientific enterprise is one which is capable of falsifying a law. This translates into the following: a set has to exhibit *undecidabilities*. This means it is not sufficient to work with an outcome space that is confined to recursive sets. A subtle modification of the definition of a recursive set to allow for an open-endedness, suggested as a requirement by Popper, will achieve it.

The intuitive idea is the following. Suppose the inferred *scientific statement* and its implied *natural law* are formalised as the hypothesis that is to be experimentally tested. The idea is that some implication of the hypothesis is to be verified or falsified. If the set of outcomes of the implication forms a recursive set, then we know that it is decidable and, hence, verifiable. Suppose, however, the set of outcomes of the implications form a *recursively enumerable set*. Then, whether or not any particular $P(s)$ is valid is undecidable in the following precise sense. Given an arbitrary predicted outcome of the experimental procedure of the law, say $n \in N$, we test whether it is the range of a Turing Machine. If it is, it can, eventually, be decided. If it is not, we will never know. The next output of the experimental setup, after say output #32786591 may well be the confirming instance. But there will be an open-endedness which means such laws can, at best, be accepted provisionally if they meet other criteria or adequacy.

There is a precise sense in which the above scheme generalises and meets objections to Popper's more classical definition of falsifiability. Even although recursion theory is based on classical logic, the exclusive reliance on *Modus (Tollendo) Tollens* and singular data and falsifiable sentences are removed to be special cases. To put it in a different way, as Glymour did, the verifiable relied on the existential form for a testable sentence (i.e. $\exists x$, s.t. $S(x)$; and the falsifiable relied on the universal quantifier (i.e. $\forall x$, s.t. $S(x)$).

In terms of Gödel's results, my suggestions can be stated in yet another, equivalent, form. The Gödel scheme shows how to transform any given proposition into one about polynomials. Then, there exist arithmetical equations, linking two polynomials representing propositions, *preceded by some finite sequence of existential and universal quantifiers* that are effectively undecidable. This is the sense in which there is no longer any reliance on singular data or singular sentences.

Transcending dogmas and intolerances

> [I]in retrospect, a concern with systematizing inductive logic has been the oldest concern of empiricist philosophers from Bacon on. No one can yet predict the outcome of this speculative scientific venture. But it is amply clear, whether this particular venture succeeds or fails, that the *toleration* of philosophical and scientific speculation brings rich rewards and its suppression leads to sterility.
>
> (Putnam 1963: 304, our italics)

Von Mises and his valiant attempts to define *place selection* rules received considerable attention in *LdF* (Popper 1972a, Ch. VIII, §50, ff.). It is, therefore, somewhat surprising that the evolution and remarkable development of that von Mises tradition at the hands of Kolmogorov and a legion of recursion theorists and philosophers[23] seemed to have by-passed the eagle eyed Popper (but cf. Popper 1972a, Appendix vi). It is particularly surprising in view of the fact that success in resolving the difficulties with defining *place selection rules*, admittedly on the basis of the *Church-Turing Thesis* and what I have called the *Kolmogorov-Chaitin-*

Martin-Lf Thesis, resulted in the *modern theory of induction*. My trans-Popperian suggestion, particularly the first part of the previous section, owes much to this development.

There is a further paradox in this sage. Popper defined, in his pursuit of a resolution of the problem of defining *place selection rules*, the concept of 'freedom from after effect' for a sequence of outcomes, say:

$$x_1, x_2, x_3, \ldots \tag{4}$$

Where the outcomes take on binary values, 0 and 1. For such a sequence, Arthur Copeland, some years earlier than Popper,[24] but also inspired by the von Mises framework for a frequency theory of probability, defined the *admissible numbers* as follows:

$$r_1, r_2, \ldots, r_k, s \tag{5}$$

where

$$1 \leq r_1 < r_2 < \ldots < r_k \leq s \tag{6}$$

$$\lim_{n\to\infty} \frac{1}{n} \sum_{m=0}^{n-1} x_{r_1+m_s} x_{r_2+m_s} \ldots + x_{r_k+m_s} = p^k \tag{7}$$

where $p \in \mathcal{R}$ *and* $0 \leq p \leq 1$. Martin-Lof, whose excellent exposition I follow here (Per Martin-Lof 1969) calls it the 'success probability of the sequence'. Now, Copeland (1928) proves that for an arbitrary p, $0 < p < 1$, the set of admissible numbers has the power of the continuum. In addition, if p is a *computable real*, Copeland's proof seems to provide an effective construction of an admissible number with success probability p.

Then, since Popper's definition of a sequence *free from after effect* has been shown to be equivalent to Copeland's definition of the admissible numbers, the problem of handling the possibility of the outcome space having the power of the continuum, as required by many physical laws and almost all economic theories, may seem to be solved, without sacrificing computable underpinnings.

However, such sequences as defined by Popper and Copeland are defined by a mathematical law, such as given above, and von Mises objected that they cannot serve as 'idealisations of sequences obtained by actual coin tossing', i.e. as truly random, i.e. impossibility of a gambling system which guarantees success. Popper himself stated that his own aims in treading that early frequentist path was for different purposes and, furthermore:

> I have meanwhile found that the 'measure-theoretical approach' to probability is preferable to the frequency interpretation …, both for mathematical and philosophical reasons.
>
> (Popper 1972a: 361)[25]

I feel that this preference, due also, naturally, to his adherence to his own, flawed, 'propensity interpretation of probability', blinded him to the possibilities of an enlightened view of the problem of induction, which would also have salvaged falsifiability, even in a broader context than that tied to *Modus (Tollendo) Tollens* and the *universal quantifier*. Perhaps it was also due to the seeming intransigence towards any concept of induction and inductive procedures.

The point I am trying to make is that Popper had all the concepts and the advantages of the correct starting points to tackle falsifiability and inductive inference in one fell swoop. Somehow, he avoided that path and, as a result, his fertile concepts and precepts have suffered interminable criticisms. I suppose all I have tried to do in the previous two sections is to return to Popperian themes, with potential Popperian concepts and tools to salvage the ruins!

I have left aside the third of the triptych that forms one set of the Popperian scientific world vision: the logic of scientific discovery. For reasons of space I must refer any interested reader, that perennially 'elusive creature', to two of my related writings (Velupillai 2000, 2002). I can, however, add that in this case I find Popper's nihilism quite unwarranted and his criticism or non-criticism of attempts to forge, for example, a (computational) theory of scientific discovery as intolerant and misguided as his attitude towards Carnap and the induction problem.

One last technical point has to be faced. In the previous section I mentioned that one assumption – that of a countably infinite observation space – may well be running against the spirit of a Popperian vision of the natural world and its laws. How, then, can a recursion theoretic resolution of the problem be attempted. The issue is something like the following (cf. for example Blum *et al.* 1998). Many are now aware of ways of constructing simple dynamical systems with complex dynamics. For example, simple 'laws' generate extraordinary complex dynamics resulting in sets that are familiar even to children playing around with computers: the *Mandelbrot set, the Julia set,* and so on. In these particular cases the domain of definition happens to include the complex plain and deciding whether a particular initial configuration of the 'simple law' which generates the Mandelbrot set retains its dynamics within the set will require considerations of an outcome space that has the power of the continuum. Is there a computable way to make such question decidable or, at least, make decidability questions meaningful?

I think there are two ways to proceed. One is to adopt the point of view advanced by Smale (in Blum *et al.* 1998) and his co-workers and define computation over the reals. The other is to remain within computable analysis and find ways to finesse the structure of the computable reals. I prefer the latter alternative but any incursion into that domain, even at an elementary level, is far beyond the scope envisaged for this chapter. I should just like to record my belief that nothing in the framework I have suggested will need to be modified, except that some seemingly sophisticated mathematics may have to be invoked. As I mentioned at the outset, I shall have to avoid going into a discussion of issues like *recursively inseparable sets* so that this chapter remains manageable.

Popper's was a lifelong voice against intellectual intolerances and dogmas of any sort. However, he does not seem to have been a great practitioner of his own precepts. Putnam perceptively noted:

> Failure to see the primacy of practice leads Popper to the idea of a sharp 'demarcation' between science, on the one hand, and political, philosophical, and ethical ideas, on the other. *This 'demarcation' is pernicious in my view*; fundamentally, it corresponds to Popper's separation of theory from practice, and his related separation of the critical tendency in science from the explanatory tendency in science. Finally, the failure to see the primacy of practice leads Popper to some rather reactionary political conclusions. Marxists believe that there are laws of society; that these laws can be known; and that men can and should act on this knowledge. It is not my intention to argue that this Marxist view is correct; but surely any view that rules this out *a priori* is reactionary. Yet this is precisely what Popper does – and in the name of an *anti-a priori* philosophy of knowledge.
>
> (Putnam 1974: 269, first set of italics added)

The pernicious influence of 'demarcationists' has resulted in intolerances and dogmas permeating all the affairs of society where the role of the narrow expert has been extolled beyond limits envisaged by the sages and the saints. The walls, whether it be the ones in Beijing or Berlin, Jerusalem or in the Ghettos of Warsaw, reflect the demarcationists' attitude in political ideology and practice. In the sciences, whole theories have been rejected on unenlightened attitudes that smack of the demarcationist: the rejection, for example, of Dirac's delta Function, the controversy over hidden-variables in quantum mechanics and the fate meted out to that impeccably erudite scientist of integrity, David Bohm. In economics, the continuing dominance of a narrow application of a narrow and irrelevant part of mathematics to formalise economic entities and derive momentous policy conclusions; and it is not too many years since Lysenko and Cyril Burt ruled wholly different political societies with equally dogmatic, demarcationist, visions.

I conclude with Edward Said's poignant call, in the fourth of his BBC Reith Lectures, for the intellectual to become, once again an amateur, thus reversing the trend towards increasing specialisation, underpinned by the demarcationists' philosophies and epistemologies:

> An amateur is what today the intellectual ought to be, someone who considers that to be a thinking and concerned member of a society one is entitled to raise moral issues at the heart of even the most technical and professional activity as it involves one's country; its power, its mode of interacting with its citizens as well as other societies. In addition, the intellectual's spirit as an amateur can enter and transform the merely professional routine most of us go through, into something much more lively and radical; instead of doing what one is supposed to do one can ask why one does it, who benefits from it, how can it reconnect with a personal project and original thought.
>
> (Said 1993)

The absence of the 'amateur' in Popper was, I think, the cause of much of the intolerance he displayed – in spite of advocating criticism and openness. These advocacies were not graced by the soft touch of the amateur's genuinely open mind.

Notes

1 Popper has noted he may have been the first to give the name *Hume's Problem* to 'the problem of induction' (*after* he had, in fact solved it): To my knowledge I was the first to call the problem of induction 'Hume's problem; though of course there may have been others. I did so in 'Ein Kriterium des empirischen Charakters theoretischer Systeme', *erkenntnis*, 3, 1933, pp. 426f., and in *Logik der Forschung*, section 4: 7. I shall, whenever I refer to this book, refer to it as LdF even though it will be to Popper (1972a).
2 I am repeating the word advisedly and consciously.
3 But, of course, we do also '*learn from our successes*' as John McCall wisely observed during the presentation of his paper at the conference.
4 In a private conversation in Los Angeles in the early 1990s, Spiro Latsis mentioned, during a discussion about the environment at LSE during his period there, that for Popper *'the enemy was Carnap'*. This, surely, reflects the intrusion of an unnecessary personal dimension – I nearly said 'subjective' – into a serious philosophical issue.
5 Among the 'titans' present at this contrived 'clash' were, in addition to Carnap: Tarski, Bernays, Church, Curry, Kreisel, Mostowski, and Kalmar. The presence of some of the pioneers of recursion theory at this contrived 'clash of titans' is interesting, given the recursion theoretic tone and content of my chapter.
6 Of particular relevance in this chapter, given my recursion theoretic approach to problems of induction, falsification and scientific discovery.
7 I am sure any number of acolytes of Popper, in the unlikely event they happen to glance at this chapter, will take me to task for suggesting that the 'openness' was 'untrammelled'.
8 As Popper himself explicitly and provocatively stated: '[I]f you can design some experimental test which you think might refute my assertion, I shall gladly, and to the best of my powers, help you refute it' (Popper 1963).
9 I accept Popper's adherence to a mathematical methodology. However, here, too, there is a narrowness of vision, to which I shall return in later parts of this chapter.
10 But, apparently, nothing else!
11 The excellent collection of essays: *The Popperian Legacy in Economics*, edited by Neil De Marchi (De Marchi 1988) is a good place to get an organised guide to the pervasive influence of Popperian ideas in economics.
12 I have often wondered why the German original 'Forschung' was translated as 'Scientific Discovery'! I am sure there must be a perfectly 'rational' Popperian explanation for the particular choice of words in English. Something like *The Logic of Scientific Research* or *The Logic of Scientific Investigation* would have been a more faithful translation of the title (and its contents). I shall, whenever I refer to this book, refer to it as LdF, even though it will be to Popper 1972a.
13 Even although it is easy to show that it is neither necessary nor sufficient.
14 The last part of this quotation formed the lead quote for the previous section.
15 I am simply paraphrasing Nozick's analogous rhetorical query: 'In what other way, if not simulation by a Turing machine, can we understand the process of making free choices? By making them, perhaps?
16 See above, the observation by Colin McGinn; however, as I proceed, I expect to be able to show that McGinn's doubts 'this [i.e. inductive inference] is not something that Popper can consistently incorporate into his conception of science' is unwarranted.

On the other hand I am not at all sure Popper would approve of my solution to this problem!

17 If not explicitly numerical then, in principle, codifable number theoretically using one of the well-known procedures emanating from 'Gödel Numbering'.

18 I shall, however, work within the framework of classical recursion theory and, hence, subject to the Church-Turing Thesis.

19 As Wise and Landsberg (1985: 461), in one of the responses to Popper and Miller (1983) put it, mildly and wisely: 'As this [i.e. the impossibility of inductive probability] would be a remarkable achievement, it is no criticism of these authors that we raise this question again. In our view the answer is a clear "No"'.

20 There are analytical ways to circumvent this assumption and allow for the possibility of a continuum of observations, but I shall reserve that analysis for another exercise.

21 I hope the careful reader will realise that the minimisation is not over a denumerably infinite sum!

22 It is seen that induction and inductive processes are intrinsically 'complex' phenomena in a precise sense. The complexity indicator is also a measure of the *randomness* of the phenomenon from which the underlying probability structure can be derived (or *inferred*). There is, thus, a kind of 'duality' between Bayes's rule and Ockham's Razor and, depending on the problem, the scientist can opt for the logic of the one or the other

23 Some of them, like Alonzo Church and Hilary Putnam, wore both hats.

24 There is hardly a single serious reference to Copeland's work in the mighty Popperian writings!

25 Almost the exact opposite path was taken by Kolmogorov.

References

Blum, L., Cucker, F., Shub, M. and Smale, P. (1998) *Complexity and Real Computation*, New York: Springer Verlag.

Copeland, A.H. (1928) 'Admissible numbers in the theory of probability', *American Journal of Mathematics*, 50: 535–52.

De Marchi, N. (ed.) (1988) *The Popperian Legacy in Economics*, Cambridge: Cambridge University Press.

Glymour, C. (1996) 'The hierarchies of knowledge and the mathematics of discovery', in P.J.R. Millican and A. Clark (eds) *Machines and Thought – The Legacy of Alan Turing*, Oxford: Oxford University Press.

Harré, R. (1994) 'Professor Sir Karl Popper', *The Independent*, 19 September: 32.

Martin-Lof, P. (1969) 'The literature on von Mises' Kollecktives revisited', *Theoria*, 35: 12–37.

McGinn, C. (2002) 'Looking for a black swan', *The New York Review of Books*, 21 November, 21: 46–50.

Nozick, R. (1981) *Philosophical Explanations*, Oxford: Oxford University Press.

Popper, K.R. (1945) The *Open Society and its Enemies*, 2 Vols, London: Routledge and Kegan Paul.

—— (1963) *Conjectures and Refutations: The Growth of Scientific Knowledge*, London: Routledge and Kegan Paul.

—— (1972a) *The Logic of Scientific Discovery*, London: Routledge and Kegan Paul.

—— (1972b) *Objective Knowledge: An Evolutionary Approach*, Oxford: Oxford University Press.

Popper, K.R. and Eccles, J.C. (1983) *The Self and its Brain: An Argument for Interactionism*, London: Routledge and Kegan Paul.

Popper, K.R. and Miller, D. (1984) 'A proof of the impossibility of inductive probability', *Nature*, 302: 687–8.

Putnam, H. (1963 [1979]) 'Probability and confirmination', *The Voice of America, Forum Philosophy of Science*, Vol. 10, US Information Agency. Reprinted in Putnam (1974).

—— (1974 [1979]) 'The corroboration of theories', in P.A. Schlipp (ed.) *The Philosophy of Karl Popper*, Vol. II, La Salle, IL: Open Court Publishing House. Reprinted in *Mathematics Matter and Method – Philosophical Papers*, Volume I: 250–69.

Quine, W.V.O. (1985) *The Time of My Life: An Autobiography*, Cambridge, MA: MIT Press.

Said, E. (1993) 'Edward Said's fourth Reith lecture', *The Independent*, 15 July.

Toulmin, S. (1971) 'Rediscovering history', *Encounter*, January.

Velupillai, K. (2000) *Computable Economics*, Oxford: Oxford University Press.

—— (2002) *The Epicurean Advantures of a Rational Artificer: Models of Simon*, mimeo, Department of Economics, National University of Ireland (NUI), Galway and Department of Economics, University of Trento, 45 pp.

—— (forthcoming) *Models of Simon*, London: Routledge.

Wise, J. and Landsberg, P.T. (1985) 'Had inductive probability been proved impossible?', *Nature*, 315: 461.

Index